*Presented by
Mrs Bardsley
to each ordinand at
Trinity College,
Bristol,
in memory of her
husband.
Spring 1993*

CUTHBERT BARDSLEY

BISHOP · EVANGELIST · PASTOR

Cuthbert Bardsley

BISHOP · EVANGELIST · PASTOR

Donald Coggan

COLLINS
8 Grafton Street, London W1
1989

William Collins Sons & Co. Ltd
London · Glasgow · Sydney · Auckland
Toronto · Johannesburg

BRITISH LIBRARY CATALOGUING IN PUBLICATION DATA

Coggan, Donald. *1909-*
Cuthbert Bardsley: bishop, evangelist, pastor
1. Church of England. Bardsley, Cuthbert
I. Title
283'.092'4

ISBN 0-00-215094-8

First published 1989
© Donald Coggan 1989

Set in Linotron Ehrhardt by
Wyvern Typesetting Limited
Made and Printed in Great Britain by
William Collins Sons & Co. Ltd Glasgow

Cuthbert Bardsley would like this book to be dedicated
to the memory of
DOROTHY (1898–1973),
his sister and devoted companion over many years,
and to
ELLEN,
his beloved wife and constant helper

"Heirs together of the grace of life."

"Cuthbert did not restrict his teaching and influence to the monastery, but worked to rouse the ordinary folk far and near to exchange their foolish customs for a love of heavenly joys . . .

"In those days, whenever a clerk or priest visited a town, English folk always used to gather at his call to hear the Word, eager to hear his message and even more eager to carry out whatever they had heard and understood. But Cuthbert was so skilful a speaker, and had such a light in his angelic face, and such a love for proclaiming his message, that none presumed to hide his inmost secrets, but all openly confessed their wrongdoing; for they felt it impossible to conceal their guilt from him, and at his discretion they blotted out by works of penance the sins that they had confessed."

BEDE: *A History of the English Church and People*,
Book IV, chapter 27

"Who are you?", asked the small girl left alone
with him in the vestry.
"My name is Cuthbert, but my niece always calls
me Custard."

Contents

Illustrations

Preface

There are lions on the path of every biographer. They are the more menacing if the subject of the book is a contemporary figure. It has rightly been said that "instant biographies are notorious for their lack of perspective, while those written at a decent distance from their subject are generally agreed to produce the more balanced portrait". There growls one lion.

Another peril arises if the writer and the subject of the book are close friends and if, as in the case of this book, the former greatly admires the latter. No less an historian than Professor G.R. Elton has reminded us that "admiration by itself produces only hagiography";[1] and hagiography is bound to be a distortion of history. Warts are part of a true portrait. There growls another lion.

Warned but not daunted, the writer has set out on his path. He has been emboldened on his journey by the words of Andrei Sakarov who, writing of his own memoirs, declared that "literature such as this is an important part of mankind's memory". That memory is like a great tapestry, to the making of which countless threads have contributed. In the case of the history of the Church, the tapestry is rich and colourful and – to consider only recent decades – has given rise to the production of many distinguished biographies. One has only to think of G.K.A. Bell's *Randall Davidson*, J.G. Lockhart's *Cosmo Gordon Lang*, F.A. Iremonger's *William Temple*, Charles Smyth's *Cyril Forster Garbett*, R.C.D. Jasper's *George Bell* and his *Arthur Cayley Headlam*, Owen Chadwick's *Hensley Henson* among a host of others.

To capture one thread for the enrichment of the tapestry is a task well worth undertaking – all too many lives go unrecorded, either because of the self-effacing modesty of the person concerned or

---

[1] In the preface to his *F.W. Maitland*, Weidenfeld & Nicolson 1985, p. vii

because rising costs prohibit production. All who know Cuthbert Killick Norman Bardsley would agree that the "thread" of his life is a colourful one, and that to leave it unrecorded would be to rob the history of the Church of a rich and distinctive element in its ongoing work. Dangers or no dangers, the task had to be undertaken.

My debt to a host of people will be obvious and, of course, to Cuthbert and Ellen above all others. Like the writer, Cuthbert never kept a detailed diary. At times, perhaps due to war damage or to the neglect of safe record-keeping on the part of local authorities, the work of the biographer has been made difficult. But many have come to the rescue, including members of the Bishop's own family.

I am greatly indebted to Canon Colin Cuttell who has contributed the major part of chapter V, and to Canon William Purcell whose share in chapter XII is of special value since it comes from the pen of one who has for many years been a close friend and often a close colleague of Cuthbert Bardsley. I must express my indebtedness to Dr E.G.W. Bill, Librarian of the Lambeth Palace Library, to Dr Brenda Hough who is in charge of the archive department of Church House, Westminster, to the Librarian of the House of Lords, to Mr N.D. Filsell, the Coventry Diocesan Information and Press Officer, and to the staff of Coventry Cathedral; also to Mrs Betty Simpson who was Bishop Bardsley's secretary.

I wish to record my gratitude to a host of people who have lent me documents and letters, who have shared memories and impressions, and who have given me lodging when I have travelled in search of information. I began to list them, but decided that "the time would fail me to tell of" them, and were I to attempt to do so, I might easily fall into the trap of invidious selection and of boring detail. I hold myself responsible for any errors of fact or judgement.

Mrs Mary Tremenheere has shown much patience and skill in the work of typing and re-typing, and I have received much help from members of the publishing house of Collins.

Winchester
Christmas 1988

DONALD COGGAN

Part One

I

HOME AND THE EARLY YEARS

Train up a child in the way he should go: and when he is old, he will not depart from it.

Proverbs 22:6

WHEN CUTHBERT BARDSLEY WAS BORN on 28th March 1907, Queen Victoria had been dead six years, and her son, Edward VII, had only a third of his short reign left – he died in 1910. Seven years were to run before Europe was enveloped in the First World War. Look at a map of the world of that day, and the enormous areas of it coloured red speak of an Empire at its zenith. If there were wars and rumours of war they did little to disturb the ordinary man's sense of security, and his confidence that, given a little more knowledge – and immense advances were already being made – Utopia might be round the corner. True, the poverty of the "lower classes", the conditions in the factories and the abysmal state of the slums in the great cities must have caused a twinge of unease in the hearts and consciences of the more fortunate. But the sun of progress had not set with the death of the great queen. "Progress" was in the air.

"Glory to Man in the highest! For Man is the master of things" – Swinburne died two years after Cuthbert was born, but he expressed the optimism of a generation glad to bask in the sunshine of a belief in the idea of progress. Only the more percipient gave heed to signs which already were beginning to point to a more serious concept of man and of the evil at work in the world – was progress *really* inevitable? And anyway what was the real meaning of "progress"?

The idea of a world cataclysm and another to follow it a generation later, the possibility of nuclear fission and of the destruction of the world as the result of men's researches seemed almost inconceivable. When Cuthbert was two years old, Blériot crossed the English Channel; when he was a boy, radio reception was obtained with difficulty by means of a "cat's whisker" set. Television was hardly dreamed of. Thomas Edison, working away in Florida – "genius is 1 per cent inspiration and 99 per cent perspiration" – invented, among a thousand other things, the phonograph, the incandescent electric lamp and the microphone. He did not die till 1931. The vicarages in which Cuthbert spent his youth were lit by gas, and the days of refrigerators and washing machines were still in the distance.

Randall Thomas Davidson had recently begun the years of his long Primacy at Canterbury (1903–28). Trusted as his chaplain by Archbishop Tait and by Queen Victoria as her chaplain and adviser, Davidson brought to his high office great knowledge and experience. He steered the ship with caution. It was said of him that, when the last trumpet sounded, Davidson would appoint a commission to decide whether in fact it *was* the last trumpet. The hand on the helm at Canterbury was steady. At York, William Dalrymple Maclagan was giving way to Cosmo Gordon Lang (1908–28). When Cuthbert was three, William Temple was a young man acting as an usher at the great Edinburgh Conference of 1910.

*　　*　　*

Cuthbert Bardsley came from a clerical family. Within three generations, twenty-nine clergy, three of them bishops, bear that surname. John Wareing Bardsley was Bishop of Sodor and Man, 1887–92, and Bishop of Carlisle 1892–95; Cyril C.B. Bardsley (cousin of Cuthbert's father) was Bishop of Peterborough, 1924–27, and Bishop of Leicester 1927–40; and Cuthbert himself was consecrated in 1947.

The beginning of this remarkable line of clergy goes back to the early part of the nineteenth century when James Bardsley, working on the shop floor of a mill in Rochdale, Lancashire, took up the suggestion of his vicar to attend some night classes with a view to eventual ordination. It cannot have been easy to do such work after a long day at the mill, but eventually he was ordained. All his sons were later ordained. What would have been lost to the Church if that vicar had not responded to the prompting of the Spirit to nudge the elbow of that factory worker and to help him with his tuition? A later James Bardsley became Rector of St Anne, Manchester in 1861, and by 1873 was an honorary Canon of Manchester and a Proctor in Convocation.

Cuthbert's grandfather, Samuel Bardsley, was vicar of Spitalfields in the heart of London's slums. He then became Rector of Finchley, at that time separated from London by a considerable country area.

He had two daughters and four sons, one of whom was Joseph Udall Norman Bardsley. Norman, as he was always called, was to be the father of Cuthbert.

Norman Bardsley, a graduate of Gonville and Caius College, Cambridge, was ordained deacon in 1882 and priest in 1883 by Bishop J.C. Ryle of Liverpool. He served three curacies in that diocese before becoming Rector of the parish of St Mary with Holy Trinity, Ulverston, Cumbria in 1896. The parish was then in the diocese of Carlisle and was in the gift of the Peache Trustees. (His uncle Charles had been Vicar of the parish 1878–93.) Norman remained there until 1909.

There was a gas works in the parish. Those who laboured there knew nothing of State assistance, and lived in constant fear of incapacitating illness. Some homes were lit by gas light, others by more primitive means. Water often had to be drawn laboriously from a well, and travel, apart from the recently built railway, was mostly by brougham and pair for the well-to-do, and horse and cart for the less fortunate.

The chief event of Norman Bardsley's incumbency was the extension of the chancel of the parish church of Ulverston. Bulmer's *Directory of Furness*, 1913, states: "In 1903, a larger church was built, which has given a very noble appearance to the interior of the church. The foundation stone was laid by Lady Evelyn Cavendish, and the work was completed, at a cost of £2000, raised by voluntary subscription."

In 1909, when Cuthbert was two years old, Norman Bardsley moved to greater responsibilities, becoming Vicar of Lancaster, where he remained until his death in 1928.

The history of Lancaster goes back at least to Roman times as its name indicates – the camp by the River Lune. Its ancient church and castle, standing side by side on the hill, dominate the landscape and look down over the river to Grange and to the hills of the Lake District. Beyond can be glimpsed the sea at Morecambe Bay. The Lune is tidal and, up to about a hundred years ago, before the bridges were built, the inhabitants of Lancaster could watch the sailing ships as they travelled up the river.

From the huge vicarage next to the church, the noise of the trains thundering their way north from London to Scotland could be heard, as could also the sound of the eight great bells which summoned the congregation to church every Sunday and on all the festivals and occasions of national importance.

Norman Bardsley came to this historic church, with its two mission churches, at the height of his powers. Two years after his arrival he was made Rural Dean, an office he was to hold for his remaining seventeen years. He became a Proctor in the Convocation of York and a member of the Church Assembly. When the diocese of Blackburn was formed in 1927 (carved out of the diocese of Manchester) he was one of the first six to be made canons by Bishop Percy Mark Herbert. Long before the word "ecumenical" came into common use, Norman Bardsley pioneered in the field of inter-church relations: he established and became president of a clergy and ministers' Fraternal, "to encourage unity amongst the leaders of the flocks in the hope that the congregations will in due time take up a similar progressive attitude, and become imbued with the same Christian spirit". Its members met for the discussion of theological subjects four times every year.

Norman Bardsley was, as his picture shows, a strong character. He did not suffer fools gladly. He thrived on controversy, enjoying the thrust and parry of debate. If he made enemies, he was soon reconciled to them, and many of them became his greatest friends. He could be outspoken; and, while coming from an evangelical background, he was not bigoted or narrow in his views. He had little love for Roman Catholicism, but included many Roman Catholic priests among his friends. He loathed the clerical voice and anything approaching a negative attitude to life. When his family asked whether they might play tennis on a Sunday afternoon, he replied: "Why not? You can walk on a Sunday afternoon; why not run on either side of a net?" Could they read a Sunday newspaper? "Why not? It was printed on Saturdays; it would be more questionable to read a Monday paper!"

He was proud to be president of the golf club, and to win the cup of the year. He was an able story-teller, and sometimes shocked his wife who tried, generally without success, to stop him as he launched into a yarn which caused him great amusement. He enjoyed taking his family to the Hippodrome.

Beneath this infectious *joie-de-vivre* lay a great capacity for sympathy – he shared deeply in his people's griefs and laid great stress on the importance of visiting, being a familiar figure in the living rooms and kitchens of the parish. He would do three hours of visiting every day, and expected his curates to do the same. At the Monday morning staff meetings, he would ask them for their visiting lists, and he himself was scrupulous in keeping notes of the families on whom he called. He was also chaplain to the Lancaster Infirmary.

A voracious reader, he prepared his sermons (rarely less than twenty-five minutes in length) with great care. He was gifted with a fine voice and had a vigorous delivery. The congregation would be about three hundred strong in the morning and five to six hundred in the evening. He sought to teach the fullness of the Faith, his message was Christ-centred and clearly related to contemporary issues and demands. On one occasion it is recorded that he stopped in the middle of a sermon: "I see a couple canoodling at the back of the gallery. *I will not have it!*" – and that in stentorian tones. His strength and firmness of character were united to a kindness and generosity of disposition which made for great leadership. He strongly supported the revision of the Book of Common Prayer. In one of six sermons on *The Church of England and her Endowments*,[1] he had declared his "whole-hearted support of the 'Disestablishment of the Church' ". He would, however, have nothing to do with its " 'Disendowment', which I should look upon as a national crime, calculated to bring God's judgement upon the country"! In later years he came to oppose Disestablishment – it "would be like the divorce of an old couple who had kept their golden wedding".

The life of the Church in Lancaster was healthy and vigorous. Norman Bardsley hoped that his church would become the cathedral of the new diocese of Blackburn, and made certain alterations in the church to facilitate its conversion. But, partly as the result of William Temple's insistence, Blackburn, not Lancaster, was to have the privilege of becoming the See city.

*　　　*　　　*

On his mother's side Cuthbert was indeed fortunate. Annie Mabel Killick's father, William Killick, was a well-to-do Liverpool merchant in the firm of Killick Nixon, which traded with India. Cuthbert's grandmother was the only married one of four girls. When they died,

---

[1] Skeffington & Son 1912

they left their money to his mother, who thus became a woman of great wealth. So we have the picture of a poor curate marrying a rich wife. Apparently this created no difficulty, for Mabel was a woman of great integrity of character who never flaunted her money. Generous herself, she taught her children the importance of tithing.

In contrast to her husband, she was reserved and shy (sex was never talked about!) and found it difficult to make friends. Those who penetrated her reserve found a depth of friendship of great value, and the members of her household staff remained with her for many years even after her husband's death. Overcoming her shyness, she became president of the deanery Mothers' Union and, for a short while, diocesan president.

She believed that home-making was her most important work. Married on 27th April 1895, she gave birth to six children, of whom Cuthbert was the youngest. She disciplined and fashioned them in her quiet way in spite of the presence of a nanny and, later, of a governess. In sympathizing with a friend on the death of his mother, Cuthbert wrote:

I still recall my own mother's passing twenty-five years ago. It felt as though a limb had been amputated and as though life could never be the same again. And indeed life never has been the same, for we were all forced to grow up suddenly. So long as a mother is alive, one tends inevitably to build around her. She is the focus of a large family, the central point to whom one turns.

Eric was the oldest of the children. Educated at Eton, he was eighteen when the First World War broke out. Within days of the outbreak he joined up, and served four years in the army in France, East Africa and Ireland. An extrovert character, he spent much of his life in France where he had a small chateau, farm and vineyard.

Then came four girls, Dorothy, Hilda, Monica and Joan. Of **Dorothy**, the eldest of the four, we shall hear more, for she was to be Cuthbert's closest companion for many years.

Hilda married Eric's best friend, with whom he had been at Eton. He became Sir Thomas Harley, senior partner of a leading firm of solicitors in Liverpool, chairman of the area hospital committee, and a prominent political worker. Hilda was no less public-spirited than her husband, being a Cheshire County Councillor, a J.P., and a tireless worker in the Girl Guide movement, for which she was awarded their medal of the silver fish. Ian, the eldest of their three sons, became an alderman and chairman of the Cheshire Education Committee. He was Lord Mayor of Westminster.

Monica married Trevor Card, an army colonel. The eldest of their three children, Petronella, is the wife of the recent headmaster of Sherborne School; and the second child, Robin Macnaghten, has been a master at Eton for a quarter of a century. Monica, a very caring woman, in many ways like Cuthbert, was a J.P. and a great worker for the Guides and for what was then known as Moral Welfare. Her younger daughter has her own promotional business in London.

Joan, the youngest of the four girls, was a young woman of great vitality. With bright blue eyes and an outgoing personality, she was loved and admired by her friends. She died at the age of twenty-six as the result of a false diagnosis following an operation. Her death was a special shock to Cuthbert because they had been brought up so closely together, sharing the same nurse and governess.

Two years after the birth of Joan, **Cuthbert** was born. His parents thought of calling the baby Benedict, but decided against it. The name Cuthbert appealed to them both; and so it was.

The name, if unusual, was a strong one, with fine historical precedent. St Cuthbert lived and served on the eastern side of the hills of the north – in Northumberland and Durham; Cuthbert Bardsley's father, as we have seen, was a parish priest to the west of those hills when his son was born. But both Cuthberts breathed the fresh and vigorous air of the north, where spades are called spades and bushes are not beaten about. Did the parents' choice of the name reflect a certain pride in and reverence for the north?

Norman and his wife Mabel could not foresee the shape of the ministry which their son would exercise. Had they been able to do so, they might have seen that the two Cuthberts had more in common than they first thought when they brought their baby to baptism.

St Cuthbert of Lindisfarne (c. 634–87) is regarded as the best-known and best-loved of the saints of the north of England. A man of charm and ability, he became a monk in 651, and was made prior of Melrose some ten years later. Seeking solitude for himself on one of the Inner Farne islands, his holiness of life was much talked of, and people sought him out for godly counsel and advice. As a reluctant bishop of Lindisfarne, he exercised a zealous ministry of preaching, teaching, visiting and healing. No wonder that a steady stream of pilgrims continues to visit his tomb in Durham Cathedral, where his remains rest beneath a simple grey stone slab. Gentle and strong, he became a centre of unity in the church, a lover of God and of God's creation, with a charismatic quality which was married to authority; he gave the kind of episcopal leadership which was greatly needed in the seventh century. He being dead yet speaks.

Some thirteen centuries separate Cuthbert of Lindisfarne from Cuthbert of Lancashire and Coventry. But there are parallels between the lives and contributions of these two men which deserve attention. They will become apparent as the story develops.

We can picture, then, a happy, rumbustious family – all six children grew to be tall – growing up in a large and roomy vicarage in spacious grounds, beset by no financial worries, loved and cared for by their parents and their staff, surrounded by happy friends. One of the latter said, many years later: "I was not a great churchgoer, but when the Bardsleys were in Lancaster it was as if a warm light glowed on the hill." Cuthbert remembers two of the staff especially. There was Elizabeth the parlour-maid, known as Bibby. She arrived at an early age to serve in a junior capacity, but stayed for over forty years to become a most important member of the household. So loved was she that her body rests in a grave alongside those of Canon and Mrs Bardsley and of Dorothy Bardsley.

Then there was the redoubtable Miss Henly, an Oxford scholar, daughter of a priest, who journeyed daily by train from Settle in Yorkshire to teach the younger members of the vicarage family. With her well-stored mind, remarkable memory and ability to make the dullest subject interesting, "Henny Penny", as she came to be known, taught the children well. A strong disciplinarian, she would take no nonsense and kept their noses to the grindstone until she left to catch her train back to Yorkshire at 5 p.m. each day. Governesses are for the most part a relic from the past, but a governess like Miss Henly left an indelible mark for good upon her pupils.

Laughter and fun were central to the life of the vicarage. The family was a happy one, there was nothing strait-laced about it. Parties provided entertainment to which people came from the whole Lune valley. There were tennis parties with officers from the King's Own Regiment and others; there were dances at Kendal and Lancaster; there were golf matches with a goose as the first prize; there was the

Lancaster Regatta on the River Lune; there were family prayers, with the family on one side of the room and the staff on the other, "all devoutly kneeling".

The Bible and daily prayer became the central source of inspiration, and visitors came constantly. Men like William Temple, Peter Green, Studdert Kennedy and Arthur Burroughs, Bishop of Ripon, made an impression on the young people at the vicarage. Religion was never forced on them, but it became natural for them to share in the services of the church (there was a splendid choir), and sometimes to go with their father on his parish visits. All Cuthbert's sisters became Girl Guides. The youngsters learned that, though their vicarage was huge and perhaps outwardly intimidating to some members of the parish, it was in fact a centre of warmth and welcome, and a base from which members of the family moved out in loving encounter with others.

Cuthbert grew up in an atmosphere which affirmed that religion was not a purely private matter. It must permeate every corner of life, civic and national.

Leaving such a happy home must have been a painful experience. In January 1916, at the tender age of eight and a half, Cuthbert entered Summer Fields, Oxford, a preparatory school which for many years held a top place for scholarships to the public schools of the country. It was run by two remarkable headmasters, the Rev. Dr C.E. Williams (known as the Doctor) and the Rev. E. Hugh Alington (known as the Bear). Both had married the daughters of the founder of the school, Mr Archibald Maclaren.

Critics might say that the staff sacrificed much in their concentration on scholastic results, but that would be an unfair criticism. The chapel played an important and central place in the life of the school. The services were well conducted – moderately Anglo-Catholic, devout and reverent. Because the war was still being waged, the masters were for the most part elderly and discipline was rigid. The food was poor and unappetising; games were subservient to studies.

Young Cuthbert was frightened; and the situation was made worse by the fact that he was ill with whooping-cough during the major part of his first term, and had to begin his lessons all over again when the second term got under way. However, he made steady progress, though he did not distinguish himself in his lessons or in his games. Some hand-written reports from his headmasters at the school survive. An early one speaks of him as "a charming little fellow, upright, frank and obedient, always willing and obliging; he is everybody's friend . . ." A year later, he is "frank and open, and he seems out to do his best . . . He has a habit of losing his head at a critical moment, whether in work or play." By April 1919, he is "a most satisfactory and charming little fellow . . . and has improved decidedly in a physical way this term – a plucky little runner". By August 1919, Dr Williams is regretting that he is unable to have "the little warning talk with him I always have with the boys leaving", and wonders whether his father could

> arrange for him to come and lunch with me . . . I should love to help, for I know the ropes (at Eton) and do think it might be valuable. We are most sorry to lose him and are parting from him with every regret. I need not tell you that he leaves us with the highest possible character and with every prospect of maintaining this if he falls into good hands: at any rate I feel pretty sure that, please God, his nice disposition and nature will cause him instinctively to shrink from anything false or unworthy of him.

Cuthbert's greatest friend at Summer Fields was David Fremantle who died early; his son Tom became one of Cuthbert's godchildren.

Clearly the years at Summer Fields had been formative and toughening, a good preparation for the period at Eton which was to follow them. He had won the junior quarter-mile and captained the victorious junior relay team. He also played football. In the realm of drama he was a Goblin in the 1917 production of *Ever Afterwards*. The editor of the school magazine recorded that Cuthbert and his fellow goblins "expressed envy, hatred and malignity by their apt and eloquent gestures – so much so that, had they not opened their lips at all, they would have by effective dumb-show supplied one with a ready cue to their diabolical intentions".

In 1964 the school celebrated its centenary, and Cuthbert, as Bishop of Coventry, presided over a service of thanksgiving in the local parish church. In a book published to mark the centenary, he wrote an article entitled *From Chapel to Church*, in which he expressed his gratitude for what the regular (and compulsory) services in the chapel had done for him. He told his readers the story of the soldier who was hauled up before his colonel on a charge of being disorderly at a church parade. In answer to questions he replied as follows: "I was christened William and after that I was known as Bill. And when I came into the army I was given a number. From that moment on it was 'Number 457 pick up your feet on parade'; 'Number 457 go and get your belt polished'; 'Number 457 go and get your hair cut'; 'Number 457 go to the church next Sunday'. Well, sir, I goes to church, and I sits down all quiet-like, and I says to myself 'peace at last', and then all at once the Padre comes in and he says 'Number 457. Art thou weary, art thou languid, art thou sore distressed?'; and I gets up and I says 'No, but I'm fed up'."

While there are some (Cuthbert said) who are fed up, at least for a time, as the result of compulsory church attendance, there are, I believe, many more who, not necessarily in the early years of life but in later days, thank God for the fact that they were forced to go to church, where they received the teaching, inspiration, and the dynamic for social service which chapel services at their best can give.

II

ETON, OXFORD AND CAMBRIDGE

Lengthen thy cords, and strengthen thy stakes.

Isaiah 54:2

CUTHBERT WAS TWELVE AND A HALF when he entered Eton in 1919. The school must have seemed to him huge and somewhat forbidding, as compared with the preparatory school in which he had become a senior boy. Now he had to begin all over again. He was shy and somewhat retiring; he did not find it easy to make friends, particularly with those whose backgrounds were very different from his own.

If Summer Fields in wartime had been spartan, Eton was to provide little relief. Wilfred Thesiger,[1] who was to enter Eton four years after Cuthbert, has given us a vivid description of the conditions which he found in 1923. He arrived at the school in a horse-drawn cab from Windsor Station. Founded by Henry VI before Columbus discovered the New World, the school surrounded him with a feeling of history, ancient and more recent – he noted 1157 names of old Etonians killed in the First World War (to which another 748 were to be added after the Second). The school was divided into twenty-four houses, each having about forty-five boys, apart from the seventy scholars who lived separately in College. Each boy had his own room, though some of them were very small. There were no fires in the houses until the boys lit them in their rooms in the evening. One house (McNeile's) had no changing-rooms or showers, only two baths and five lavatories; each boy had two baths a week. Birchings by the Lower Master were "reminiscent of a beheading on Tower Hill". Things must have been very similar to this when Cuthbert entered the school. Though Eton was thought to be a place for the privileged, it could by no means be called a place of luxury.

The centre of Eton life is the House to which the boy is assigned. Cuthbert's housemaster was R.F. Kindersley. He was elderly, and

[1] *The Life of My Choice*, Collins 1987, pp. 68ff.

had never recovered from the shock of seeing his house destroyed by a fire which had cost the lives of several boys. Charming but shy, he found it difficult to keep discipline or to make contact with the boys. Morals were not what they should be. Bullying was rampant. On one occasion, after a semi-final, all the members of the junior football team were hauled up before the captain and told that if they did not win the final, he would beat the lot of them. They lost. They were all beaten.

Kindersley's place was taken by E.V. Slater, a keen disciplinarian who soon cleaned up the Augean stables and transformed the house. He cared about the progress of the boys and would visit them in their rooms. Some of the boys admired him, but Cuthbert found it difficult to make any close contact with him. He appeared to have little religious faith, if any, as may be illustrated by the story of Cuthbert's confirmation which took place in the college chapel.

Somewhat illogically, his father mistrusted clerical schoolmasters, and insisted that he go to his housemaster for preparation for confirmation. "But, father," said Cuthbert, "I am not sure that he is a Christian." "Of course he is", was the reply. "He could not be a housemaster at Eton if he were not a Christian." So in filial obedience Cuthbert knocked at the study door. "Come in", said a voice. He entered. "What can I do for you?" "Sir, my father wants me to be prepared by you for confirmation." "I have never prepared anyone for confirmation in my life", said the housemaster. To which Cuthbert replied: "I am sorry, Sir, but my father insists on it." "Come to my study on Sunday afternoon and I will see what I can do." The entire preparation for confirmation consisted in the reading of a book by H.G. Wells on the book of Job, and Cuthbert was confirmed together with 163 other small boys. It meant nothing at all to him.

Later he told his father that his confirmation had had no meaning for him, and added that if ever he were to become a bishop (which he thought extremely unlikely) he would try to ensure that it meant much to those who came before him. "Boy," replied his father, "you must never become a bishop, for they tend to be pompous, and of all sins pomposity is the most inexcusable." He remembered that in years to come.

Cyril Alington, later to be Dean of Durham, was headmaster (1916–33), though to young Cuthbert he must have seemed a remote figure, at least in his earlier years at the school. Three men influenced

31

him considerably. One was Eric Powell, the art master, whose enthusiasm and power of communication kindled in him a love of painting which was to prove lifelong. One day he came to Cuthbert's room and, looking at a picture on the wall, said: "Who did that?" "The master at my prep school, sir." "You could do it better than that, boy." "I've never painted in my life", replied Cuthbert. "Then you'd better start, for I think you have it in you. Meet me tomorrow and I'll give you some special tuition." In hours of private tuition, he helped the boy to see beauty and to capture it. He taught him the love of nature.

The second was Henry Marten (later Sir Henry, who was to tutor the future Queen Elizabeth). He brought history alive, and Cuthbert found himself sitting on the edge of his chair participating in episodes of long ago.

The third was Edward Bell, brother of George Bell who was later Bishop of Chichester. Edward instilled into his pupils a love of words and of poetry, and triggered in Cuthbert a desire to speak, to write, to communicate.

Cuthbert was a "wet bob", that is to say he rowed while at the school. He was never a member of the "Library" (what, in other schools, would be called a prefect). He never really enjoyed Eton. He himself called his career there undistinguished, and he felt himself to be unappreciated. As for religion, the beauty of the services in the ancient chapel appealed to him, but he left Eton with religion meaning less to him than when he entered it. No one, he felt, went out of his way to develop the faith of the growing boy. One man – from outside the school – did make a lasting impression on him and on his religious development. He was Robert Howard, headmaster of Liverpool College, who conducted a Lent course at Eton chapel. Attendance was voluntary, but Cuthbert went regularly and began to realize, as he put it,

> that religion was a matter of personal relationship to God through Jesus Christ, and that prayer was a means of deepening that relationship. I realized also that this relationship depended on personal commitment. But this I was not ready to do. Love of popularity, the desire to be liked, to be a pagan among the pagans, an aesthete among the aesthetes . . . and a Christian among the Christians – the desire to be a chameleon, changing my colour

according to the company I was in . . . was a flaw in character which I was not ready to change. So I left Eton, still a nominal adherent of the Lord, but far from being a committed follower. This was to come two years later, when I was twenty-one.

To Oxford he went, in 1926. He was nineteen.

* * *

Life at New College, Oxford, proved exhilarating to Cuthbert as his time at Eton had never done. He began to feel his wings. He enjoyed the camaraderie of friends, not always Old Etonians, but often men who had gone up from Winchester and other schools. He found himself able to go deeper in making friends than he had done before. Among other Wykehamists who came up to New College were John Sparrow (later to become Warden of All Souls) and Richard Crossman. Sir William Hayter, who came up in the year after Cuthbert and later became Warden of New College, remembers him as "good looking and sporty but given to fashionable enthusiasms" (no doubt a derogatory reference to Cuthbert's connection with the Oxford Group). There must have been plenty of intellectual and political stimulus at the College at this time.

He had digs in the same house, 92 High Street, with William Hayter, Humphrey Wright (killed in the war), John Witt, Anthony Lousada, the artist, and Edward Bradby, who was to become Principal of St Paul's College, Cheltenham (1949–72). The latter remembers Cuthbert as "a thoroughly nice chap, but a bit naïve . . . Years later he came over and preached for us in the chapel of St Paul's College, Cheltenham, and it was delightful to find how his personality had deepened and filled out, and what an inspiring and firmly grounded evangelist he had become."

Cuthbert continued to row as he had done at Eton, and was a member of the Leander Club. He rowed in the College second eight in 1927 and 1930, and in the first eight in 1929.

The College chapel services appealed to him, as those at Eton had done, for the beauty of their music, but made little impact on his life. He was President of the Student Christian Movement in the University.

When he came to take his degree in 1930, he took a poor class.

That may be attributed to several causes, the main one being the autocratic decision of his father as to the subject he should read. Cuthbert would have liked to read Theology. His father said, "No: I don't want you to be a man with a one-track mind." He urged him to read Modern Greats, and so he did, but without enthusiasm. He studied German and French, philosophy, economics and modern social history. The range was too wide for him, though he enjoyed exploring the social history, thanks very probably to the influence of Henry Marten's teaching at Eton.

Then there was the death of his father when he was in the middle of his course. And, no doubt, his wholehearted enlistment in the activities of the Oxford Group detracted from attention to his books. The four years at Oxford, however, disappointing though the class of his degree proved to be, opened doors of intellectual interest which he was to enter in later years. He had a love of history, of words, of poetry; and this love was never to leave him.

Like many other people who were distinguished in their careers, Cuthbert would seem to have been a late developer. Good wine matures slowly.

*   *   *

Motoring home from Oxford on Sunday, 8th July 1928, Cuthbert noticed that the flags on the buildings in Lancaster were at half-mast. On arriving at the Vicarage, he learned the reason – his father had died that morning.

Norman Bardsley's health had been showing signs of deterioration for some time – he had, for instance, been compelled to sit while delivering his sermons. He was taken ill just before he was due to celebrate the Holy Communion at 8 a.m. He reached home, but died as the result of a heart attack before the 10 o'clock service. He was only fifty-nine.

The funeral took place on 12th July and was conducted by the Bishop of Blackburn, Dr P.M. Herbert. Every seat in the church was occupied, and there were more people outside the church than in. "No assemblage so large or so representative of the town has ever been seen before at a funeral in Lancaster", declared the *Lancaster Guardian*. It is significant that when, in January 1930, memorial gates were dedicated by the Archdeacon of Lancaster "to the glory of God

and in loving memory of Canon J.U.N. Bardsley, Vicar 1909 – 1928",
they were "erected by the people of Lancaster" – the people of the
town, not only the congregation of the church. (In 1968, Cuthbert was
to come back to Lancaster to dedicate a cross and candlesticks, a
credence table and communion rails, in memory of his father, and of
his mother who died in 1939.)

The whole town seemed to go into mourning when Canon Bardsley died. Many of the shops closed on the day of the funeral.

His father's death made a profound impression on Cuthbert. He
had a deep respect for him as a man of God devoted to his people.
"Class" mattered not one bit to him – he was the pastor of them all. If
Cuthbert's relationship with his mother was closer than it was with his
father, he none the less recalls how the green baize door of his father's
study, which was shut on weekdays to keep out the invasion of his six
"hooligan" children, was always open on Sunday evenings, when the
activities of the day were over. Then it was that, as a small boy,
Cuthbert would climb up and sit on his father's knee, open up his
problems and receive something of the wealth of his wisdom. As he
grew older he would often accompany his father on his walks through
the town, notice how frequently he would stop to enter into conversation with his parishioners, and then pass on to visit them in their
homes.

It says much that Cuthbert's book, *Sundry Times Sundry Places*,[2] is
dedicated:

In Piam Memoriam Joseph Udall Norman Bardsley sometime
Vicar of Lancaster and Hon. Canon of Blackburn; a beloved Father
who taught me the meaning of the ministry.

He writes of him with affection in *Him We Declare*.[3]

Though Cuthbert had perforce spent much time away from home
during his first two decades – at Summer Fields, at Eton and at
Oxford – the Vicarage at Lancaster had been his base, and the
influence of his home had been powerful and formative. Now his
father was dead, the man whom he venerated, his hero. He could
never be quite the same carefree young man again.

His mother moved to Lunecliffe, a large house a few miles from

[2] Mowbrays 1962
[3] Mowbrays 1967, pp. 62–4

Lancaster, taking with her some of the staff who had helped her run the big vicarage, and there she lived for the eleven years of her widowhood. That house became Cuthbert's home base during the coming years which were to prove so eventful for him.

The death of his father affected him in several ways. Death became a reality to him in a way it had never been before. When, only a few years later, his sister Joan, nearest to him in age and affection, died at the age of twenty-six, he had to face that reality once again. "In the midst of life we are in death."

> When my youngest sister died . . . (he wrote) I was inconsolable. After my father's death, she had been a close companion, gay and vital. Suddenly, she was stricken. Within days she was dead. Before the funeral, I went into a village church to mourn, and be alone. A long time I sat there, deeply distressed. And then, quite suddenly and unemotionally, I saw that He was there, comforting and encouraging. There took place in that church in fact an encounter with the risen Lord which has often put me in mind of the experience of Mary Magdalene in the garden. I knew that my Redeemer lived, and because of that, that my sister lived.[4]

After his experience in the village church, Cuthbert realized that he had to return home and comfort the other members of the family. In attempting to do so, his sorrow was eased and he himself found comfort.

Then there was the relationship with his mother, always one of deep affection but now calling for an attitude of responsibility which he had had no occasion to exercise while his father was alive.

His father had a strength of character which could at times be somewhat dominating. He had a streak of obstinacy which had shown itself in his decision about Cuthbert's confirmation and about the subjects he was to study at Oxford. Had he continued to live as Cuthbert entered the twenties of his life, that very strength might have proved to be inhibiting and in some ways to have limited his freedom of development. Now Cuthbert was left on his own. There were other influences knocking at his door.

*   *   *

[4] *Him We Declare*, p. 74

A few months before his father died, Cuthbert had come into touch with a lively group of people whose activities at Oxford were creating a considerable stir. They were members of what later came to be called "The Oxford Group". (According to Garth Lean,[5] the name owes its origin to a sleeping-car attendant on a South African train who, seeking to put a name on the compartment occupied by six Oxford men pursuing the aims of Dr Frank Buchman, called it the Oxford Group. The press picked up the title and it stuck.)

Frank Buchman was born in 1878 in Pennsylvania, USA. His father was successively road builder, farmer, store merchant, hotel keeper, restaurant proprietor, and owner of a wine and liquor business. Against this unlikely background, Frank entered a Lutheran theological seminary, ambitious "to make the name of Buchman shine forth. By earnest toil and labour I can accomplish it." A visit to the Northfield Student Conference, where John R. Mott was in charge, "completely changed" his life, and he decided that winning people to Christ must be his main objective. In 1902 he was ordained, and parish work was followed by hospice work for young men who were away from home. This lasted for some years, but Buchman ran into difficulties and finally, on a matter of principle, he offered his resignation. It was accepted, and Buchman left, bitter and down at heart.

He sailed for Europe and, among other activities, attended the Keswick Convention, an annual gathering of evangelicals held in the Lake District. There, in a little stone-built chapel, at a small meeting conducted by a woman, he had an experience of Christ similar to that which John Wesley had, when, in a room in Aldersgate Street, he felt his heart "strangely warmed". The cross of Christ, which Buchman had so often discussed as a matter of doctrine and about which he had so often preached, became the focus of his life. "I was the centre of my own life. That big 'I' had to be crossed out." With great pain, but with a pain that brought him peace, he wrote letters of apology to those who he felt had wronged him and against whom he had borne strong feelings of resentment. A very different man returned to America.

After some hesitation, he accepted the post of YMCA secretary at Pennsylvania State College in 1909. It was a post of peculiar difficulty, and Buchman found himself confronted with much

[5] *Frank Buchman: A Life*, Constable 1985, p. 138

opposition, although the lives of some students were altered to the good. "But," he said later, looking back on his work, "the changes in their lives were not revolutionary enough to be permanent." It was at this juncture that he began to give one hour each day, between five and six in the morning, listening to God. As he thought over the names of the men in the college, he believed that during those quiet times God led him to approach particular students. Again and again, as he acted in obedience, he found that those students were in special need or were particularly ready for his ministration. A wide impact was made on the college during Buchman's seven years there, and he trained a great many students to engage in the kind of work that he was doing. Other colleges took note – a new form of evangelism was finding its way into many other campuses. Buchman was busy leading teams of men whom he had trained.

For some years he travelled the world, spreading his message, training and enlisting others, building teams of helpers. Oxford and Cambridge came within the orbit of his activities, and he came to love England. In 1922 he was given two rooms in Christ Church for a couple of weeks; on a later visit he stayed at University College. More and more he felt impelled to concentrate on Oxford. In 1928, during the long vacation, six Oxford men went to South Africa to spread the work. In the Universities his work was beginning to tell, and was becoming more and more a centre of controversy.

In Oxford itself and in wider circles of Church and society, the debate spread. What was this new-fangled movement from America? Who was this Buchman? What was all this talk about the four "absolutes" of honesty, purity, unselfishness and love? Of quiet times, of "guidance" and "checking your guidance"? And what did the groups do when they met? What was this talk about confessing one's sins, and was there a special interest in sexuality? Religion, hitherto rarely introduced into polite society, now became a subject of animated discussion, rather as it was to do years later when Billy Graham came on the scene.

Oxford was puzzled. Here was Canon L.W. Grensted, chaplain and fellow of University College and a University lecturer in psychology (later Nolloth Professor of the Philosophy of the Christian Religion), throwing in his lot with these people. Here was B.H. Streeter, New Testament scholar of distinction, later Provost of Queen's College, inscribing his Warburton Lectures to Frank Buchman. Here was Julian Thornton-Duesbery, later Master of St Peter's Hall, at first opposed to Buchman but later quietly and consistently upholding what he stood for.

On the wider front, here was Cosmo Gordon Lang, Archbishop of Canterbury, weighing things up and writing (in 1938) to congratulate Buchman "on the great work he has been able to achieve in bringing multitudes of human lives in all parts of the world under the transforming power of Christ". But here also was Herbert Hensley Henson, Bishop of Durham, keen of mind and master of the sharp phrase, admitting to an "almost physical repugnance" to the kind of movement he thought the Group to be. He devoted part of his Third Quadrennial Visitation charge to a sustained indictment of the Group and, abandoning his usual care for accuracy, compared Buchman's "dictatorship" in the movement to the dictatorship of Stalin.

What was Cuthbert to think about this movement, this centre of controversy in the University? Behind him, he had the immense advantage of a Christian home, the solid teaching, mainly from his father, of the Christian faith, a widening appreciation of Christian history and art and music. Moreover, as we have seen, he was president of the Student Christian Movement. But he was conscious of a lack which perhaps he could hardly define, a timidity of faith, a lack of reality in his relationship with God. It focused on a fear of ridicule, of unpopularity, of making a fool of himself. Two incidents, small in themselves, smote his conscience – his refusal to sign a notice about an SCM meeting while others were in sight, lest they should mock him for being a Christian; and the night at Henley when, sharing a bedroom with other oarsmen, he slipped into bed without openly saying his prayers.

It was at this juncture of his spiritual development that he came into touch with members of the Oxford Group. At first, he thought they had little to offer him – after all, was he not president of the SCM? Then a member of the Group, an American, Kenaston Twitchell, asked him to tea at his house. As he walked there, Cuthbert had a strange feeling that a decisive moment in his life was about to occur. As he talked with this young man, he realized that Twitchell had a personal courageous faith in Jesus which he himself lacked. With little or no emotion he knelt, and, in his own words, "gave as much as I saw of myself to as much as I saw of Jesus", prayed for forgiveness, and sought courage to bear his witness. Great joy followed. Religion came alive. Not only was his relationship with God changed, but so was his relationship with others. It was "the greatest single adventure" of his years at Oxford. He was deeply thankful, in later years, that that experience of God in Christ became his just before the shock of his father's death.

Cuthbert delights to add the story that, the day after this spiritual encounter, he met one of the men with whom he had shared that bedroom in Henley. "How are you, Bardsley?" "Fine. I want to apologize." "Whatever for?" "Well," said Cuthbert, "I let you down." And he told him the episode of the prayers said in bed. "That's very interesting", said his friend. "I had the same thought that night as well!" That brief conversation proved to be fruitful – the man lived to be a missionary.

For the rest of his time at Oxford, Cuthbert found himself caught up in a stream of what he called Christianity with a purpose. Bible studies under the direction of Canon Grensted, and meetings in the Randolph Hotel and the Town Hall fanned the flames of his newly discovered faith. Little did he dream at this stage that five years of his ministry would be given to the work of the Oxford Group. Meanwhile, partly through his recent experiences and partly through the impact made on him by the funeral of his father, he felt the call to ordination and responded to it. Westcott House, Cambridge, beckoned.

*   *   *

Cuthbert was fortunate in having as the Principal of his Theological College a man who probably influenced the Church of England more than any other teacher in this century. Certainly he influenced Cuthbert deeply. Bertram Keir Cunningham, known affectionately by his friends as "BK" or "The Professor", became Principal of Westcott House, Cambridge, in the spring of 1919. Owing to the war, he and his vice-Principal, H.E. Wynn (later Bishop of Ely), had only eight students at first but the number increased to over forty as men were demobbed. BK's aim for the House was clearly expressed in the first Embertide letter that he wrote:

I am most eager that this place should help the men to be, not indeed like one another nor like those on the staff, but to be each his own best self as God intended. I am anxious, too, that men ordained from this place, to whatever school of thought they may belong, should be above all else *real* in character and belief and worship. It is, as those of us who have been chaplains know well, the strong and wholesome demand of this generation. I hope, moreover, that we shall be able to have here the minimum of discipline imposed from without, together with a maximum suggested and worked out from within. For it is, I am convinced, by treating men as sons of God and English gentlemen that the best in them is called forth.[6]

So it was that Westcott House welcomed men from all strands of churchmanship within the Church of England, and the chapel worship reflected these differences. The Principal was deaf, very deaf. What might have been a fruitless trial BK made into a positive gain. His deafness gave him a certain detachment from life, and the little box which he carried about to aid his hearing could always be turned off when a boring speaker went on interminably. Not always did he realize that what he himself thought was a whisper was in fact heard by all. When Frank Buchman came to speak at Westcott, BK's question, "When is Mr Moral Uplift going to stop?" rang across the room.

BK's sense of humour was a joy to his students. Taking Matins one day, he began: "We praise thee, O God – Oh, no we don't, it's the *Benedicite* today." Cuthbert recalls oversleeping one morning and arriving unprepared to take the service in chapel. The psalm appointed was 136, whose twenty-six verses have as their refrain "For his mercy endureth for ever". After Cuthbert had said the refrain some ten times, BK interrupted: "I think his mercies have endured enough. Start again."

Cuthbert entered Westcott House in the Long Vacation Term 1930. Among the students there were a number of men who, like himself, were deeply under the influence of Buchman and his friends. The Movement first struck the College with full force in 1931. BK's biographer[7] tells how BK wrote in his diary:

[6] Quoted in *B.K. Cunningham, A Memoir*, by John R.H. Moorman, SCM 1947, pp. 96–7
[7] John R.H. Moorman, *op. cit.* pp. 161ff.

"This has proved to be quite the most wonderful term in my experience of thirty years." Then he went on to say that this was due to the fact that "six of our best men went through a deep spiritual experience in and through the 'Oxford Group House Party' which was held at Selwyn in the week preceding Term". Two of them early in the following term, described what they had been through and "the effect was electric, and for some days the situation was difficult and dangerous". In the following April BK himself attended a three-day house party at Selwyn, and was deeply impressed, not so much with the methods of the Groups as with their results. He wrote in the Ember Paper at Trinity 1932: "It is easy to criticise these 'Oxford Groups', but the fact remains that God is using them in many cases to his greater glory, and their watchwords 'surrender', 'sharing', 'guidance', 'witness', contribute a challenge to a more direct evangelistic effort on the part of the Catholic Church. Be critical if you must (and I, too, am a critic), but first of all understand and appreciate. We shall indeed be doubly condemned if, after the warning given in Methodism, we by our prejudices force another schism."

BK, wise man that he was, was at once appreciative and critical.

"My general impression is that in cases when a man has no background of corporate Christianity the position of a 'Group' convert is dangerous. On the other hand, when a man has such a background of Churchmanship, and just in proportion as it is strong and intelligent, nothing but good can result."

In that last sentence he may well have had Cuthbert in mind. BK gladly acknowledged that the movement was being used by God – they must not be frightened when they see him at work! But he saw the theological weakness of the movement and the dangers of over-emphasis on personal experience alone. Meanwhile, it was his task to hold together the unity of the College, a unity which the enthusiasm of its Oxford Group members sometimes threatened.

A contemporary of Cuthbert's at Westcott tells of how Cuthbert persuaded him to attend a house party of the Oxford Group at Selwyn College. Those who attended came strongly under its influence.

After this house party, as a group of six including Cuthbert, I am afraid we caused a division in Westcott House which caused much concern to BK as well as to other members including Forbes Horan (later, Bishop of Tewkesbury) and Ken Carey (later Bishop of Edinburgh). Some of us became very aggressive; but somehow Cuthbert, who was I think entirely under the influence of the Group at this time, and had a very great respect and admiration for Frank Buchman, always retained his loving spirit and gentleness.

What that loving spirit meant in the life of the College is hinted at in a personal record which has survived in the Principal's handwriting:

Long Vac. Term, 1931. An exceptionally happy term even for W.H., thanks, under God, to a very strong group of arrivals from Oxford, especially Sydney Linton, Ken Carey and Cuthbert Bardsley.

The main cohesive force at Westcott during these difficult years was the person of the Principal. Living in the closest contact with his students, he gave himself wholly to them; and his long talks with them, his down-to-earth spirituality, and his strong sense of humour did much to overcome any possible rifts.

The eighteen months spent in Cambridge were happy ones for Cuthbert. He rowed in the Westcott House eight which beat Ridley Hall. He took on two duties as one of the "officers of the Moot" (a quaint title given to the holders of various posts within the College): one connected with Toc H and one as almoner. He extended the circle of his friends, meeting men of other shades of churchmanship than that of his father, beginning to enter into the riches of Anglican thought and devotion. His Vice-Principal was John (Jock) O. Cobham (later Archdeacon of Durham); and among his contemporaries in addition to those already mentioned, were W. Launcelot S. Fleming (later Bishop of Norwich and Dean of Windsor), Joseph W. Poole (later Precentor of Coventry and a close colleague when Cuthbert was the Bishop), Graham R. Sansbury (later Bishop of Singapore and General Secretary of the British Council of Churches), Leslie E. Stradling (later Bishop of Johannesburg), and Geoffrey L. Tiarks (later Bishop of Maidstone).

He read theology, the subject he had wanted to take for his Oxford degree but from which he had been diverted at his father's wish. Just how much theology he read we do not know – as we have seen, the activities of the Group made demands on his time which perhaps should have been given to study, and home responsibilities conse-quent on his father's death no doubt made further demands on him. But Westcott gave him much, especially in the realm of the devotional life, the life of prayer and meditation and sacrament which he learned to regard as the very heart of Christian discipleship and ministry.

The months passed quickly. To what diocese should he go, and where should he be ordained?

III

ALL HALLOWS: THE OXFORD GROUPS

The Church and Congregation whom you must serve, is his spouse and his body.

The Book of Common Prayer
The Ordering of Priests

WESTCOTT HOUSE WELCOMED a steady stream of visitors, some of whom would lecture, some give an address at compline, some mix informally with the ordinands. Among those who came to the House during Cuthbert Bardsley's time there was a rotund, Pickwickian figure, only five foot five inches in stature, with large head and sensitive features, a bundle of humour and activity.

Philip Byard Clayton, known to everyone as Tubby, had come to the attention of Archbishop Randall Davidson – and of the world – as the man who had founded, and was the moving force in, Toc H. During the First World War, Poperinghe in Belgium had been the centre of his work among the troops, and the men loved him. The living of All Hallows on Tower Hill was in the gift of the Archbishop, and what better appointment could be made than to instal Tubby Clayton as vicar of this ancient church, with authority to pursue the work of Toc H and travel the world on its behalf? So it was that Tubby began his work there in 1926, and things began to hum. A lunch club for city workers, with lunches initially consumed in the church itself (to the raised eyebrows of conservative and less imaginative church members); a "soap-box" erected on Great Tower Hill, where the Christian case could be argued; the enlistment of a posse of curates and other colleagues (including a small cocker spaniel named Smuts, who went visiting with the Vicar and was described as "the best curate I ever had"); all these things put All Hallows on the map in a way it had not been for a very long time.

Cuthbert had a horror, as he once confessed, of becoming "a curate of a parish where I would spend my time having tea with old ladies". On Tubby's visit to Westcott Cuthbert approached him – would there be the possibility of a vacancy on his staff? "I was going to ask you if you would come", Tubby replied.

46

When Cuthbert joined him in 1932, little did either of them imagine that a few years later a second World War would take place, that the lovely church of All Hallows would be destroyed, and that in 1948 Her Majesty the Queen (now Queen Elizabeth the Queen Mother) would lay the foundation stone for the church to be rebuilt, bearing the inscription:

Ethelburga founded me in 675, Samuel Pepys rescued me from the Great Fire in 1666. 1940 the enemy wounded me, 1948 loving friends restored me.

Tubby was still in charge when the church was rededicated by the Bishop of London in the presence of Queen Elizabeth the Queen Mother on 23rd July 1957. Tubby died in December 1972.

Cuthbert was made deacon at Michaelmas 1932 and ordained priest a year later. His Bishop was Arthur Foley Winnington-Ingram, consecrated as Bishop of Stepney in 1897 and enthroned as Bishop of London in 1901 (his long London episcopate ended in 1939). Perhaps because the Bishop knew Tubby and his work well, he saw more of Cuthbert than he could do of others of his ordinands. On at least three occasions, young Cuthbert went to see his Bishop. On every occasion the Bishop bade him kneel and gave him his blessing. The place where he prayed in his study was lined with photographs. "These are my boys", said the Bishop. "When I see their photographs I can pray for them" – boys he had met in boys' clubs in the East End of London, men he had met in his travels around the world, men like Cuthbert himself whom he had ordained. Cuthbert learned his lesson – years later anyone entering his chapel at Coventry could see by his prayer-desk, on the floor, a large pile of photographs of his clergy, their wives and families. They helped him to remember them in his prayers. Winnington-Ingram may have delayed his resignation too long – it was said of him that he had every gift but the gift of resignation. He may have left his successor a hornet's nest of problems unsolved. But no one could deny that the man who ordained Cuthbert was not only a man of consummate charm and grace but also a man of God and a true shepherd of his flock.

The world which Cuthbert entered as deacon and priest was one of which he had known very little before. It was a world alienated from the Church. Tubby believed in visiting, and particularly in visiting two by two. Cuthbert and he would go out together and visit offices and warehouses, fish market and Port of London Authority. Cuthbert noticed that Tubby had a way of spotting the essential goodness in the people he met, and in drawing that goodness out. Thus, he would find a man whose gift was carpentry. "You are the very man I want. Would you make a crucifix for me?" – and the man found himself, very unexpectedly, involved in the life of the Church. Another thing that Cuthbert learned from Tubby was never to go visiting empty-handed, but always to take leaflets with him. They were good points of reference next time – "Did you read my leaflet?"

Then there was Tower Hill. It was the Hyde Park Corner of that part of London, a place in which Cuthbert and his colleagues spoke from an improvised (soap-box) pulpit, and learned how to deal with tough people and tough questions ("If God made the world, who made God, padre?"). Cuthbert dreaded this ordeal, at least at the start. It was a baptism of fire. But it proved to be an ideal preparation for the work he was later to do with men in the Forces.

Then there was the liturgical side of his work. Here again he learned much from Tubby, who gave great care to the preparation of services. No detail was too small for attention – though when it came to the point Tubby was totally unpredictable in the conduct of the service itself. Sunday services were well attended, though the City emptied itself at weekends. Tubby was well-known as a preacher, and Toc H supported the church. Lunch-hour services provided great opportunities for worship, for preaching, for contact with City workers.

Tubby needed little sleep. He even had two secretaries, one to work by day, and one by night. He expected the impossible of his curates – after all, he pointed out, our Lord promised rest only to those who travailed and were heavy laden! Some of Tubby's young men got to the point where they were too tired to love or to think, and one of them is recorded as saying: "Tubby, I would gladly die for you, but not after midnight". Cuthbert came near to breakdown.

But they were wonderful years, those two and a half years in the slump and depression of the early thirties, years of working with a team of at least four curates under the leadership of a man of extraordinary power and love. For the rest of his life Cuthbert looked back to that time with gratitude. His book *Bishop's Move*[1] was to be

---

[1] Mowbrays 1952

48

"dedicated with gratitude to the Rev. P.B. Clayton, C.H., M.C., who first taught me to love the Evangelical Catholic Faith".

*   *   *

In spite of his absorption as a curate in the work of All Hallows, Cuthbert was not forgetful of the ongoing activities of Frank Buchman and his colleagues and followers in the Oxford Group. Their influence on him at a critical period of his development at New College and his spiritual experience through them had been too deep for this ever to happen. Indeed, Tubby Clayton had given him a month off from his work in London to take part in a great campaign in Vancouver. This was followed by a house-party in Victoria, also organized by the Group. In a wider context and in a different continent, he was able to see at first hand that the Group had lost none of its vivacity since he came down from Oxford.

A conviction grew in him that his next period of service as a priest might well be spent as one of their full-time workers. He consulted the Bishop who had ordained him and in whose diocese he was working. Winnington-Ingram was not averse to the suggestion that Cuthbert might take a share in helping the members of the Group, many of them young and with little Church allegiance, to remain in the Church and not to form a "sect". "But", said the Bishop, "I urge you to do this as a curate at All Hallows, and with that church as your base." Tubby was no happier than the Bishop at the thought of Cuthbert leaving All Hallows after only two and a half years' work. Cuthbert refused the advice of his Bishop and disappointed his vicar by resigning his curacy, so strong was his conviction that this course of action, at this point of time, was right. He was launched on five years of intensive work under the banner of Frank Buchman.

A letter (undated but presumably late in 1934) to his friend Sydney Linton shows how Cuthbert's mind was working:

... At the moment my own vision is in the rather upsetting stage of *becoming* clarified along certain lines ...

A. 1. The machinery of the church *is* assuredly cumbrous.

2. The parochialism ... of the Church is deadening in its effects on priests.

3. The Church is, generally speaking, wholly failing to evangelize the masses . . .

He then touched on the possibility of communities of priests living together, but free to go out on missions conducted by bands of priests and laymen. He went on:

My own future:
1. Do not feel that I am called to essentially parochial work.
2. Feel that my job is evangelical, i.e. 1. prophet, 2. priest. But necessity for scope for 2.
3. Feel like you that a period with the Group team is very necessary – other vision will come later.
4. Only know at present that I stay at All Hallows till Christmas: after that blank, but I'm not worrying!
5. The vague possibility that a city church may be my more distant future – a city church with none of the All Hallows encumbrances.

In a further letter to Sydney Linton, written from his mother's home, undated but presumably about Christmas 1934, Cuthbert wrote:

At the moment I feel almost dazed – All Hallows a thing of the past: the new life of a roving Friar not yet here. But I look forward with eagerness to 1935; setting forth with the blessing of the Bishop of London and on his commission. When I went to see him, he was most interested in the venture and agreed most cordially that I should go. I am going to remain very near to him and consult him very frequently because thereon holds my churchmanship among a band of prophets. I had a 4-day retreat at Glasshampton, which is very glorious and received much instruction and counsel from Father William and from Geoffrey.

By late February 1935, he was already engaged in the work of the Group and wrote to Linton with his early impressions:

I am regarding myself as I would were I a missionary, evangelizing new tracts of country where as yet there were no churches. I am chaplain to these people in the sense that I am an ordained minister among a band of prophets and *slowly* already in a week since I joined *this* team, they are beginning to see me as this. But it must of necessity be a slow business.

As regards discipline, I am reading my offices, keeping my devotional times in the morning, making *spiritual* Communion twice a week and I hope to go to the Lutheran Communion service and to their High Mass whenever possible.

As yet during this week I have had no opportunity to celebrate and this is being a real *experience of the Cross* (I believe this to be true and not exaggerated). God will give us opportunities, I know. But at present, like Father William, I must be willing to enter in the (? world) offering of the Eucharist – spiritually I am finding this a very real and very wonderful experience.

We are fortunate in having from Cuthbert's own pen a review of a year's work. The year was 1935, the first year he spent wholly at work with the Group. He visited Norway, Denmark (twice), and Switzerland, as well as engaging in the activities of the Group at home and especially at Oxford. We shall let his review speak for itself, and in doing so, shall listen to the enthusiasm of a young man who saw in the Group the hope of a new society and a renewed Church. Note the military language – their work is a "campaign"; "an attack" is made on "three salients"; in Denmark "the Christian siege of a country was planned" . . . If we are inclined to be critical, we shall notice the emphasis on big names and important people, and shall be tempted to think that the writer over-simplified the issues with which he and his companions sought to deal. But through it all there breathes a zeal for the things of God, and a passion to share with others the new life which the writer had found at Oxford, which he had enjoyed in the rigours of his London curacy, and which he believed could and would transform not only individuals but nations.

Here, then, are brief extracts from his review:

A team of four hundred collected in Copenhagen from all parts of the world. This in itself is significant when one realizes that four hundred people are prepared to come at considerable expense and personal sacrifice to witness in a foreign country to what Christ has done for them. Certain things stand out from these early days. I look back to crowded meetings in Copenhagen. I recall a great house party held in two of the famous schools in Denmark attended by about two thousand people. I remember another great house party held over Whitsuntide at Marienlyst culminating in an unforgettable open air demonstration on Whitsunday afternoon in Hamlet's Castle at Elsinore attended by about twelve thousand people. One might summarize these early days by saying that it was a Spiritual Springtime in Denmark. From there we moved to Oxford.

In Oxford I saw in July the concentration of men and women from more than forty countries, thinking out together the answer for nations in the present world crisis.

I saw men come from all five continents to prepare and train in leadership for work in their countries in the months ahead. From New Zealand came people to prepare for work there. From Canada came a whole team to get a European picture of the situation. From Bulgaria came one who is spending six months with the teams, in preparation for leadership among the Balkans. . . .

The army of life-changing Christians that was forged in these four weeks in Oxford is now at work in more than fifty countries of the world. But it is such that it can be mobilized for decisive action at strategic centres where the world is looking for a solution, and is expecting the Church to give her answer now or never.

August was spent in a return visit to Denmark, where the Group had been from February to June. In these months the work had been carried through in Copenhagen and the islands. August was given to the capture of Jutland, the mainland of Denmark. . . .

In these campaigns, the huge public meetings are always followed up by personal contact between members of the team and townsfolk, in cafés, in hotels, and in their homes, so that accurate detailed personal work is always done. The city begins to take on a new appearance as everywhere, sitting, standing, walking, there are groups of two talking intently or listening in silence to the voice of God. . . .

There stands out from Denmark the memory of the spiritual hunger of a people. Wherever the teams went, great numbers came to the meetings; they said openly that they came to be changed; whenever there was a meeting in the churches, they were full, often long before the meeting began. But in the churches they listened with a still hungry silence, devouring every eord as if this was a message for which they had long waited, and had long been starved.

I have seen too in Denmark the strategy with which the Christian siege of a country was planned. The vision for the work was far beyond a wide scale revival; it was that of the emergence of a new national life; a national life that should be God-centred, God-controlled, God-driven. . . .

From Denmark we moved to Geneva. Our guidance to visit Geneva came some time ago, but we never knew how important it was to be. Over a hundred of the team, trained for action by the Denmark campaign, travelled together by a special train to Switzerland. On arrival we were greeted by a message from the President of the Swiss Confederation, who has given statesmanlike consideration to the work of the Oxford Group. Later, the Government in Berne received a team of sixty, who travelled over especially. Another week, seventy-five of us visited Berne for a meeting with the twenty-five picked leaders of the Parliamentary parties, in a committee room of the House of Parliament.

At the end of his review, Cuthbert asked: "What of the future?" This was his reply:

During the past twelve months I have been privileged to see the miracle of a nation reborn. But the significance of this lies not so much in the fact that small countries like Norway, Denmark and Switzerland can be given – through a national spiritual awakening – a new direction in their national life. Rather does it lie in the fact that if this can happen in these countries through the instrumentality of mobile teams of active Christians four hundred strong, there is no reason why teams of two to three thousand should not bring just such a needed reawakening through the Church to the larger countries of Europe. Many of the problems are identical, the time is ripe and people on all sides are crying out for just such a reawakening – not revival merely but something so intensive that we begin to see the reconstruction of national life.

Already widespread undermining work is being attempted in every part of England – I pray that what has begun to happen on a large scale in South Africa, Canada, Norway, Denmark and Switzerland may happen shortly in the larger countries of Europe.

Travel, meetings, house parties, interviews – so the work went on. In an article written for the *Church of England Newspaper*, Cuthbert gives an outline of "a typical day" during his time in Denmark, where he had made a particularly close friendship with the Dean of Copenhagen, Paul Brodersen:

> During the course of one day I was present at a luncheon for businessmen at which seventy of the most prominent businessmen in Copenhagen were present. One newspaper representative said afterwards that it was the most remarkable luncheon he had ever attended. Nearly all stayed till three o'clock, our host concluding the proceedings with a magnificent speech in which he described what he would do if he were Bishop of Copenhagen. O clergy, beware! That man's change is reverberating throughout the town, and he will soon be a force for Christ instead of a good layman taken for granted. During the afternoon I was present at a tea party given by an old aristocratic family at which were present many of the Danish nobility. Later I had supper with an ex-Communist bricklayer. I completed the day at a meeting given by a hundred employees of an electrical firm. A few days later we met the head of the firm, who was amazed at the change in some of his clerks.

In the same article, Cuthbert tells his readers that:

> Every morning we have a Team Meeting at which we hear stories of miracles which should be the normal life of the Church. Here are a few: The Editor of a great newspaper has made a decision to run his paper under guidance. God may well use that man to lead a national awakening. The owner of another great newspaper – who would certainly not have described himself as a churchman – sees in this message the answer to the problems of his country. A medical student has been changed whose father has been for many years the leading opponent of the orthodox church because he had seen it too full of cold dogma. I was present at a small dinner party a few evenings ago, at which one business director got three other business directors to meet the team; one of them had said when asked, "Oh, but it's not my line of country", to which our host had replied, "Well, anyway every well informed man ought to know about it". Before the evening was out they began to share. A

barrister described how he had been asked to take a part in a divorce case. Shortly before the hearing of the case, both parties in the case had been changed. The barrister was so gratified that he was willing to remit his fee. He himself is on the point of making a decision.

Cuthbert wonders:

> if the readers of the C.E.N. have really appreciated the significance of this work? Nearly three hundred men and women from thirteen countries have come at great expense and sacrifice to Copenhagen to witness for Christ. A whole town has been set ablaze by their coming. Lives have been changed; churches have been crowded; the papers have been treating the Christian Gospel as front page news for days; leadership has been created, the whole country has been shaken. Is not this something for which to be thankful? We hear news from Norway which simply sends one to one's knees in sheer gratitude.

In July 1936, he spoke at a great gathering of the Oxford Group at the Albert Hall in London. He told the audience of the time he had spent in Scandinavia seeing "the beginnings of the reconstruction of national life through changed lives". He told them of a vision he had had of 7,500 people going into the Albert Hall on crutches – "and I was one of them, a Christian cripple, leaning on things rather than on God". He told them how he was enabled to throw away his crutches. "One night in Oxford six years ago those barriers of pride, which I used to call reserve, came down, and I was honest about myself in the presence of another person. It was only then that I found the experience of the Cross – not as a vague dogma, but as a concrete fact, and with it came God's abundant forgiveness. It means being concrete. I did not believe, at that time, that God could guide me, but I made an experiment. I asked him to show me where I had to begin, and he showed me five concrete things which I had to do: I had to write a letter, I had to tell a friend that I had been a coward, I had to be honest with my family, I had to identify myself with the Oxford Group, and I had to be prepared to tell people that I had given my life to God." He challenged his audience to "surrender".

In 1938, he was still travelling with the Group, this time visiting the Mediterranean countries, to study their problems and to visit the

Groups of various nationalities. From England he went with Frank Buchman, through Holland to Bulgaria and to Greece, where at Athens they joined an Hellenic Cruise, "hard at work getting to know our fellow passengers: these included people like the Dean of Durham, Dean Inge, Mr H.V. Morton, the Bishop of Southwark, Sir Henry Lunn etc. . . . The whole boat was seething with interest by the end." On they went to Egypt where "many lives were changed". They met the Coptic Patriarch, the Greek Patriarch and the Anglican Bishop. Thence to Palestine – "an armoured car went before us, and an armoured car followed us" – Syria, and Trans-Jordan. To him the Oxford Group stood "as a beacon of hope". In Jerusalem he found an old Oxford friend, Julian Thornton-Duesbery, taking a prominent place in the "team which includes every kind of outlook, nationality and background". On the way home he stopped again in Greece, where he remained for six weeks "hard at work" in a little team of five "aiming at nothing less than national Renaissance".

From this distance, he looked at the country of his birth and at the British Empire. Writing to a friend, he asked:

What of the British Empire? I have been impressed once again by the vast ramifications of the Empire – the greatest Empire the world has ever seen. But frankly I am deeply concerned as to her future. We are not loved. We seem to govern on a basis of isolated aloof patronage: small English communities living in a country not their own tend to regard everybody as "foreigners". Our cold British pride needs to be broken: we need to be born again into a passionate faith in God out of which will come the salt of true inner discipline (badly needed in democratic countries), the fire of true patriotism, and the glow of a steady, unsentimental, constructive, life-changing love. We need to begin by admitting that at times we have been wrong.

He returned to England "grateful for this unique experience and more than ever convinced that we in the Oxford Group have within us the vital spark of national spiritual awakening. On us rests the awful but glorious responsibility of bringing that to pass in every country of the world."

*   *   *

The Group could scarcely have had a more devoted and enthusiastic ambassador than Cuthbert Bardsley. He had learned much from association with its founder and with its members. Their greatest gift, under God, had been the enkindling of his own faith.

> I owe an enormous amount to Frank Buchman – a very remarkable man, a prophet, but not a saint. It was through his friends that my religious life came alive . . . It was in a very poor way. Father died, my hero. I realized my religion was secondhand, it was not mine. God was remote, not accessible. Then through one man in the Oxford Group I was led to discover Christ as my personal friend and God and Lord.

For that experience he could never be thankful enough. It was to influence his whole future life and ministry.

Then there was the gift of fellowship with other like-minded Christians, friendship of a depth of which he had known little before. He learned the meaning of quiet waiting on God, of listening, of guidance, of "sharing" (a much used word) and "checking" his guidance with that of others.

Again, he learned much about how to help others to give their lives to Christ – the winning of their confidence, conviction of sin, the liberation which comes from confessing, the moment of surrender . . .

These were substantial gifts and he never underestimated them. Even after his break with the movement, we find him writing to "my dear Frank" (Buchman) in September 1940:

> Thank you so very much for your last letter which arrived some weeks ago . . . despite the fact that our paths have in the past six years lain somewhat apart, I do want you to know that I never cease to be grateful to you. You helped me to find the guidance of God as a living reality. I hope and believe that my life and work for God is still a credit to you. Life-changing is, as it has always been, of paramount importance to me. Only the week before last I saw God mightily at work in the lives of ninety clergy from the Rochester diocese – some glorious miracles were taking place in the Retreat-Conference in which I had the privilege of taking part. Tomorrow I am taking a Quiet Day for the leaders of the Church Missionary Society . . .

The friendship between the two men never ended.

*   *   *

F.A. Iremonger, in his biography of William Temple,[2] has a passage in which he tells us of the Archbishop's attitude to "the Buchmanite Movement". It is a passage of particular significance as we seek to understand the misgivings which began to assault Cuthbert, at first with no great strength but later with increasing vehemence. Temple, though he saw the limitations of the movement, found it possible to commend it.

> It did sometimes effect what it claimed to do, which was to change men's lives. But there were "dangers of a serious kind" to which its disciples were exposed, chiefly the ignoring by members of the admitted limitations and consequent supposition that the Groups can be substituted for the Church. That, of course, is bad, because the Groups make no provision for worship in the sense of adoration, and the activity of the Groups is almost confined to what members can personally accomplish – so that if there is no religious interest beyond what the Groups cater for, the social reference of the Gospel largely drops out. When I took that Mission in Oxford last year I came to the conclusion that the best folk in Oxford were those who had got into the Movement and had then got partially out again – not with any repudiation of it, but simply going on to a wider fellowship and outlook. For someone already active in the Church there would be no occasion to get out again because he would never be "in" in the sense of having no vital religion outside.

Those perceptive words were written in 1932. Cuthbert's own hesitations were to develop some seven years later. At first, the cloud was no larger than the size of a man's hand. Gradually it became bigger and darker as he thought more deeply about the Movement and its developments. Was he to be like those folk in Oxford who, in Temple's words, "had got into the Movement and had then got partially out again"? He pushed the idea from him – how could he "get out" of a Movement to which he owed so much? But the doubts

[2] O.U.P. 1948, pp. 489–90

persisted. They would not go away. He was assailed by a battery of questions: was there a danger, as Temple had seen, that "the Groups can be substituted for the Church"? Was the impression a real one, that to disobey the guidance of the Group was to disobey the guidance of the Holy Spirit? There certainly were disturbing instances of unwillingness to accept criticism and to attribute, somewhat arrogantly, any such criticism to moral failure on the part of the critic. Was Christ himself becoming less than central in the teaching and experience of members of the Group? Here was the very nub of the matter. Did Cuthbert recall how Augustine, many centuries before, in his search for truth, could not rest content with Cicero's *Hortensius* precisely because "the name of Christ was not there . . . and whatever lacked that name, no matter how learned and excellently written and true, could not win me wholly"?[3] And if Christ were less than central, where was the power whereby those standards of absolute honesty, purity, unselfishness and love might be attained?

The Oxford Group was becoming the Moral Rearmament Movement (MRA). Did this mean that the main thrust of the Movement would be on morality rather than on Jesus as Saviour and Lord? If this were so, would it not lose its cutting power, its challenge, its demand? Frank Buchman would have his followers take a leaf from the communist doctrine of infiltration rather than direct frontal attack. But was this right? And the new stress on processions, banners, flags, did this detract from the simplicity of the Gospel and of the truth as it is in Jesus?

As Hitler's grip on Europe threatened to grow rapidly stronger, Frank Buchman and other leaders of the Group were in America, the headquarters were in some disarray and, at the moment when some clear note of leadership was desperately needed, there was no voice, no clear rallying cry. At least that was the impression which many members of MRA gained – with consequent dismay.

As the questions persisted and the doubts increased, Cuthbert had to consider the possibility of a break with the Movement to which he owed so much, and with it the parting from friends with whom he had worked so closely. And if he did pull out from full-time service with the Group, where should he go and what should he do? One thing was clear: he would not leave England at this critical juncture of her history.

---

[3] *Confessions* Book III, iv

Two friends, Lewis J. Davey and his wife, who owed much of their spiritual development to Cuthbert's ministry and who were deeply committed to the work and thought of the Oxford Group, were themselves passing through a similar period of doubt and disillusionment at this time. Davey records:

In our quiet time we found ourselves thinking about Cuthbert, for we had not heard from him for some weeks. We felt concerned and prayed for him. A few days later a letter came from him, but with no address, asking us to meet him in London the following Sunday and not to tell anyone about this. We met in St James's Park on a raw, misty November day. Cuthbert looked drawn and tired and soon we knew why. He had come, full of anxiety on our behalf, to break the news – which he feared would cause us consternation – that he had left the Oxford Group, basically because Christ had ceased to be central to it. We stopped him and said, "We too have taken the same step and for the same reason, and we have been wondering how we could break the news to you." Then he told us how, in his Quiet Time a few days previously, he felt strongly that he must meet us . . . and tell us of his decision which had been very costly, and had brought in its train very determined pressure to make him change his mind.

One can understand the regret with which the leaders of the MRA viewed Cuthbert Bardsley's decision to leave the movement. Cuthbert was young, vigorous, attractive, a compelling speaker, in touch with "influential" people. He had given devoted service over a period of years. His departure would arouse much comment and lead, no doubt, to others following his example. The pressure to make him change his mind did not end with his taking up new work. It persisted even into the period of his work as Bishop of Coventry – to his distress and, it must be said, his annoyance.

This was a bleak period in Cuthbert's life. He was barely thirty-three. He decided to withdraw for a while, and chose the Community of the Resurrection at Mirfield for the place of his withdrawal. Saul of Tarsus, after his shattering experience on the Damascus road, had to withdraw to the deserts of Arabia to sort things out with the Lord who had called him so compellingly. Perhaps Cuthbert was looking for a like opportunity. At Mirfield he could not easily be "got at". There, in the daily rhythm of the Offices of the Church, he could quietly wait upon God and avail himself of the "ghostly counsel and advice" of priests more experienced than himself. He is a wise man who "retreats" before he advances to new work.

IV

ST MARY MAGDALENE, WOOLWICH

Feed my lambs . . . Tend my sheep

John 21:15,16

HIS YEARS WITH THE OXFORD GROUP and the brief period at Mirfield behind him, Cuthbert was at a loss to know where his next sphere of service should be. The early months of 1940 were part of the year of the "phoney war", that uneasy lull which gave opportunity for the rallying of our forces before Hitler's bombardment began. It was clear to Cuthbert that he could not leave Britain at its moment of peril for any work abroad. But where should he serve at home?

He was on holiday in Cornwall with his sister Dorothy when, out of the blue, came a letter from the Bishop of Southwark, Dr R.G. Parsons, asking him to consider becoming Rector of the parish church of St Mary Magdalene, Woolwich – it was in an unhappy condition, very few people attending the church, the vicarage temporarily uninhabitable. He went to see the parish. From North Woolwich, he "looked across the river. I thought one would never find anywhere closer to Dante's *Inferno* – factories, warehouses . . . eighteen thousand people . . . no curate." He was young and inexperienced. He accepted the Bishop's offer or, perhaps he would say, God's challenge.

He was joined by his sister, and so there began a period of thirty-two years in which they lived and worked together in close co-operation. He was often to speak of his indebtedness to her, through the weary years of war and its aftermath, and the constructive and exciting years at Croydon and Coventry. From a somewhat sheltered life, she came straight into the rough and tumble of a south London parish waiting for the opening of the German offensive. She never turned a hair. On one occasion, she and her brother were out in the street when an enemy plane was heard overhead. There was no shelter nearby, so they threw themselves flat on the pavement. The bomb fell uncomfortably close with an almighty crunch. Brother and sister stood up and looked at one another, glad to be alive. "Isn't it maddening," said Dorothy, "I've laddered my stocking!"

The church was a fine one, set in a lovely churchyard in the middle of a densely industrial area. The congregation numbered about eleven, "mostly old ladies", scattered over the big building. Cuthbert erected a large curtain five pews from the front – any who insisted on sitting behind it saw nothing at all. The obstinate soon learned their lesson. Slowly but surely the congregation grew, and the curtain moved further and further back. There was also a mission church, St Anne's, with one of the curates mostly in charge.

There were a few months of "phoney" peace between Cuthbert's institution in the spring and the beginning of the bombardment in September. By that time Norway, France, Belgium and Holland were under the Nazi heel. Dunkirk had given only a brief breathing space. Then came the Battle of Britain. The Germans wanted to get the Arsenal. On 7th September there was a tremendous raid. A pall of smoke rose into the sky. Cuthbert, who was visiting people in Greenwich, wondered whether his church and home had gone. Two hours' interlude and the bombs started to fall again, and they continued to rain down day and night. There were shelters under the Town Hall, under the station and elsewhere, and there the people went until the All Clear sounded. Cuthbert saw these shelters as providing a great opportunity for his work – he had a captive congregation. There he worked, in and out among the people, ministering to them, heartening them, bringing hope and comfort. Many were killed. Many were called up to join the Forces. Many mothers and children were evacuated. But many remained, and to them Cuthbert gave himself by day and night, in the streets and homes, among the rubble and in the shelters.

In spite of blackout and bombs, the congregation increased to some two or three hundred every Sunday night. Occasionally, because of the bombing, they would have to crowd into the crypt chapel, standing or sitting on the floor. It was always open – a haven of peace and power and, it was hoped, of safety. There was never a dull moment. Cuthbert learned many lessons during those months and years; among the most important was the necessity of getting into industry. He realized that it was no good waiting for the workers to come to him or to his church. He must go to them.

"Industrial Mission", as we have come to know it, was in its infancy in the early 1940s. At Swynnerton, in Staffordshire, "Ted" Wickham (later Bishop of Middleton) was Chaplain of the Royal Ordnance Factory 1941–44, before going to be Diocesan Missioner to Industry in the diocese of Sheffield, a post which he creatively held from 1944 to 1959. To Bishop Leslie Hunter and to Ted Wickham much of the credit for this industrial work must go. But not all of the work was being done in the North. In the diocese of Southwark and in the parish of Woolwich, in addition to the Woolwich Arsenal were Siemens' works with twelve thousand employees, all of them doing work of vital importance to the nation in the sphere of electrical engineering. With the Bishop of Woolwich (L.H. Lang) and others, Cuthbert determined to see what could be done in their own area – and on an ecumenical basis. So Industrial Mission began in Woolwich Arsenal.

About this time, Cuthbert had to pay a visit to his doctor. In the course of conversation he told him what had happened in the Arsenal, whereupon the doctor said: "Why don't you do the same thing at Siemens where I visit?" "Because I have not been invited." The doctor said: "I will have a word with the directors." Very soon afterwards the Managing Director rang Cuthbert up and invited him to lunch. Now let him continue the story:

When I arrived I prayed outside the main entrance that God would open the way; by the end of lunch with all the directors I had received an invitation to become Industrial Chaplain. Having expressed my gratitude I said that I could not begin my ministry without the consent and full support of the Trades Union leaders. Immediately I was taken to a room where the six Trades Union men were meeting. The chairman asked me to explain my plans. I said that I hoped to do what every Service chaplain did – to be available to visit the sick; to keep the men in touch with their families when they, the men, were at work during the air raids; to mediate in cases of misunderstanding between employers and employees; and possibly to conduct short lunch-hour services. The chairman, after consultation with his colleagues, agreed that I be introduced to the men. The vice-chairman, who was a Roman Catholic, said: "Realizing that you are coming as a Christian and not primarily as a Church of England parson, I will introduce you to all the foremen which will take some weeks." At this point another

T.U. committee member said: "Padre, you must make yourself known to as many workmen in this factory as soon as possible; otherwise the sight of a parson in the factory will arouse suspicion. I advise you to introduce yourself tomorrow to all the men eating in the work's canteen during the lunch break." After a somewhat sleepless night, I arrived at the canteen, an enormous building holding upwards of a thousand men and women. The noise was deafening and clearly there was only one thing to do. I stood on a chair and shouted one word: "Silence." There was a deathly hush! I told them who I was, and that I had been invited to come to the factory as chaplain by the directors and T.U. leaders – and I outlined what I hoped to do. They received my words in silence and then burst into applause. I knew then that I was "home and dry".

So started a chaplaincy which lasted till I left Woolwich and was later continued by my successors for seventeen years till the factory closed down.

Every Wednesday I set aside for a visit to the factory. A room was provided for me to talk with any who wanted to speak to me about some problem. A large room was made available for two lunch-hour services at 12.30 and 1.15. These were well attended. In those dangerous days, men's hearts turned to God; they sought to discover a working faith for their life.

Gradually Cuthbert became part of the furniture of the factory. Men brought their problems to him. He visited many of their homes, and helped to unravel domestic problems. He became a member of the Absentee committee.

Remarkable stories could be told of his work in the factory. For instance, a leading Communist agitator, who regarded Cuthbert with great suspicion, would not speak to him or respond to his work. Cuthbert bided his time. One day the man approached him shyly: "Padre, my little boy is gravely ill. My wife and I wondered if you would come and visit him in our home." Cuthbert went and ministered to the boy and his family. Before long the man had moved towards the Christian faith. On another occasion, as the result of a bomb falling on the factory, a young man had lost a leg. Cuthbert visited him and the family in hospital, and helped the lad to overcome his distress and to adjust to life. So the work went on, a work of quiet pastoral concern which slowly made its impact on the whole factory.

No doubt, the lessons learned there were to stand Cuthbert in good stead when, as Provost of Southwark, he had much to do with the initiation of the South London Industrial Mission, and, later, with his work with industry in Croydon and in Coventry.

*   *   *

The main service of the week in the parish church was the Sunday 9 o'clock Eucharist, which was followed by breakfast in the nearby school. This, together with the Monday night team training meeting for prayer and forward planning, was the power centre of the work. A family relationship grew up in a community where differences of age, background and intellect ceased to matter. From that fellowship emerged a group of lay people who were prepared to knock on doors and "bring the Church to the people". Drama, too, was important, and Cuthbert himself wrote the play, *A Sword shall Pierce*, which was performed not only in Woolwich but also, later, in Southwark Cathedral and elsewhere.

Patrick Ashe, who was to assist Cuthbert Bardsley with his work among the Forces and, later, in some of his Missions, was one of the curates at Woolwich during Cuthbert's time as Rector. He has described what it was like to be under his guidance:

> Cuthbert had been a member of the Oxford Group Movement, and I also had been greatly helped by its insistence on the daily Quiet Time, the use of a notebook, the four absolute standards of honesty, purity, unselfishness and love, and the readiness to "share" with one another. On this basis, we saw many lives changed. Each morning we met for prayer and sharing. . . .
>
> Cuthbert's preaching was always challenging, his presentation simple and clear, easy to follow, and easy to remember . . . He would read through one of my prepared sermons, a jumble of ideas, and in a few strokes produce a simple pattern into which the ideas fitted. He took a lot of trouble in teaching us how to present the Gospel in sermons, and how to help a person surrender their lives to Jesus Christ. He was a highly experienced and successful spiritual midwife bringing people to rebirth.
>
> Those who made the decision, and wanted to go further in the Christian life, used to meet together on Monday evenings in the Rectory Room. It was there that I learned the meaning of team-

68

work, and how to train people in the Christian life. Everyone used a notebook in their daily prayer time. At a fellowship meeting when someone started preaching sermonettes, which were not allowed, Cuthbert would say gently, "Let's just hear what you have in your notebook".

One of Cuthbert's often repeated phrases was "Expect great things from God", and there is no doubt that great things happened. He took infinite trouble in preparing all the "Special Services" even if only a handful of people were expected to come. We had them at every possible opportunity, and they were always beautifully printed out. There were Civic Services, Dedication Services, Candle and Carol Services, and each time the numbers grew. His enthusiasm was infectious, and one got caught up in it.

Another expression of his was "Think big". To him life is big. One sees something of that in his paintings – mountains are higher, trees are larger, houses taller. He sees things larger than life, and somehow passes that vision on. He made you feel important, because he thought you were important. He made everyone feel they were the one person in the world he wanted to talk to. Sometimes I knew he had an engagement in a few minutes, but he would go on as if he had all the time in the world . . .

Another "feature" of the life at St Mary's was the plays put on in church. It was surprising what talent was to be found amongst those who had started worshipping there. One play that Cuthbert wrote was *Victim Victorious*, which had a tremendous impact on those who saw it.

Those days in the "blitz" were like the Acts of the Apostles – lives changed, a constant series of little miracles – days full of sadness, yet full of fun and laughter that no amount of bombing could destroy.

1941 was one of the grimmest years of the war. Two documents help us to gain an impression of what life was like in South London, and of the kind of ministry which Cuthbert exercised. In the first, we have an account from a young woman which shows his sensitivity to God's guidance – we can watch him at work. The second is a letter which he sent to bereaved parishioners.

Kathleen Bristow (now Mrs Gibson) was almost twenty-one when the incident occurred of which she tells:

During the relentless bombing of Woolwich it had been the custom of my family to go with several friends to spend the night hours in the Public Air Raid Shelter specially constructed underneath the Town Hall. This provided good comfortable bunk-beds, First Aid Room and adequate facilities of all kinds which made life just "bearable" for many.

My father was working in the Royal Arsenal and I was commuting daily to London to the Admiralty. Neither of us knew our time of arrival home each night, so we were grateful to have friends who would take my mother with them to the Shelter. We would come home, change into "shelter gear" and then join my mother as soon as we could.

In March 1941 my father had been unwell and we two had stayed at home in our own Anderson shelter for several nights. But as the bombing increased in violence and my father was getting better, he insisted that I joined Mother in the Public Shelter on the night of 19th March and he stayed at home.

That night there was a merciless bombing attack when land-mines were dropped all over the town and we knew that one was fairly close. After the All Clear in the early hours of the morning of 20th March I was leaving the Shelter with a friend to find out whether my father was all right. At the precise moment that we reached the front door of the Town Hall, Cuthbert arrived with his Curate and Churchwarden to meet me. They had been out all night (as was their wont) visiting the Shelters, comforting the distressed and dying etc., and had returned to the Rectory exhausted and hoping to have some rest when Cuthbert suddenly had a most vivid "message": "Go to the Bristows'." He knew that our road had been badly hit and he remembered that we normally went to the Town Hall Shelter – so he "obeyed" and came in search of us . . . and met me face to face at the door!

He then took over and gently guided me back to my home warning me that things were not good. When we arrived we found a scene of utter horror – practically half of the road had been flattened and our house was just about holding up but highly dangerous. After exhaustive enquiries of police, wardens etc., there was no news of my father. But I was taken back to be with Mother, and Cuthbert and his colleagues took over and pursued enquiries. After many police visits etc., the Chief Warden ordered his men to pull our house down brick by brick until they found my father – which they did eventually after many harrowing hours of waiting – dead, of course.

You can imagine what Cuthbert meant to us then! My mother and I literally had nothing left except the shelter gear we had on. It was a devastating experience and without Cuthbert's help I don't know how we should have survived. We never ceased to be grateful for the loving care of both Dorothy and Cuthbert.

Here is Cuthbert's letter to the bereaved:

My dear friends,

During this year sorrow has come your way. I am writing to you as one friend to another, as a friend who has known a great deal of sorrow in his life and who, therefore, can speak with understanding.

The more that sorrow comes into one's life, the more value does one place upon Easter. Easter stands like a ray of light in a dark world. Easter reminds us that at least one Person has been through death and returned to show us that death is not the end of everything, but really the beginning of a new kind of life, freed from the sin and tragedy of this world. At this season of Easter the trees are coming out, the flowers are budding and the whole world is shouting to us, if we can only hear, that

> Spring is risen, is risen again,
> Love is risen, is risen again,
> And Love is Lord of all.

This springtime reminds us that the world is not just a mockery, that we don't just appear for a few years, only to pass into nothingness. Somebody once said very beautifully "this life is for the making of friendships, the next life is for enjoying them". Our bodies may die, but that "I", the eternal "I", which is really me, lives on. They killed the body of Jesus on a gibbet, but they did not kill His "I". In fact He said to the penitent thief on the cross: "Today shalt thou be with me in paradise". We do not know much about the next life, but if our loved ones are in the closer presence of Jesus, then surely that is all we need to know.

You will ask perhaps whether we are able to get in touch with our loved ones who have gone forward into that life. Yes, I believe from time to time we are granted in a very real way the sense of their presence with us. But this is only granted to us occasionally and must not be sought. Let us remember that though we are not able to see them, we are, nevertheless, like a huge orchestra playing the Symphony of Life; some are playing in this world and some in the next, but we are all united under the baton of the Divine Conductor.

Jesus is the link between this life and the next life. He stands on the threshold of death to welcome those who go forward through the narrow doorway into the next room of God's house. The more closely we live in His presence, the closer we shall be to our loved ones.

Easter comes to us this year, more than ever, with a note of victory, assurance and hope. Try to get to at least one of the services on Easter Day, particularly His own divinely instituted service of Holy Communion. If you would care to make a little act of remembrance and rededication, I suggest that you buy a lily in memory of him or her who has passed over, and that you bring or send it to the vestry during Saturday, Easter Eve. At 6 p.m. that evening, Easter Eve, there will be a short Devotional Service in preparation for Easter Day, during which I shall talk on the subject "The Communion of Saints" or "Fellowship with our Loved Ones".

May you be led forward, through Easter into a deeper experience of fellowship with your family on the other side, because of a deeper experience of fellowship with Him, who is the Master of the household and the Father of the family – Jesus Christ.

Your affectionate Friend and Rector,
Cuthbert Bardsley

Another of Cuthbert's curates, Michael Meredith, writes of his insistence on mission, not maintenance, as the chief purpose of the Church.

This was still the day of large Sunday night cinema queues. There was one regularly just opposite St Mary's Church. With the constant thought in mind of "outreach", summer Sunday evenings after evensong found Cuthbert leading us all, congregation, choir and clergy, out on to a convenient space to hold a short open-air service of witness. Standing on a chair, Cuthbert would give a short address which could be heard by all in the queue.

. . . Another of his early projects was to establish a soldiers' club, canteen and social centre in a large house . . . which became available next to the Rectory . . . Another project was the establishing of the Weathercock Club for men which met . . . every Saturday night, with a varied programme of discussions, talks, music, recreation, slide shows.

Cuthbert produced a regular weekly article for the local paper, and gave several series in the BBC "Lift Up Your Hearts" programme at 7.55 a.m. His voice was becoming known beyond the bounds of Woolwich.

Parish magazines can make boring reading. Many of them went up in flames during the bombings by the Nazis, which was perhaps no great loss. Two bound volumes of *The Parish Magazine of St Mary with St Anne's Mission Woolwich* have survived. Surprisingly, they are full of interest; indeed, they are difficult to put down. They reflect the tragedies of the war years – some of the burial lists are long. But they are full of humour – the courage and the laughter of the men and women of South London shine through. Large parts of these issues of the magazine are contributed by lay men and women, and are by no means confined to parochial affairs. Clearly, the man at the helm of the parish had his eyes looking out over Europe: with the aftermath of the Versailles Treaty in mind, as early as January 1941 he pleaded for generosity when peace terms had to be concluded with the Germans.

From the pages of the magazines one can trace the growth of the Church in Woolwich – "we have increasingly become a family. Now we must aim to become a team". (That language would be understood by followers of the Arsenal football team.) There are "upwards of fifty people learning about prayer, and praying for three-quarters of an hour every Saturday night". There are letters and articles in plenty from the Rector and his colleagues, full of teaching about the Church (including a long one from Cuthbert on the value of sacramental confession).

During the last two years I have stressed the vital importance of a Gospel of personal salvation which Christ brings to every individual ... But the message ... is not only personal; it is corporate and social ... new conditions of labour ... the right kind of education ... old inequalities must go ... the old profit motive must disappear ...

The magazines give glimpses of the Rector at work: "The Rector has again broken his record from the Rectory to the church – this time on a bicycle. 'That's the Rector, that was'." A touch of humour brings a point home: "West End clubs are full of old bores who sit in armchairs and snooze. The West End of most churches is full of old bores who sit in pews and snooze." Cuthbert's love of alliteration finds full scope: here is his five-point programme – "Awake: Alert: Arise: Atone: Attack" (the substance of a BBC broadcast in July 1941). His Passion play draws over two thousand people to the church in May 1942. Things are moving in Woolwich.

Sometimes things moved so rapidly that Cuthbert's diary could not keep pace with them, and disasters were only narrowly averted. The following story from Sir Thomas Harley comes from Cuthbert's days at Southwark Cathedral, but might equally well have occurred during the Woolwich period. On his return to Streatham one Saturday night from a short break in the Cotswolds, Cuthbert's sister Dorothy

confronted him with that day's newspaper announcement of Sunday's London Services. These showed Cuthbert as down to preach at St Paul's next morning and (apparently at the same time) at All Souls Langham Place. Dorothy was in a great state of perturbation but Cuthbert calmly enquired at what time the respective two services were to begin.

"Yes", said he, "I see St Paul's is at 10.30 while the other at Langham Place starts at eleven. That's all right; I think I'll be able to do it!" Well, all was still not quite right. It was Dorothy's custom to lay out on the hall table two suitcases (somewhat alike); one contained Cuthbert's off-duty grey flannel trousers, shirt and shoes, the other contained his vestments. It seems that Cuthbert in his hurry next morning seized one of the cases and proceeded to St Paul's to be ready for the service at 10.30. Getting there at 10.20, he was indulging in a friendly conversation with the Dean when his Verger reminded him that they should be robing. With that, Cuthbert snapped open his suitcase only to discover his grey flannel bags and, to the acute embarrassment of his Dean looking on, remarked: "Deans are frequently accused of being forgetful, but it would seem that perhaps Provosts are apt to be even more so!" However, the Verger promptly rose to the occasion by enquiring "Oxford or Cambridge?" To which Cuthbert replied "Oxford" and was at once adorned with his appropriate hood and surplice. "Can I borrow these?", he enquired. "You see, I'm due to preach at Langham Place later on this morning and I will have to leave here directly I've delivered my sermon."

He did so, and mercifully, as he related to me, "the green lights along Oxford Street were all in my favour, and I just got to Langham Place as the last verse of the hymn preceding the sermon was being sung; so I was just in time to make it"!

*   *   *

The summons to Southwark came at a time when the blitz was particularly severe.

"It grieves me bitterly to be leaving you at such a time", he wrote in July 1944. "I console myself with the thought that I am going to a neighbourhood just as vulnerable as Woolwich, perhaps more so." He pointed his people to "a Friend and Saviour who has been through all the suffering that you are going through. He has 'inside information'. He knows, he cares, he understands, he cures by carrying the load with you."

In August, Dorothy Bardsley wrote to the parishioners: "Thanks to you my stay of four years in Woolwich has been one of the happiest periods of my life." Cuthbert echoed her words.

His time at Woolwich was short – a brief four years. The desperate state of the church when first he became its Rector, and the strains and demands of the blitz, the shortage of clerical help, all meant that he had had to concentrate his energies on his work in South London. That was wholly right. But he could not be totally immersed in his parish – that would have been impossible after those years when he had roamed the world. One Sunday, he shared with his congregation the vision of a new venture which had come to him on a visit to North Devon. He had seen a large country house set in ample acres overlooking the sea; what might be made of that? It was the beginning of Lee Abbey. Of that, too, we shall hear more later on.

Cuthbert left behind him a strong congregation – people who, under his example and teaching, had at least begun to grasp the absolute priority of worship, of prayer (the "quiet time" of the Groups could never be forgotten) and of witness to one's faith. And the parties – he enjoyed those times of relaxation and fun – were riotous! No wonder that he and his three curates were locally known as "the Bardsley circus".

V

SOUTHWARK CATHEDRAL

Our eyes fixed on Jesus . . . who, for the sake of the joy that lay ahead of him, endured the cross.

Hebrews 12:12

MOST VISITORS TO LONDON who want to see its main sights make straight for Westminster Abbey or St Paul's Cathedral. Many end their visit without being aware that on the South Bank of the river Thames, at the southern end of London Bridge, there stands another cathedral. It is smaller than the Abbey or St Paul's, and its setting is less imposing than either of theirs. Its title speaks of its modesty – it is the Collegiate and Cathedral Church of St Saviour and St Mary *Overie*, the latter word hinting that, if you want to find it, you will have to look *"over the water"* from the great City of London. But if you do, you will find a treasure. The church nestles comfortably among a variety of buildings, close to the water. It is a real "incarnational" church by the look of it. It says to any who would listen: this is precisely where you will find God, Emmanuel, God with us, among the hurly burly and the smells of trade and industry.

If you are interested in the great figures of the past, you will find the remains of the Bishop of Winchester's palace nearby. He had a status comparable to that of the prince bishops of Europe. Here lie the remains of Lancelot Andrewes, bishop, theologian, preacher, writer, courtier, man of prayer. If you are interested in literature, you are right in the environs of Shakespeare and his Globe Theatre, and of Dickens, too. If you are interested in industry, here are warehouses and docks aplenty. Even today, with most of the old buildings pulled down or in process of demolition, your eyes and, yes, your nose will tell you that you are in the midst of a hive of activity. Here is real life.

It was to this Cathedral Church of the Diocese of Southwark that the Bishop, Bertram F. Simpson, invited Cuthbert Bardsley to come as its Provost. (The title is given to the head of a cathedral chapter when that (new) cathedral is also a parish church. His duties correspond to those of the Dean of an ancient cathedral.) The summons came in 1944, when Cuthbert had been at Woolwich only some three and a half years. How could he leave his people while the war was still on and the bombs were still falling? But the inter-regnum at the Cathedral had been long – their previous Provost (F.D.V. Narborough) had left almost three years before, and the need for strong leadership at the mother church of the diocese was imperative. Cuthbert could do no other than accept the Bishop's invitation. He was "instituted and installed" on 5th August 1944, aged thirty-seven. The condition of the Cathedral at that time could scarcely have been worse – it was an act of courage to undertake the task.

We have seen that Cuthbert was a man of prayer. He had noticed how our Lord worked through a small group of followers, and how he commissioned them to operate in twos. Immediately on arrival at the Cathedral, he began to pray for the right colleague. He soon found him. Walking down Oxford Street one day, Cuthbert ran into a man whom he had known in his days at All Hallows by the Tower, Colin Cuttell, who had recently returned from mission work in Canada. "What are you doing here?", Cuthbert asked. "I am back in England and looking for work", replied Cuttell. "You are the answer to my prayer. Come and work with me at Southwark Cathedral." He came, and a very fruitful partnership followed. Cuttell became Priest Vicar of the Cathedral in 1945, and Industrial Missioner of the diocese in 1948, a post which he filled with great energy and distinction until 1963. He was the motive power behind the South London Industrial Mission (SLIM) and became its senior chaplain.

Most of the rest of this chapter shall be given to Colin Cuttell's own story of Cuthbert's coming to Southwark Cathedral and of his work there. We are fortunate in having the story straight from the lips, as it were, of a close colleague, though written modestly in the third person.

*   *   *

When Cuthbert came to Southwark Cathedral in the gloom-drenched autumn of 1944, leaving behind him the warm fellowship of Woolwich parish church which he had transformed, it would be fair to say that, humanly speaking, everything was against him. Things were going badly across the Straits of Dover. In London, rockets had been added to flying bombs as a further test of morale on the home front.

People were still being killed daily on our streets or in their beds. All honour to a faithful remnant which had maintained the daily round of worship through the years of endurance. Unlike St Peter's, the old parochial centre, St Saviour's had survived the bombing but had lost all its windows; the board substitutes rattled an accompaniment in high winds to the detriment of worship within. Assorted litter from the fruit and vegetable market eddied and settled about the Cathedral steps, into the nooks and crannies of the desolate churchyard with its forlorn plane trees and anaemic scrub grass. To the north, the begrimed warehouses of the Dickensian riverside served to emphasize the extent and depth of the gulf separating the Church from the world of work. The prevailing odour in the vestry on the north side was not of incense but of cheese – to that extent, Church and World were one. To the south, it was impossible to ignore the rumbling railway viaduct, for without glass there was no insulation against sound at service time. As one Canadian soldier on leave remarked: "If you liked railways, Southwark Cathedral was the right place to come on Sundays".

A preliminary "recce" had convinced Cuthbert of two facts of life at London Bridge foot: he must learn to live with noise and airborne dirt: and in the matter of dirt, the Southwark of 1944 claimed to have the heaviest tonnage of soot per acre of any London borough. Secondly, a bridge must be built between the church and the surrounding wharves and businesses which supplied the daytime commuting parishioners. There was something reassuring about that sturdy Bishop Fox tower standing foursquare above the smoke and mist following a night of alarms. But did it mean anything more to the average worker than a bit of ancient history – beautiful, yes, but irrelevant? If five per cent of the working population of riverside London had home ties with any church at that time, we were doing well.

The Bishop, Bertram Simpson, was a realist. It was precisely for this reason that he had called Cuthbert to a cure at the very hub of the diocese. Dr Simpson said:

There is very little animosity towards the Church on the part of the Trades Unions: but only a sense of living in a different world. The plain responsibility of the clergy was to go to them in their place of work. On the other hand there was a growing realization among the thinking half that our need for bread, our need for one another and our need for God were interdependent. More than that, not a few folk untouched by Christian ministry were ready to admit that the crisis of our age was a spiritual crisis: Christian values must somehow get a firm footing in our economic life and that would mean a new pastoral strategy and a new kind of outreach; out from the pulpit and pew to the market place and factory.

It was because Cuthbert agreed wholeheartedly with the Bishop's understanding of "mission" that he moved from St Mary's, Woolwich, to St Saviour's Cathedral and Collegiate Church by London Bridge while the war was still raging in Europe; and he declared his position in the first number of his new outreach magazine *Over the Bridge*. We were called to be bridge-builders.

> The Church has an immense part to play in the life of the nation. The greatest danger is that the Church should be exclusive, narrow, "cliquey", parochial . . . Far too many of us clergy are content to minister to an ever-declining number of the faithful, while the masses remain unchurched.

Cuthbert stood firmly with Gilbert Shaw of Soho in his definition of Evangelism as the activity of making known the Gospel, in the course of which the Evangelist is cheekily challenging the whole world order of "money, things, man, God (if time)" to make it read: "God, man, things, money". "What will make our message cogent is the sincerity of our living and our own spiritual conviction", said Shaw. Cuthbert carried that conviction. And it was as a direct consequence of this conviction on the part of Bishop and Provost that Colin Cuttell was called to initiate an auxiliary ministry and, wrote Cuthbert in his first Provost's Newsletter,

> . . . he has begun to move around amongst the offices in the district, getting to know people and making friends. I have been going when time permitted . . . As a result of these visits, a fellowship of men now meets every Tuesday in the Cathedral and numbers are growing.

Out of such personal relationships grew closer contact with the railway workers, the telephone engineers, the local wharves, the hop merchants, the Borough Market, the big brewery and the smaller engineering firms. It was to be the genesis of SLIM (the South London Industrial Mission) which was officially launched in December 1952 by the Bishop of Southwark, some five years after Cuthbert's departure: but he had provided a fertile soil.

Meanwhile, there was no adequate office base. When the need was known, the chairman of a large wharfing business offered the Provost the top floor of a partly-blitzed building, the seventh floor of which, though minus its glass, was at least waterproof. When the time came, they were not lacking willing volunteers to wash down the walls, clear away the broken glass and reglaze the windows. Another local businessman covered the cost of furniture. Cuthbert, Colin, Renée Copsey and (later) Kay Islip the secretary moved in. Meanwhile Colin was wearing out shoe leather distributing some one thousand hand-bills giving information about midday services and meetings. Cuthbert's Thursday addresses attracted congregations of rarely fewer than two hundred; speakers of the standing of Dr Donald Soper, Lord Elton and Dr Max Warren ventilated the issues of a grey postwar Britain. As for music, well of course there was a great musical tradition already established under Maddy Richardson and E.T. Cook, and they had attracted many famous names to Southwark: Vaughan Williams, Kathleen Ferrier, Eric Greene, Elsie Sudaby, Albert Sammons ... *hoc genus omne*. There was the memorable "moment musicale" on a grey drizzly Saturday in February 1946, when the queue for Handel's *Messiah* stretched across London Bridge as far as Fishmongers' Hall on the City side. Kathleen Ferrier was at her sublime best – no less Isobel Baillie, the lofty Gothic nave enhancing the beauty of two rare voices. And of course there were the great Diocesan occasions when it was "standing room only", with Cuthbert always the warmly-welcoming, vital host. It should also be remembered that the new Provost had inherited a lively parish centre at St Michael's on Lant Street, which was still much as Dickens knew it. The church was served by the devoted and greatly-loved Peter Hand. Later, that redoubtable scholar priest (later Canon) Donald Bradley came from Purley to join the staff, and together with Victor McClaughny, Chaplain of Guy's Hospital, completed a singularly happy ship. This "household of faith" was mothered by faithful Winnie Spicer at 85 Mint Street, a former lodging house which, although it had escaped direct bombing, was known to let in water at inconvenient points. Cuthbert would often join the inmates at meal times. Food was of the simplest but laughter unrationed.

Hitler's robot bombings (the V1 and the V2) went on well into 1945, and the new office eyrie on the seventh floor of Empire Building was rocked more than once by high explosive (H.E.) detonations. In late 1944 one V2 killed many people on the Borough High Street and rocked the top of the office premises. Cuthbert was already a veteran of the heavy raids on Woolwich when he was Rector and seemed unaware of the big bangs of this final Nazi attempt to break our morale. Shelters were not for him: he took his share of the fire-watching at the Cathedral, which meant an all-night vigil and "sleeping rough"; these all-night watches went on until the spring of 1945. The new Provost was also a familiar figure on the platforms of the deep tube tunnels of the Northern Line, where hundreds of Borough people were still spending their nights in odoriferous propinquity – without benefit of sanitation.

What was the Provost like to work with? Well now, *difficult* – but in a charming way. You gave up trying to keep pace with Cuthbert. Physically, he did everything on the run; and he drove in the blackout like a Jehu, as members of the Metropolitan Police, kindly fellows, had occasion to note. Spiritually, you had to be very wide awake to follow. Flaming ideas – he was always burning up with them and, as in chess, invariably two or three moves ahead. And there were times when the patience of the somewhat conservative and non-resident elderly Chapter was stretched to the limit.

Cuthbert kept the Woolwich link. He had established lunch-hour services in the deep shelter of Siemens Brothers, the vast engineering works five miles down river, as early as 1941, and he had been asked to keep them going. Thus, every Wednesday, he and Colin would take the train to Woolwich, and share both the Siemens services and pastoralia. As Colin acknowledged again and again, to watch Cuthbert at work was an object lesson in pastoral concern; more than one of his privileged colleagues faced the plain, unvarnished truth that they could never take his place. For one thing, it seemed to his heterogeneous *ad hoc* parishioners of the factory that he prayed as if God Almighty was present and heard and cared.

In the weeks before Christmas, December 1944, Cuthbert and Colin had teamed up for a visitation of some hundreds of offices in the London Bridge area, carrying with them an attractive Christmas card.

On all sides, the warmth of the welcome was palpable. And there was an extra visitation at Siemens with its eight thousand employees, including two packed lunch-hour carol services in the deep shelter chapel, for which there was a welcome respite from the V2s, though one had dropped (mercifully) on the perimeter in October; and (wait for it!) the salvaged parts carried the unmistakable imprint of a Siemens (Germany) product! In the Cathedral itself, chilly as it was, Christmas Eve drew a congregation of some two hundred and fifty people; while on Christmas Day the service was broadcast to our Forces overseas. It brought many letters of appreciation from as far away as India, not least of the boy choristers and of Howard Reed the soloist, with his memorable "O Little Town" . . .

Cuthbert's particular concern was that the church should offer sanctuary to "the weary, frayed and overworked". And he was constantly exercised over the question of "What kind of Church will meet and greet our men home from foreign fields of battle? Will they find God's life there? Or shall we 'mouth the same phrases', preach the same lifeless words to our returning soldiers? It is possible for a parish to have any number of organizations on the books but few Christians in them . . . We must be a welcoming family."

Cuthbert's "manifesto" is encapsulated in *Over the Bridge*, April 1945. That magazine was already finding its way into hundreds of offices in the workaday world; to the commuting parishioners of St Saviour's weekday ministry.

The prophetic Cuthbert wrote at Easter 1945:

> . . . Out from the ruins of Rotterdam, Warsaw, London and Berlin will march the real Christians – the men and women who in the dust and tragedy of collapse have kept close to the crucified Christ, have been identified with the sorrowing Love of God and who have been available amid the ruins to bring comfort and healing to the war-weary, sick at heart and dying . . . their symbol the empty cross, their text the words of the Risen Christ: Behold I go before you into Galilee – they will follow him into the Galilee of the new world and in his strength build anew. They will build homes where Jesus is the Unseen Guest; build industries where man is not just a cog in the machine but an immortal soul, and profits are subordinated to man's welfare; build again civic life in which the Will of God is fearlessly sought. For such Christians the horror and the hate will

be seen as the inevitable judgement upon men's insensate folly as they become "other Christs", binding up wounds and pouring in the oil of love.

With the sound and fury of the last great drive against the foe still raging, Cuthbert staged his own Eastertide drama *A Sword Shall Pierce* in the Cathedral. The Editor of *The Bible for Today* was there. He wrote:

> I came with an open mind, more fearful than critical lest everything should not be quite right; yet hoping for the work's sake that this daring effort should succeed; I was not disappointed. The acting and the settings, the music and lighting, were so good that I could hardly believe it was an amateur production. In the vast body of the church, throughout the whole performance, there was a breathless silence. The Provost had taken the liberty of making the very pillars and pews, the choir and mediaeval screen, the rails and the sculptured figures – everything belonging to this ancient house of the Lord – contribute to the Proclamation. A bold step, but it was worth it.

The Cathedral was packed to the doors night after night. Only one other person present would have taken any particular note of the Flying Officer in air force blue. This Canadian airman went away deeply moved, to join his squadron for a night mission over Hamburg – from which he did not return.

In June this came from the Provost's pen. He would return to the theme again and again.

> Peace has come. Will it last? We must learn from our mistakes from 1918 onwards. Grasping sectionalism; the impatience which expected "Jerusalem" to be built in six months; apathy on the part of those who might have built but didn't, who preferred comfort to responsibility; blatant materialism which ignored the things of the spirit – such was the face of our new enemy. We should remember the evils of Buchenwald, when the lid was lifted on unregenerate human nature. Equally we should remember the valiant offering of those who gave their lives that these things should not happen again. Peace will depend on the right use of memory.

It all served to intensify Cuthbert's overriding determination to create a Christian family at the centre of the Diocese. Her Majesty the Queen's visit for the Shakespeare Commemoration Service, to honour the Bard on his birthday, seemed to set a seal upon the Provost's vision of that New Jerusalem coming down out of Heaven from God: to transfigure the mean streets of Southwark. Thus he wrote:

> The Church's main task is the re-creation of people – caring, loving, responsible men and women whose reverence for God issues in a reverence for their fellows. As the Hebrew prophets foresaw, religion and social righteousness are closely inter-related. Those churchmen of the last century who divorced soul from body and made no protest when people were housed in slums, underfed, underpaid and overworked, had laid the foundations of the present alienation.

Cuthbert's arrival took on the nature and spirit of a crusade. "Unite to put right the postwar world" was spelt out on flamboyant posters hanging from the Cathedral railings. A Church Missionary Society speaker at a lunchtime service took the words out of Cuthbert's mouth when he said:

> Christians of 1945 are called to be the shock-troops of humanity; with a Faith that will be getting them *into* trouble not out of it.

VE Day did not catch the Borough napping. It knew how to celebrate. The parishes of St Michael's and St Peter's (bombed in October 1940) were still thickly populated and were under the pastoral wing of the Cathedral clergy. These inner city parishes had suffered as much as any in the bombing, and so many of the folk now *en fête* had suffered personal loss: the Guildford Street disaster, with its scores of casualties, was fresh in their memories of the blitz. There were many gaps where had been houses – and in those gaps already flowered many-coloured long-forgotten "weeds" giving bright promise of resurrection; promise of a new quality of life. Meanwhile in the back streets of Southwark in June 1945, the sun smiled down upon street parties which went on far into the night. There were flags and bunting, bonfires and fireworks, not forgetting an astonishing abundance of food conjured out of the meagre rations of parishioners along Union Street, Park Street, Lant Street and Redcross Way. Drama was not lacking. A Mrs French, straight out of George Belcher's *Punch*, stood in a Union Street shopping queue, when up came Mrs Wiggs all breathless like. Says she, "Oh Mrs French, I don't want to frighten you, dearie, but I just seen a man climbing through your winder." Mrs French went like the wind; well – as fast as avoirdupois permitted. It was Papa French, lately POW in a German Stalag, freed by the Americans, and home, sweet home! Cuthbert never forgot that he had taken on a parish church-cathedral, and despite the demands of reconstruction at the centre, he was a welcome visitor in the old houses, flats and less salubrious tenements of St Saviour's parish. On VE Day he was part of the Victory jubilation of those warm-hearted folk; having got to love them, they loved him back, for he had no side though he knew how to cut an impressive figure when vested for a Sunday Eucharistic procession.

Provost Bardsley was thinking about his second Lent in Southwark as he looked down from the seventh floor of Empire Building, upon the scurrying multitudes in London Bridge station yard. The emergent message is as simple and direct as ever. He had never claimed to be either a New Testament scholar or a theologian – it was the contagion of his enthusiasm for God and the "paschal fire" that went with it that commanded attention.

In Lent we do not merely throw off a coat of worldliness which during the winter we have acquired, but we put on the coat of Godliness . . . by concentrating on Jesus – and as we do, we shall find God and be found of him . . . And the 9.15 is just coming into London Bridge.

As was said of Chaucer's "povre persoun",
. . . *Cristes lore, and his apostles twelve*
He taughte and first he folwed it himselve.
In so doing, our Cuthbert would be found in complete accord with that Neo-Platonist Dean Inge:

We must believe the explorers of the high places of the unseen world when they tell us that they have been there – and found what they sought.

Not such strange bedfellows after all; for Cuthbert, too, saw Man as he is in history; and God in Christ, our Redeemer. All his emphatic preaching hung upon that axis; too emphatic for some.

St Saviour's other great tradition, the boys' camps, was revived in August 1945, when living standards were still those of wartime Britain, and every commodity including bread was rationed. In August some fifty boys and their leaders were away to Dorset, the guests of Mr R.C. Sherriff, the playwright. The group included Cathedral choristers and those of Westminster Abbey's wartime choir. Among the half dozen guests was a Polish boy, who at twelve years of age had fought at the defence of Warsaw and been wounded. Cuthbert lent a car which made possible the camp supply line – and he was a welcome visitor, making one of his earliest water-colours of Thorncombe Beacon, for he had just taken up painting as a hobby.

A few weeks later he was leading a hectic autumn programme which began with a hundred-strong pilgrimage to Canterbury. In those postwar years the link with Guy's Hospital was very close; Provost and clergy were in conference that autumn with medical students and nurses on "the spiritual factor in healing". It was conceded that Fear is the greatest obstacle to wholeness: the most frequent factor in a variety of breakdowns, physical as well as mental. Cuthbert continued to practise the laying-on of hands with anointing, and set up a prayer group in support of this ministry.

The Cathedral laity were also rallying to the urgent call for help from relief organizations fully engaged in Europe, where hordes of refugees were in imminent danger of starvation. Eye-witnesses said that the coming winter would bring certain death to thousands of German children if nothing were done. The Provost responded with all the force of his personality; indeed, it began to look as if the laity would need a new eight-day week to keep pace with this pied piper who never took "no" for an answer. At the same time, he was pleading for more "Crusaders": "Men and women who have learned from Jesus to put 'Give' before 'Get', to take some part in the immense social reform waiting to be done . . . a crusading family going out from the altar of Communion to capture the pagan world for Christ." He saw signs that Britain was already slipping back into a comfortable rut. "Christ does not ask for our support; He demands our obedience. To this end we Christians should always be in training; the words 'athletic' and 'ascetic' had the same root." Almost all of the Provost's preaching and writing in those early postwar years at Southwark could be summarized thus. And one of the most significant pointers in the renewal going on at the centre was the growing number of people slipping into the Cathedral between seven and nine in the morning, to be quiet before the beginning of the working day.

Cuthbert had again raised an insistent question in the summer of 1946: "Are Christian forces strong enough to resist those subversive forces which are already undercutting attempts to rebuild the nation's life upon Christian foundations?" Alexis Carrel, the scientist and Nobel prize-winner, expressed the dilemma of our times when he declared that the supremacy of matter and dogmatic materialism were destroying a Christian-based culture more surely than war. A moral dimension was almost completely ignored in contemporary society. It was significant, noted the American Walter Lippman, that the only serious challenge to the Totalitarian State had come from men of deep religious faith. Such was the climate in which the Church worked towards a revival in its own bit of the vineyard, in sprawling South London.

There was some personal anxiety at this time. Cuthbert's sister Dorothy, the pivot of a stable home life, was only just turning the corner in a prolonged illness, in the course of which her life was despaired of. The practical ability to "turn to" in the kitchen was not among Cuthbert's many gifts, but friends rallied to the house on Streatham Common, and made sure that his ministry and health did not suffer.

In May, Shakespeare's birthday was celebrated in a great service in the Bard's own church (St Saviour's is a stone's throw from the site of the Globe Theatre). Among the participants were Robert Donat, Irene Vanbrugh and Flora Robson. But it was the singing of South-wark school children that made the day.

Another "sight for sore eyes", remarked Cuthbert, was the 1946 rally for men of the diocese. The procession, led by three spirited bands, stretched from the old "Elephant and Castle" right to the doors of the Cathedral, where they were welcomed by Provost and Chapter. "Never held up traffic for the likes of this before", said a traffic cop. And the moral support of thousands lining the route was a clear indication that ordinary folk wanted to see the Church active, militant and generally at action stations.

In the same month, July, his Cathedral Scouts were entertaining thirty-five boys from Holland, sleeping them on the floor of the Chapter House and introducing them to real food after five years of privation. Several of these young Dutchmen had fought in the Resistance Movement. There was a return visit later in the year, when the Southwark boys gave a concert of English folk songs in Eindhoven, sang at the Court of Queen Wilhelmina in Appeldoorn, and led the very first remembrance service at the Arnhem War Cemetery. Parachutes still dangled from trees, and the adjoining fields were strewn with wrecked gliders of the Airborne Regiment. It was the first visit of a British choir since the cessation of hostilities. There were not many dry eyes.

It is August 1946, and Cuthbert is again calling his people back to the priority of prayer – that is, if "peace" is to be anything more than a brief respite from armed conflict. In all his forward-looking plans for the Cathedral, we have already seen that the prophet in him was acutely conscious of a Europe facing its last chance. "We must set our own house in order while there is time", is a recurring theme: "this Island's only ultimate defence lay in those moral and spiritual values which we were in peril of losing for ever." He found himself in accord with Victor Gollancz, who in the same month had pointed mankind's choice in his book *Our Threatened Values*. In effect Gollancz was saying that the ethical principles which the Greeks had announced, the Christians developed, the Humanists endorsed and the "plain man" had borrowed from all those sources, were being rapidly lost. It was this deep awareness of a "Day of the Lord" that brought Cuthbert to his knees; and his flock with him. He was constantly taking them back to Evelyn Underhill and her view of prayer as "a long intercourse with God". Thus, one of the earliest ventures was a fellowship of prayer which met weekly in the Harvard Chapel. But of course it didn't stop there.

This was the year of the official report *Towards the Conversion of England*. Donald Bradley, who had joined the Bardsley team at the outset, concentrated his scholarly mind on the philosophical and historical issues which that report could not grapple with in detail: and he contributed some fine editorials on the impasse in Europe to *Over the Bridge*. In November 1946, Donald was writing in the shadow of Remembrancetide. As we prayed for the fallen, he reminded us, we were paying tribute to much more than their gallantry. There was also the beauty and dignity of their manhood as God's creatures. Not to do so would be to dishonour God. The fallen were being restored through Christ to a condition even more wonderful than that which they originally enjoyed. Truly, they were *of* the Church though not visibly *in* the Church. Donald went on to take issue with the Report in seeming to dismiss "Humanism" with such scant qualification:

> Modern science has encouraged man to think of himself as little more than an animal; the tonic of *true* humanism might assist the bestial groveller to recover his posture, proper to him as a human being.

The end product of this view of man had led men of science to lend themselves to sordid experiments revealed at the Nuremberg trials. Many who gave their lives so generously in the late war may not have recognized that their humanity had been grafted into Christ by his death; but their deeds proclaimed them his. Cuthbert endorsed every word, and then carried Donald's thesis to its logical fulfilment in the New Testament when he wrote in the same issue:

> The Church family exists primarily to worship God. All worship involves obedience and service. For worship will be mere words unless we love both God *and* his children (1 John 3:18).

And that for Cuthbert meant commitment to a kind of bridge-building which brought him to see "industrial mission" (so called), not as a specialist ministry for a few who couldn't fit into the normal parochial pattern, but as an essential part of the Church's mission; an area of outreach where priest and layman must work together in double harness. Well, there were already close links with the business community in St Saviour's parish, notably in the adjoining historic borough market, along the riverside wharves, in the great Barclays Brewery, at London Bridge Station, in the Provision and Hop Exchanges and in the Fire Service. In the south transept there is one moving token of this bond, a fine example of the monumental mason's art. In the height of the London blitz, a Southwark fireman saw three of his comrades die beside him. (Nearly three hundred and fifty firemen of sub-area 37 on Southwark Bridge Road were killed or seriously injured.) There and then he made a vow that he would use his skill as a sculptor to raise a memorial worthy of them – and so he did. And the Chief Regional Fire Officer, Mr (later Sir) F.W. Delve unveiled it in the presence of a great company of National Fire Service men. A sad postscript is the fact that ten years later, a tidy architect, on instructions from a tidier Chapter, mutilated this marble memorial to "greater love".

Out of such human contacts, five years after Cuthbert's departure, would arise that lay venture in Christian witness, the South London Industrial Mission – SLIM for short. It must go on record for posterity that without his early invasions of the Siemens factory, it might never have been. Underlying the venture was his fervent conviction that without the apostolate of the laity, the Church of England was doomed to languish in sacred islands of piety. He wrote:

> The priest must stop thinking of the average layman as pew-fodder; the layman must stop thinking of his vicar as the harassed director of a religious organization mainly concerned with home and family. As Tubby Clayton of Toc H reminds us, the initial impact of the first-century Church upon a pagan society was that of a *lay* movement of utterly committed working men.

Early in 1947 Cuthbert's hopes for a year of consolidation were rudely disturbed by a letter from the Archbishop of Canterbury – not so much an invitation as a command to undertake a pastoral visitation of troops under BAOR (British Army of the Rhine) auspices. *Not* the best time for Provost or Cathedral.

Of the Germany of 1947, Victor Gollancz had written, one detractor said, hysterically:

> If English people could know the truth about postwar Germany and see for themselves the widespread misery and want, they would rise up and with a single voice demand immediate action of the Government . . . the present muddle is preparing the country for anarchy and another war which would finally cure our island of its insular spirit by engulfing us.

Of a class of forty-one in one Ruhr school, twenty-one children had had nothing to eat till lunch – a single bowl of soup per child. The prospect filled Cuthbert's sensitive soul with horror, and he did not accede to Geoffrey Cantuar's peremptory request without much heart-searching, though the schoolmaster Primate was used to having his way, charm notwithstanding. Providentially, the Provost was able to win a postponement; which meant his being able to see the Lent programme through to its conclusion.

The principal item on the spring agenda was the Methodist-sponsored Christian Commando Campaign, in which Provost and Cathedral team were deeply involved. Said Cuthbert after the dust had settled:

It is easy to criticize but I believe that the last ten days have seen a solid advance for the Kingdom in this area.

There were meetings of dockers, postmen, engineers, firemen, railway and office staffs, mostly in the lunch hour, in workshop, canteen and office premises.

Many were asking: was the Commando Campaign, Methodist inspired and led, worth the effort? Cuthbert thought so. For one thing, it was a clear witness to the healing of some old wounds, since the supporting speakers, more often than not, were Anglicans. And Cuthbert himself took the initiative in Southwark. It was a preaching of Christ in the market place, the offices and factories and canteens. At Question Time there was little criticism of the Christian way, though plenty of the Church – as it appeared to the outsider. "Why couldn't we be more like Christ?" was an over-simplification of the great alienation of the twentieth century, but the question veiled a genuine *cri de coeur*. And there was general agreement that standards were slipping so fast as to threaten the very survival of Western civilization. Questions came thick and fast. A minority of speakers used the language of nineteenth-century street-corner evangelism: Why, it was asked, had so little time and money been spent on the *training* of the lay commandos to utter in a contemporary idiom? But sincerity and a sense of humour often won the day. There was the commando who was all but silenced in the market. One intransigent hearer wished the speaker in hell. He replied in a rapid-fire retort, "And I wish you in heaven"!

Cuthbert summarized the campaign thus:

The secularization of Britain goes deep. I see the way of advance in a closer partnership between all clergy, ministers and congrega-

93

tions; for there are certain things which can only be tackled effectively by a united body of Christians. I visualize cells of Christian laity cutting across denominational divides, praying and training together in a common concern for people in need beyond the bounds of the local Church.

He quoted Captain B.H. Liddell Hart, the military commentator, when he wrote:

As a student of war, I have come to see that world peace depends upon a new moral order. The division of the Church into "churches" is a hindrance to a common moral order.

Inter-church co-operation of this sort and at this depth was still something of a daring innovation, a novelty.

A few weeks later, in June 1947, Provost Bardsley was writing his first impressions from occupied Germany. In his extended visit to the British Zone, part of his mandate from the Archbishop was to seek out first-class candidates for the ministry:

The faces of the people reflect malnutrition, more obvious in the town than country. Nerves are edgy, fuel scarce and T.B. rampant. Shops are almost empty. There is quite incredible selfishness and a flourishing Black Market. No German appears to take any responsibility for any other German. The problem of refugees is acute. Over two million were uprooted overnight from East Prussia – one suitcase per person! Thousands of bodies still not recovered from the ruins of Hamburg, and some 50,000 are still living in cellars and underground shelters. In another town 13,000 out of 20,000 inhabitants were killed in half an hour. Our padres are doing a magnificent job. All of them agree that sending every (National Service) recruit out here for his first period of training is an utterly mistaken policy, and the effect upon the morale of our future British citizens may well be disastrous.

In the course of the three-month visit, Cuthbert visited thirty-three regiments, made many broadcasts on the Forces network, took part in several Anglo-German discussion groups, conducted a four-day course on Christian Leadership, and drove nearly seven thousand miles. But he found the German people full of self-pity, expecting everything to be done for them. How he squared this verdict with the speed of their remarkable rehabilitation is difficult to understand, for within ten years, cities like Hamburg and those of the Ruhr had risen from the ashes and were well on the road to prosperity. He thought that BAOR should stay long enough to forestall "another Hitler waiting in the wings"; nevertheless, Britain should step up relief supplies of food and clothing for "a hungry body makes a disturbed mind". We had been granted a breathing space to help build a better Germany. For all Europe it was a race between the givers and the getters, he said.

With the searing experience of the grim consequences of Nazi totalitarianism fresh in his mind, and conscious of the looming threat from its communist counterpart, equally ruthless in its way, Cuthbert had come to this typically forceful, sweeping conclusion:

At this most dangerous moment in history, it is the duty of all Christians, at all costs (even persecution), to stand firmly for the free development of the human personality. We must watch jealously all threatening violations of freedom. The Battle of Britain is over; the Battle for Freedom is only just beginning.

The Provost's remarks on the threat to freedom did not go unchallenged in print by those who saw the Church of England as the Tory Party at prayer. "Will he not forsake generalities, half-truths and innuendoes and get down to particulars", wrote one local pillar of the Labour Party. It must be said that public debate was not Provost Bardsley's *forte*. The storm blew over. But to be fair, the "attack" (if attack it was) was not directed against any government whether Left or Right. And Professor C.E.M. Joad (of all people) rallied to the Church's support.

To be sure, he had awakened among his Southwark flock a new concern for the kind of values that would shape "our battered, bewildered, postwar society", and in particular made them aware of the evil forces pitted against the builders of postwar Germany. There already, "in the misery of famine and ideological discontent if not downright despair, were the seeds of a third world war". That autumn the Chapter House was crowded for an encounter with a party of German students, led by the Rev. Michael Meredith, lately chaplain at Kiel and one-time curate under Cuthbert at Woolwich. A profound impression was made by a former Luftwaffe pilot and Nazi youth leader, still carrying the marks of battle – an empty sleeve and scarred face – as he spoke about his conversion.

The German assignment had drained Cuthbert to the dregs – he was always going flat-out anyway – though it was plain to all concerned that he possessed just the right qualities for the task, and the evident success of his mission was not lost upon Geoffrey Fisher, Archbishop of Canterbury, who had been looking around for an emissary, an *episcopal* visitor to the Forces. Upon the first approach to the Provost of Southwark, he (the Provost) felt obliged to register a firm "No"; he had by no means finished his job at the Cathedral, he wrote; and there the matter rested – or so he thought. But Geoffrey Cantuar had always been more accustomed to directives than negatives; not for nothing was he known in private as "the headmaster". The Archbishop waited awhile but soon returned to the attack. At that point, six months later, Cuthbert gave a qualified assent – that he should see the year 1947 out at Southwark. The autumn programme was in full spate when the news broke.

Never a dull moment. Queen Mary was investigating the Cathedral and environs in depth on a day visit late in September; and wanting to see everything *comme d'habitude*. The church was twice filled for Harvest Thanksgiving in early October; once for the worshipping community, and again for the world of industry and commerce – the wharfingers and dockers, the Tooley Street provision traders, the hop merchants of the Borough, the electricity and telephone engineers, not forgetting the delegates from a large number of small businesses within the Cathedral's day-time parish. In addition, the banks, the insurance offices, the railway terminus and the post office all had their appointed delegates. It was the culmination of many months of visiting in the business community – and at the cost of much shoe leather. In mid-October the matchless voice of Kathleen Ferrier was heard again in *The Dream of Gerontius*. Then at the end of the month the Cathedral was filled by Diocesan Youth; and yet again for the South London Church Fund. In short, you could say of St Saviour's that there was always something going on, always people in the building during the day and often well into the night, with every kind of human need.

All in all, it hardly seemed the time for the chief minister to be moving on. But he did. Cuthbert was consecrated Suffragan Bishop of Croydon on All Saints' Day 1947, and wrote in his last Provost's Letter (January 1948):

In three short years a bond of friendship has been built which I hope nothing will destroy; just because we are human, we depend much on friendship . . . As you meditate within the Cathedral upon the enduring greatness of the Church, the comings and goings of Provosts count for little – your loyalty was not for me but to Almighty God.

All very well, but many followed Cuthbert about on account of his personal magnetism and charm; many came up the line from Woolwich, his old parish, because they still needed that inner security of which he had been the catalyst in a highly insecure world, for he had an ability to make you think you were the only person who mattered in a moment of encounter. "Certain lewd fellows of the baser sort" called it "blah" – certainly he was, first and last, an Etonian, with all the urbanity and *savoir faire* belonging to the breed. And certainly he was ambitious, albeit ambition sanctified by a deep love of the Lord and a genuine caring for ordinary folk. Years after leaving Southwark, he had been known to break a journey between London railway stations to call at some tenement block – just to keep an old pastoral bond intact. Yet he was a meteor, and like a meteor, a rare flash of light and warmth in the somewhat stuffy ecclesiastical firmament which prefers what Fred Hoyle has called "the steady state". For Cuthbert "like a comet burn'd" – and Southwark got a brief passing glimpse of one who by temperament was forever "splashing at a ten-league canvas with brushes of camel's hair". Such a soul needed an outsize setting, a stage larger than life. Thus, Southwark was always, to change the metaphor, a staging post – and we all knew it.

The editor of *Over the Bridge*, Colin Cuttell, attempted an evaluation of Provost Bardsley's three years at Southwark, from which the following appreciation is taken:

In the late autumn of 1944, flying bombs were giving place to rockets and this more terroristic weapon began to weave, with increasing tempo, its scientifically-conceived pattern of destruc-

97

tion upon an already hard-hit city. CKNB, veteran of the London blitz, hardly gave them a passing thought as he concentrated with feverish intensity upon the new work. At the close of the first year it was evident to all there could be TNT in ideas as well as bombs. For ideas came pouring out of Cuthbert's fertile mind in a manner calculated to disturb and budge even the sworn advocates of Anglican *status quo*. We the members of the team could be both breathless and cross in our attempts to keep up; to read his mind; to anticipate the next *fait accompli* with a mixture of charity and admiration, rather in the mood of "theirs not to reason why".

Soon the farthest parts of the Diocese registered a quickening of the pulse, catching the infection of the new Provost's enthusiasm, for nothing succeeds like dramatized success. And one of the tokens of a tide taken at the flood was the revival of Drama on a grandiose scale (was this not Shakespeare's church? he reminded us).

Behind all his lavish outpouring of creative energy, we did not fail to sense his overriding ambition to create a family of God, a magnet for the unchurched. Thus, the Sunday evening service grew remarkably. Through this particular channel he brought to bear his personal gift of warm, compassionate caring for the individual. The first dark November Sundays left an indelible memory; a score or so of people gathered in the gloomy windowless nave against a background of detonating V2 warheads, the sound of the siren's wail and falling glass. The signs and portents were, to say the least, unpropitious; yet before the winter was over, those twenty worshippers had swelled to two hundred. And then one remembered how, going back a hundred years or more, this very nave had stood open to the elements, a roofless ruin hired out to a keeper of pigs and hens, the lovely retro-choir a bakery. This postwar resurrection could scarcely be less than "the Lord's doing: and marvellous in our eyes".

There was the inevitable price tag; the times when CKNB suddenly looked much older than his years; the times when this ministry seemed to be getting on top of him. His gifts were personal rather than administrative, and he did not relish the steady round of committees which threaten to drain if not destroy the essence of ministry. Yet he disciplined himself into the routine and never complained, except perhaps to God – for he really believed that dipped in prayer, the stuffiest meetings could be sanctified – "and there the heaven espy".

On his last visit to Southwark, the Archbishop of Canterbury said, "This Cathedral feels prayed in". Looking back over the many red letter days; the great diocesan occasions; the plays and pageantry of the great festivals; the crowded schools services; the notable oratorios with their famous names, and the royal visits, nothing speaks more eloquently of faithful stewardship than the place St Saviour's Southwark had made for itself at the heart of the workaday world as, first and foremost, a House of Prayer: as the shadow of a great rock in a weary land. The secret of that Presence is related to the fact of a thousand years of worship on this site. There were periods in history when the Light seemed about to be extinguished for ever. In his turn, Cuthbert rekindled a Light that has never really failed – to guide, cheer and warm "them that come after".

*   *   *

Colin Cuttell's vivid account has given us a clear idea of what happened in Southwark as a result of the prayer and action of a group of worshippers under their Provost's dynamic leadership. In the sermon which he preached at his installation on 5th August 1944, he had expressed the hope that the Cathedral would hold out a hand of fellowship to commerce, to industry, to civic administration in the South London boroughs, and would be a home in which even the casual visitor would feel that he mattered and was wanted. Their vision must be *outward* – to serve and to help to save the national life. He had four main aims in view when he began his work: he wanted to reach the people in their homes around the Cathedral – Cuthbert was a parish priest as well as the Provost. He wanted the Cathedral to be seen to be the mother church of the diocese, where there would be a welcome for all the parishes. He wanted the Cathedral to be alive in the lunch hours for music, lectures, services. He wanted a ministry of the Word on the Sunday evenings, where the Faith could be expounded, learned, and appropriated.

Against the forbidding circumstances of the immediately postwar years, food rationing, lack of building materials, and so on, much was accomplished in achieving these ends, and the minutes of the

Cathedral Chapter, as well as the Bishop's letters in the Diocesan Gazette, reflect a resurrection and an outreach which were remarkable. Much had been achieved in the years 1940–44 at Woolwich. A similar revival, on a larger scale, took place at Southwark in the years 1944–48. No doubt everyone hoped that the Provost's ministry, there in South London, would continue well into the 1950s.

But, as we have seen, that was not to be. That special mission to the Army of Occupation, which took Cuthbert to Germany in May, June and July of 1947, was to have repercussions in his own life and ministry which he could not foresee. Archbishop Geoffrey Fisher knew a good man when he saw one. The man who had successfully fulfilled so difficult an assignment with the Forces was surely the man to continue that work, on a far larger scale, in the next few years. The Archbishop would have him based at Croydon as one of his suffragans, combining his episcopal work there with a continuing mission to Army, Navy and Air Force.

The Chaplain-General (F.L. Hughes) had written to Archbishop Fisher (25th July 1947) about Cuthbert Bardsley's visit:

> It is very striking to see how "A Man with a Message" is received. He is given pin-dropping attention during his addresses. Then there is a rush of senior officers to date him for a meal. Personal conversations follow which, I believe, achieve even more than his addresses – especially among young subalterns in Messes . . .

And F.R. Barry (later to be Bishop of Southwell) in a letter to the Archbishop refers to

> the magnificent job that Cuthbert Bardsley has done in the BAOR. It makes me very thankful that you sent him.

Against that background, the Archbishop wrote to Cuthbert on 16th September 1947:

> . . . The Bishop who represents me to the Forces must be acceptable to the Chaplain in Chief, that I know is true of you. This co-operation is, of course, essential. But more than that he must be the right man to make the impact on chaplains, officers and men. There is no shadow of doubt that you are the right man to do this.

Every report I have had of your visit to Germany is overwhelming evidence of it . . . It is for this reason that I not only invite you but urge you to accept my proposal.

On 18th September, Cuthbert replied:

> . . . the whole idea of it appeals to me enormously, though the prospect of leaving Southwark after only three years saddens me . . . The work is exactly the kind of work I would love to tackle – both the pastoral and civic work at Croydon and the wider responsibilities with the Forces.

It is hardly surprising that the Bishop of Southwark, on being consulted by the Archbishop, uttered a protest: "Our poor diocese is having a thin time struggling to regain its vitality and having our men taken from us." But the Archbishop won the day. "It is with something like consternation that the diocese has heard of the new appointment of the Provost", the Bishop wrote in his letter to the diocese in November 1947. ". . . We hoped that he would be left to see us through at least three more years during which his work would be firmly consolidated . . ." His sentiments were echoed by a very large number of men and women in an area well beyond Southwark.

On All Saints' Day 1947, in his own Cathedral of St Saviour and St Mary Overie, Cuthbert Bardsley was consecrated Bishop of Croydon by the Archbishop of Canterbury, Geoffrey Fisher, assisted by ten other bishops. At forty he was certainly one of the youngest bishops in the Church of England. He continued his work as Provost during November and December, and left to take up his new work on 8th January 1948.

VI
CROYDON: THE THREE
ARMED SERVICES

In journeyings often.

Corinthians 11:26

TWO THINGS DID NOT CHANGE when the Bishop took up his new work. The first was his home. He had travelled daily from 21 Southside, Streatham Common, SW16, to Southwark Cathedral. This house was only just outside the boundaries of Croydon, and so there was no need for him to move. The other constant was the presence of his sister. The lady who had stayed by him during the air raids at Woolwich, and through the difficult years at Southwark, remained with him during his time as Bishop of Croydon and eventually went with him to Coventry. A woman of strong convictions, a member of the Church Assembly, she obviously felt that her main task was to provide a gracious home from which her brother could go to his work and to which he could return, especially from his long overseas journeys, for renewal and refreshment. Dorothy was a caring and loving colleague.

Croydon, in diocesan terms, is (or, rather, was), an island separated from the rest of the diocese of Canterbury. (The anomaly ceased in 1985 when Croydon became part of the diocese of Southwark.) To go from Croydon to Canterbury, one had to pass through the diocese of Rochester – such are the illogicalities which history leaves to succeeding generations. The other Suffragan See within the diocese of Canterbury was that of Dover, whose Bishop, A.C.W. Rose, was Cuthbert's colleague throughout his years at Croydon.

When the Bishop of Croydon, Maurice H.H. Harland, was appointed to the See of Lincoln in the spring of 1947, the Archbishop had to consider how best to allocate the work which he had been doing. Harland had combined his diocesan work with that of being Vicar of Croydon. Fisher decided to end this union of offices – "the duties of a Vicar of Croydon in relation to the parish church and to the Borough are more than enough for one man", he wrote in his November Letter to the diocese. He went on:

> I must add, however, that having relieved him of parochial duties in
> Croydon, I am charging him with other duties which are wider than
> the diocese. The Archbishop of Canterbury has certain respon-
> sibilities in relation to the Chaplains' departments of the three
> services and to the Church of England chaplains therein which it is
> quite impossible for him to discharge adequately himself. As
> Archbishop Temple saw, he must have an Episcopal lieutenant
> who can give special attention to these responsibilities as the
> Archbishop's representative. It is with these duties, formerly
> carried for a brief time by a Bishop of Maidstone, that I am
> charging the Bishop of Croydon. He is peculiarly fitted by his own
> gifts and by his experience to discharge them, as he showed
> conspicuously when earlier this year he spent, at my request, some
> months with BAOR in Germany. We must see how things work
> out; but I have every hope that these duties can be combined with
> his duties in the diocese and in Croydon without detriment to
> either. I ask your prayers for him as he enters upon his episcopate.

The next eight years and a half were to be a period of intense activity
in two distinct spheres, in the diocese and in the armed services. In
both Cuthbert was responsible to the Archbishop, whose "Episcopal
officer" he was. He was devoted to Geoffrey Fisher, "a wonderfully
loving, caring, sometimes frightening man", who never ceased to be a
"headmaster" but was so much more. The Archbishop was a pastor –
the last to leave the parish hall after a confirmation because he wanted
to make informal contact with individual men, women and children.
His great administrative gifts found full scope in the postwar years, in
his diocese and far beyond. In spite of his worldwide responsibilities,
the Archbishop would always make time to see Cuthbert; and the
latter was not allowed to exceed his own responsibilities, for example,
in the disciplining of chaplains!

Unless he was on one of his overseas tours, Cuthbert attended the
diocesan staff meetings, at which, under the chairmanship of the
Archbishop, the Suffragan Bishops and the Archdeacons met
monthly for the major part of a day at Canterbury. The Archbishop
appointed him to a Canonry, "the only way of securing that he should
have his own place in the Cathedral with which otherwise he would
have no official link".

In his January 1948 Letter, the Archbishop comments that "the new Bishop of Croydon is getting quite busy in the town and deanery, and popular too, both in civic and ecclesiastical circles, and from all accounts he will be a welcome preacher". "Quite busy": that surely was an under-statement. In the early months of 1948, we find Cuthbert taking on the chairmanship of the Youth Council, and of the Diocesan Board of Women's Work (the latter a somewhat surprising appointment for a bachelor, but one did not say "No" to Archbishop Fisher nor to Mrs Fisher). The Archbishop drops in to a Conference held under Cuthbert's chairmanship at Kent College, and comments: "the right combination of gaiety and hard thinking, of cheerful exploration and of serious purpose, of talk and worship". Things are beginning to hum already.

Here are some almost random flashbacks. In Lent 1950, about nine hundred people each Wednesday night come to hear Cuthbert's addresses. ("He has the lifting power of a cheerful spirit and the drive of an intense enthusiasm", the *Croydon Advertiser* notes.) There are frequent *courses* of sermons, where some continuity of teaching could be ensured – Cuthbert noted the abysmal ignorance of even the basics of the Christian faith among the young men in the Forces. There are performances of his Passion Play, *A Sword Shall Pierce*, in St Mary's, Addiscombe, and other churches. There are indications that, in spite of his activities at home and abroad, he is attempting to keep up his reading – in October 1953, charged by the Archbishop to write the monthly Diocesan Letter, he devotes it to a plea for the reading of books and gives a list of "the twenty or thirty books that I have read during the past few weeks".

Nor did he forget the importance of industry and the Church's ministry to those engaged in it. He had learned his lesson at Woolwich and at Southwark, and pursued this ministry in Croydon. In that Borough, with a population of more than a quarter of a million, there were over a thousand factories, large and small. Why not have *Industrial* Thanksgiving Services in the Parish Church, on the analogy of Harvest Festival Services but more closely related to the interests and skills of urban workers? And so it was, with the Bishop preaching and the Archdeacon (C.F. Tonks) receiving token gifts from the many sides of industry and commerce. At Christmas 1949, we find Cuthbert making a tour of workshops and factories in the Croydon Deanery; and in January 1952 we note that recently, directors and representatives of thousands of workers in factories and shops in Croydon were guests of Messrs Grant Bros. on the occasion of the Annual General Meeting of Croydon's Industrial Chaplains' Committee. The Bishop of Croydon, who with a group of businessmen initiated the scheme in 1949, said that although there were other Industrial Chaplains in the country, nowhere else is the salary of the Chaplain found by the firms served . . .

Little did Cuthbert know how good a preparation he was receiving for the years to come in Coventry, that centre of industry in the Midlands. There he would be able to continue this particular form of ministry which, in three different areas, he had promoted. Though he loved the country, he was essentially an urban man.

So Cuthbert pursued the ordinary pastoral work of a bishop, confirming, instituting new incumbents, interviewing clergy and laity, presiding at meetings, visiting parishes, entering into the joys and griefs of his people. It was work after his own heart and he loved it, and could have spent all his energies on this alone. There are no limits to such work if the love of God is in your heart and if you care for the people committed to your charge.

Perhaps the last words about Cuthbert at work as a Bishop in the Croydon area should come from two clergy who served under him there. The first writes:

I had been in my first living . . . for only a short time when this young, handsome, immaculately turned out Bishop of Croydon arrived. With a splendid quality of voice, attractive personality, enormous vigour and enthusiasm, he swept all before him. He was a truly great popular (using that word in its best sense) preacher though by no means, one would judge, an academic. Those early postwar years were what I have always called "the golden years" for the Church in this country when the congregation queuing to get in was by no means unusual. At that time, after all the years of struggle, pain, deprivation and so on, when people were open to the Gospel in a most remarkable way, Cuthbert swept into Croydon and at once they knew they had a Bishop around! . . . It was as if a mighty, fresh and invigorating wind of the Spirit was sweeping through Church and Borough. A "bit much" for some, it must be

admitted, who found this enthusiasm not quite Church of England!
But I would say they were few in number. . . .

The members of the church,

> after all the problems of wartime and two previous vicars who
> between them had stayed for seventy-nine years, took their new
> Bishop to their hearts when he came to confirm, preach or give a
> series of addresses in Holy Week . . .
>
> Here was true, loving care for clergy and people. On many an
> occasion when he came to our vicarage for a simple evening meal,
> he would sit down and say, thinking of the work of the parish,
> "Come on now, tell me all about it". And we did, with not a little
> laughter more often than not, all the time knowing that here was a
> truly interested and trusted *listener*. Though only four years older
> than I, he was a true Father in God. He was deeply concerned with
> spiritual healing as I, having contracted polio at the age of thirty-
> eight, with a wife and three young children, had cause to remember
> to the end of our lives. . . . After my recovery it was my privilege
> to lend a hand with this facet of Cuthbert's ministry in the
> Borough . . .

The writer of the above sentences asks the question, "What
motivated him throughout his life?" He answers it as follows:
"a. single-minded; b. *deeply* converted; c. above all, he has become a
truly Christ-centred person."

The second clergyman recalls a mission held in one of the parishes
in the diocese, to which Cuthbert came on the final night. The church

> could hold nigh on a thousand and that night they sat on the steps
> up to the choir and up the sanctuary and all round the pulpit. I can
> recall nothing in detail except Cuthbert's great enthusiasm and
> telling preaching which he ended in his own quite simple and
> impulsive way: "There is no other way to end this evening – let us
> all sing 'Onward Christian Soldiers'." This the congregation
> obediently did. Cuthbert announced the hymn and "flung wide his
> arms in the fervour of the moment. The glass of water on the pulpit
> edge went flying over the heads of those seated on the steps below."

*   *   *

Then there was the other side to the Bishop's work. Cuthbert was the Archbishop's Episcopal Representative to the three Armed Forces. That was his official title, though he was more generally known as "the Bishop to the Forces". In certain quarters, his appointment by Geoffrey Fisher met with a somewhat mixed reception – surprise and an element of apprehension. Some recalled that when, after Dunkirk, Leslie Owen, Bishop of Maidstone and later Bishop of Lincoln, had been given special responsibility for the Forces, there were difficulties between him and the Chaplain General – perhaps the Bishop's brief had not been well enough defined. The Royal Navy had its Chaplain of the Fleet, the Army its Chaplain-General, the Royal Air Force its Chaplain-in-Chief. (Today they have the rank of Archdeacon and are members of the General Synod.) What need was there for this new young Bishop to interfere in their particular patch? Cuthbert's position was a very delicate one – he himself described it as a "tightrope job".

From the start he took good care never to offer advice on administrative matters which he recognized as being the responsibility of the senior chaplains, nor to intrude into the matter of the postings and promotions of chaplains. Slowly but surely he won through. Let him tell the story in his own way:

No one could have begun his work feeling less well equipped for the task. I had never been a Forces' chaplain, I had never mingled among Forces' personnel, I had never shared their discomforts or assumed uniform except as an OTC cadet. I was, and, thank God, realized that I was, clueless and incapable, but I had learned three important lessons: (i) admit your incompetence and put yourself at others' disposal to be trained by them; (ii) in all strategy start at the top; and (iii) work through small numbers.

With these somewhat frail convictions I arrived in BAOR (the British Army on the Rhine, Germany). Having surrounded myself with prayer – an indispensable preliminary – I began my work. I placed myself unreservedly at the disposal of the Senior Chaplain, the Rev. Geoffrey Druitt. He said I must not open my mouth for at least a week, during which time I must watch, listen and learn. This I did. Indeed, it was all I could do. First impressions are often the most enduring. It was soon borne in on me that the army was suffering from a postwar hangover. Men were impatient for demobilization. They had done the work they had been called to do, to defeat the Germans and put an end to threats to liberty, and to make the world a slightly safer place to live in. Now they wanted to retire from the combat, to put away their uniforms and to go home.

This could not easily be achieved – (a) because of massive unemployment at home; (b) because a police force was still required in the defeated Germany. With such a postwar hangover, morale was low, tempers were frayed, criticism was rampant. It was at that early moment in my work that my second conviction forced itself into my mind – I must start at the top. So I asked if I could have an interview with the Commander-in-Chief, BAOR, General Sir Richard McCreery. I found a tall, distinguished, rather for- midable character, with a long neck, a beaky nose, stern eyes, and a reputation for a quick and at times ungovernable temper. He asked me straight away what I thought about the morale of the Forces. I said bluntly that I felt it was low. I described my initial conviction that the men were suffering from a hangover and that they wanted to go home. He said, "Yes, I agree, what do you propose?" This was the first of three or four occasions when he made the same comment: "What do you propose?" I said, "General, I don't think it is much good talking about morale and trying to raise it. I think we have got to talk about the Christian faith out of which morale comes; we have got to rekindle faith." Again he replied, "Yes, quite right; what do you propose?"

I said, "I have not given it a great deal of thought, but I think we must start at the top". There was a rather ugly pause at that point, and I said, "I think it would be a very good thing if you were to invite many of your senior officers to come for a long, unhurried weekend to one of the Church Houses and to listen to a series of lectures on the Christian faith." After a long pause he said, "Yes, I agree, what do you suggest?" I said, "I believe that it should be done soon, and of course you will come yourself?" A still longer pause, and he said, "Yes, I think that is right. I will lay it on."

About three weeks later I received an invitation to go with two other friends to one of the big Church Houses, where I found about sixty very senior officers, ranging from General to full Colonel. Most of them had not wanted to come. They were sitting around the room looking bored and, in some cases, annoyed. They had had long journeys, they were tired, and they felt that they were going to be totally disinterested in the subject. Most of them had a nodding acquaintance with the Christian faith, some of them indeed were regular churchgoers, but many of them sat very lightly to the faith. So difficult was the atmosphere that I said to the General that perhaps we could lay on the first lecture rather sooner than had been arranged. So it was agreed, and it was laid on for immediately after tea, when I had to wade into this somewhat cold and hostile atmosphere.

I started, as I always did, on a subject which concerned us all, namely the state of the world, because that is where they were living and where I was living – we had that at least in common. I talked about the world of that day, the postwar difficulties etc., speaking about fifty minutes, filled, I hope, with a certain amount of humour. At the end the atmosphere was less tense, and when the evening came and the opportunity for lecture number two, the atmosphere had begun to change. They were more prepared to listen and so I could give the second of my main talks, the subject of which was proofs of the existence of God and the nature of God. That was listened to and we all went off to bed.

Sunday came with early morning Eucharist, followed by lecture number three, and this was always, in all of my series of lectures, the main central talk on which everything else depended. It dealt with the person of Jesus and that lasted 45–50 minutes, listened to in total stillness. I can still remember one man coming up to me and saying at the end of the course, "Bishop, we had a long way to come, but it would have been worthwhile if only to listen to that talk about our Lord."

And that taught me something. It taught me that one must not mince matters, one must not compromise, one must go right to the very heart of the Christian faith.

Subsequent lectures related to the Holy Spirit, the Church and the Sacraments, Prayer and, all told, I think about eight to ten lectures.

On Monday afternoon they left. I heard afterwards that as they went home they passed the next group coming to the Church House. Cars were stopped and the great question of those coming was, "What was it like?" Apparently the answer was not too unfavourable, so that the next lot came in a slightly better atmosphere, less critical, more prepared to listen and to learn.

This was the beginning of a series of lecture-courses that were to go on for the next nine months, going right away down the whole list, until we came to the warrant officers and petty officers. That was quite a tough assignment, but like everybody else, by the end, they were at least grateful that they had come. Then a series for other ranks was laid on.

I realize what a deep debt of gratitude I owe to the rather shy, formidable, powerful leader of men, General Sir Richard McCreery. I cannot sufficiently thank God for his courage in laying on something which could well have been criticized by senior authorities.

Word of what was happening reached the ears of the Navy, and I received an invitation from the Commander-in-Chief, Mediterranean, to visit Malta and to give a series of lectures to the personnel there. Again accompanied by two others, I shall never forget my first sight of the first course. Sitting in the front row were admirals including the Commander-in-Chief himself and Lord Louis Mountbatten (it was before he became Viceroy of India). Altogether there were thirty to forty very senior officers.

Precisely the same thing was laid on, the same subjects, the same talks and, thank God, with the same result. They went away and spoke about it positively to many others. So that was the beginning of a series of lectures that went right through the personnel of the garrison in Malta.

Word of what was happening reached the ears of the Royal Air Force. I received an invitation from the Commander-in-Chief of the Air Force throughout the world, Air Chief Marshal Sir William Dixon. A small, powerful man, he met me in his London office and said that he proposed to lay on a weekend at Dowdeswell Court, near Cheltenham – the Church House of the Royal Air Force.

The day came when, again accompanied by two others, I arrived within a mile of Dowdeswell and found military police standing there saluting as one went past. My heart began to move a little more rapidly as I realized the tremendous significance of what we were going to find. Sir William Dixon had issued an order that his senior men should come from all over the world for a long weekend at Dowdeswell Court to study the Christian faith. Nowhere else could this have been laid on – not in civilian life. There they all were, from Singapore, Malta, Middle East, Germany, far and wide.

They again experienced the same lecture course. This proved to be the prelude to similar courses held in different places and different parts of the world for the RAF personnel.

A copy of the talks which Cuthbert gave on Christian leadership at Celle Church House in February 1948 survives. The audience consisted of senior officers and padres. Cuthbert sought to discover with them "how best to deal with the lads of eighteen who will be out here in Germany shortly". He reminded his hearers that these youngsters' education had been wrecked; they had been moved from their homes into the country, brought back during the phoney war, moved again during the blitzes, sent to different schools and, as a result, were "very undeveloped". How could they help them? Cuthbert planned seven talks. In the first, he would consider the world of 1948; in the second, the character and conduct of the lads; in the third, belief in God; in the fourth, the revelation of God in Christ; in the fifth, man management in the light of the Christian faith; in the sixth, the meaning of the Church; and in the seventh, practical suggestions in "getting this across".

The language of these talks is basic and untechnical. It had to be. Illustrations from life and experience are plentiful – doctrine is closely related to life. The relevance of the Church – the Bible, the Sacraments, the Ministry, the Creeds – is spelled out. No officer who heard these talks could be unaware of the need of strong Christian leadership as these boys passed through his hands. The work of the padres must have been greatly aided.

The pages of the Royal Army Chaplains' Department Journal give some idea of part of his work. In January 1951, together with the Rector of Stepney and the Rev. T.J. Savage (London Diocesan Missioner), he conducted a series of courses for warrant officers and sergeants in the three Church Houses, in Ostenwalde, Iserlohn, and Verden; in August 1952 he paid his second visit of the year to Germany, and took two retreats for the Chaplains of the Rhine Army in the peaceful setting of Ostenwalde Church House; from 21st April to 8th May 1952 he conducted a series of courses for senior officers from formations throughout BAOR – they were declared to be of "outstanding spiritual value" and "well worth attending". 1953 saw him spending fifteen days touring Hong Kong, Singapore and Malaya – his first visit to the Far East; in February 1954, with the Rev. T.J.

Savage and the Rev. R.G. Strutt, he conducted a series of special Christian leadership courses at the three Church Houses, returning in April to conduct confirmation services for some who had attended the courses; in November 1954 he met the Royal Navy based on Malta, and units of the Mediterranean Fleet; also in November he spent a fortnight in the East Africa theatre of operations. In May 1955, following a tour with the Second Tactical Air Force, he conducted a special course for Commanders and Senior Staff Officers of BAOR at Verden Church House; in November he visited BAOR to conduct a mission at the Joint Headquarters of the Northern Army Group and Second Allied Tactical Air Force.

Cuthbert learned the value of humour in catching and holding the attention of the men he addressed. He sought never to talk down to them but, starting where they were, to think with them.

Sometimes the gatherings were huge in number – in hangars, on airfields, on battle ships and on parade grounds. At other times he ministered to individuals, often under unusual conditions. He tells of two such instances. The first occurred in "the Officers' Mess in a barracks in Germany":

There had been the normal drinks party, prior to dinner, followed by the meal. I retired early for the night; exhausted, I went sound asleep. Suddenly I heard a tap on my door. I put on the light, looked at my watch and found it was 1.30 a.m. The door silently opened. My heart beat rather fast: I wondered who was at the door. A young, diffident and scared young officer came in and said, "Bishop, I am terribly sorry to trouble you. I have been walking up and down outside your room plucking up courage to come in. I was deeply moved by what you said and realize only too vividly that my life is in a mess. I don't know which way to turn, I don't know what to do." So I told him to come and sit on the end of the bed and we would talk. There ensued a talk lasting about half an hour in which he told me exactly what had happened, his moral compromises which had led him to the brink of disaster. I told him that there was only one person who could bring him the answer to his problems and that was Jesus, and I tried to introduce him to the person of our Lord. I cannot say what happened because I lost touch with him, but I hope that that night he was set on the road home to God.

A second illustration comes from one of my brief visits home from a trip to the Forces. I was running along London Bridge Station trying to catch the last train from Southwark Cathedral to my home in Streatham. As I arrived, the train was moving out, but I managed to grab the last door and stumbled in, to the fury of the ticket collector. I sat down panting, looked around and found there was one other occupant of the compartment. I turned to my newspaper and was engrossed in it when suddenly the man moved across to occupy the opposite seat. Immediately my mind remembered murders that had happened on trains and wondered what was going to happen to me, and only hoped that whatever was going to happen would happen quickly. To my astonishment, he made the last comment I ever expected him to make. He said, "Padre, can you help me to find God?"

I realized that I had twenty-one minutes before I reached my station in which to help him to find God!

These two interviews taught me that one never knows when one is going to be suddenly called upon to help people to a living awareness of the living God. One must be always alert and available and attentive and ever pointing people to the living, loving, liberating Lord of today.

Then there were the confirmations, with anything between five and a hundred and fifty candidates, services held mostly in battalion chapels, but sometimes in big garrison churches.

And there was the ministry to the padres, a task to which Cuthbert gave high priority. Sometimes they were lonely, feeling themselves misunderstood. Sometimes they were bewildered by the war and its aftermath, feeling they were getting nowhere. Hence the need for quiet days and retreat conferences at Bagshot Park in Surrey and in the Church Houses in Germany. And there was the ministry to ordinands. It was a ministry which Cuthbert loved.

Cuthbert was fortunate in the men who helped him with his work, men of the calibre of R. Gordon Strutt (later Bishop of Stockport), Mark Green (later Bishop of Aston), F. Patrick B. Ashe, Algy Robertson, F. Evered Lunt (later Bishop of Stepney), Eric S. Abbott (later Dean of Westminster), T.J. Savage (later Bishop of Zululand) and others.

Two little notebooks, used by Ronald Bowlby, the present Bishop of Southwark, survive to show the kind of work which went on under

Cuthbert's guidance. The first contains notes of a Christian Leadership course held at Iserlohn Church House in June 1947 when Cuthbert, as Provost of Southwark, was assisted by Pat Ashe; and notes of a Retreat in 1952 held at Cerne Abbas conducted by Father Algy. The second contains notes of a three-day "semi-retreat" for ordinands conducted by Cuthbert in July 1947, and notes of two Quiet Days conducted at Westcott House, Cambridge, the first by Evered Lunt in 1950 and the second by Eric Abbott in 1951. As one examines the notes of Cuthbert's addresses, one is impressed by the orderliness of presentation which enabled the hearer to grasp and to jot down the essentials of the addresses; one notes, too, Cuthbert's use of alliteration as an aid to memory (the "evil agency" at work "divides, derides, dissipates, discourages, deceives"); and one catches the sound of the influence of his years with the Oxford Groups. None of the ordinands could forget his talks on, for example, the life of prayer or on the Holy Communion (the Lord's Supper, the Eucharist, the Mass). All the teaching was centred firmly in experience of God in his glory and of men and women in their need.

Let three men give their impressions of Cuthbert's work. The first is Ronald Bowlby:

In the summer of 1946, I guess (when Cuthbert was still Provost of Southwark), he came to speak to a large gathering of my regiment (the 2nd Household Cavalry) at a place called Menden, near Iserlohn. I think I am right in saying that he had been asked to do a tour of our army and airforce units in the occupation zone, where boredom was rife and morale rather low! I can still picture all these men in the main canteen (was it compulsory? probably), and wondering what it would be like to address such a meeting "from cold". (I had just become an ordinand.) I don't remember what Cuthbert said, but I do remember the attractiveness of the man, the conviction with which he spoke, and the attention he was given.

And so when I heard that he was to lead a short residential course at one of the local "Church Houses" (there were three for the Army in BAOR, at Preetz in the North, Alfeld near Hanover and Iserlohn near the Ruhr), I applied to go. I think this one was called "Christian Leadership". I subsequently went to another for ordinands at Alfeld. At both, Cuthbert's addresses were memorable for their directness and effective illustration. He had the evangelical's ability to use a good story, and to know a good many. But what was particularly important to me at that time, he came across as someone who loved the Sacraments as well as the Bible. He took me and someone else to his room, and helped us to do Bible study with him: an example of his personal interest and care, reinforcing the more general teaching. But he also knew about sacramental confession and valued it, so that in Cuthbert I caught a glimpse of an Anglican spirituality which was wide and inclusive – something less common then than it is today.

Our paths therefore crossed three times in 1946 and 1947, and it was to Cuthbert that I owed the rather firm suggestion that I should apply for admission to Westcott House for theological college training later on. One can see there one of the roots of his own spiritual formation, and I am still grateful for the advice (which I followed!). When I came out of the Forces at the beginning of 1948, I felt the need for a spiritual director or counsellor, and after a while I found my way to the house on Streatham Common where he lived as Bishop of Croydon. Again I look back gratefully to the mixture of infectious warmth, encouragement and guidance which he gave me over several years until it had to come to an end with my departure for a curacy in Sunderland in 1952.

The second impression of Cuthbert's work comes from J.H. Lloyd Morrell (later Bishop of Lewes). He, together with Gerald A. Ellison (later Bishop of London) helped Cuthbert in the series of Moral Leadership courses in the Rhine Army. Lloyd Morrell had considerable contact with the three Chaplaincy Departments during the war.

As I look back (he wrote many years later), I am inclined to think that one of Cuthbert's greatest achievements at the period of which I am writing was the initiating and carrying through of these Moral Leadership courses. I do not at all wish to imply that the heads of the Chaplaincy Departments were difficult people to deal with, but the whole plan must have been a very novel department.

Lloyd Morrell refers to Cuthbert's great personal charm; to his genuine love of all human beings; to his tireless use of his imagination to meet the needs of those to whom he was ministering – he "was equally good with all ranks . . . The impression was made by the holiness, complete sincerity and personality of the speaker."

The third memory comes from the pen of Colonel (later the Reverend) H.A.R. Tilney who writes of Cuthbert's visit to British troops in Germany during the late summer and early autumn of 1946:

In retrospect I feel that this visit was inspired, for it had a most definite and beneficial effect at that time, and who knows but that what was received then has not been passed on many times since?

As C.O. of a Regular Armoured Regiment one of my chief concerns was the several hundred soldiers from disbanded wartime-raised Regiments who were awaiting demobilization and who were attached to us meanwhile. Our own Regiment's strength was considerable, and inevitably when it was difficult to employ troops gainfully without the purposefulness of military training, one had to be very concerned about the impact on morale.

Maybe other Regular Regiments and Battalions were likewise concerned. Maybe too, we were preventing ourselves from seeing the situation clearly owing to seeing the alleged difficulties too clearly, at the expense of evaluating them calmly!

We were told of Cuthbert's impending visit. That his aim was to meet as many soldiers of all ranks as possible. That he intended to hold a series of two-day courses centrally which he hoped would truly represent Senior and Junior Officers and similarly Other Ranks. After which he hoped to visit Formations and Units in their respective locations.

For our part we looked forward to the coming of this prominent cleric and felt that he certainly had his work cut out! I imagine that for most people he was an unknown person. But that supposition did not last long. He, like Julius Caesar, came; he saw; and he conquered!

The venue for the series of two-day courses was Church House, at Verden, located between Hanover and Hamburg. This vast house and its surroundings had been of considerable importance to Nazi engineers and scientists working on ballistic missiles, notably V1s and V2s. (The doors of all the rooms had spy-holes so that the occupant could be watched!)

So far as I remember very little if any preparation was required of us who were attending a course. In retrospect it came to me that

Cuthbert preferred to have us as we were – "warts and all" – confident that the impact of what he had to say to us was even more telling if received quite raw! He expected that much of additional value would appear during the discussion periods. I believe it did so work out.

His theme was "History", but spelt His Story, *God's Story*. It was fascinating how the Old Testament line was followed and fulfilled. Clearly, enormous interest was shown and long before the course ended it was obvious that Cuthbert had completely held his hearers, to a man. He was seen to be, quite simply, a Man of God. He was delightfully happy; loved his work and his fellow men, was absolutely natural and normal, and was great fun! In short he was a rare man and certainly and evidently, a real channel of God's grace.

I do not think that many who met and talked with Cuthbert and had an opportunity to refer a problem to him, would not have been greatly helped; both at the time and strengthened for the future.

Of course Cuthbert's visits were not confined to Europe. He was invited to go to the troops in Korea, where he has vivid memories of sleeping in Monty's caravan, and being picked up by the C-in-C, General West, in his helicopter and flown to the front line, where he talked with men in advanced positions. Afterwards he was able to write to their families, conveying greetings and messages. He was deeply impressed by the morale of the Forces in that distant country.

Another visit was paid to Kenya at the height of the Mau Mau trouble. Constantly he was flown by the RAF to units deep in the forests, where they were busily engaged in mopping up communist infiltration. He visited on a number of occasions General Sir Richard Erskine, the GOC, and stayed with the Governor, Sir Evelyn Baring, a devout Anglican and a keen mountaineer. He took part in services in their private chapel and was grateful for the inspiration brought by the shining personal faith of the Governor and his wife.

All through the years of his work among the Forces, Cuthbert had kept the Archbishop informed of his activities – writing sometimes in considerable detail. The Archbishop was aware of the inevitable strain incurred in the combination of the duties of a Suffragan Bishop with those of his representative to the Forces. As long ago as March 1949, Geoffrey Fisher had written encouraging Cuthbert in his work, and then added: "I forbid you to regard all your time at home as mortgaged to Croydon, and I order you along with this list of visits overseas to set aside proper intervals for holidays . . . " – a nice combination of headmasterly authority and pastoral care.

But the strain was bound to tell. It was in Kenya that Cuthbert's health began to deteriorate. He suffered a minor thrombosis behind one eye. This was not helped by continuous activity day and night, visiting battalions in different parts of the country, by lectures and discussions, by Quiet Days for padres, by constant travel over dangerous mountain terrain. On returning home, he was sent to the Middlesex Hospital and told to rest for three weeks. With careful nursing, the trouble cleared, but broke out much later in the same place. The strain of his work contributed also to a duodenal ulcer, the intense pain of which constantly recurred over the next twenty-five years. The signs were clear that his two-fold responsibilities of work in Croydon and with the Armed Forces must soon cease.

When Cuthbert's appointment to the See of Coventry was announced, the Chaplain-General, Victor Pike, wrote:

It was with a sense of real personal loss that we learned of the translation of the Bishop of Croydon to the See of Coventry, though many of us felt that it was inevitable that the parting of the ways must come when he would be called to the responsibilities of a diocese.

Without qualification it can be said that to no other does the Department owe the same depth of gratitude as we do to the Bishop for all he has been to us, and for all he has done for us, since his appointment nine years ago as the Archbishop of Canterbury's Episcopal Representative to the Services.

So willingly and so unsparingly has he given himself in furthering our work and sustaining each one of us by his counsel and prayer, that he has come to occupy a unique place not only in the affectionate regard of Chaplains of all denominations, but also in the esteem and respect of Servicemen of all ranks.

For long he will be remembered among us for his great contribution to the work of the Church in the Army, and for the winning way in which he has made plain to all sorts and conditions of men the relevance of Christianity to their present situation. Through his ministry many have recovered a lost faith, and many more have been won to Christ and his Church, while Chaplains everywhere have been inspired by his precept and example.

In her Birthday Honours List in 1952, Her Majesty the Queen had conferred on Cuthbert Bardsley the honour of the CBE.

*   *   *

On 22nd April 1956, Cuthbert, then Bishop of Coventry, returned to Croydon for a reunion service for those confirmed during his eight years as Bishop there. There was no church big enough to contain those who came, so the Davis Theatre was taken. Four thousand three hundred people crowded in, and another thousand were unable to gain entrance. Five hundred of these went to an overflow gathering in Croydon Parish Church.

The Archbishop sent a message to be read out. It began: "Could there be a better farewell party for Bishop Bardsley as he leaves us for Coventry than this reunion party of people whom he has confirmed while Bishop of Croydon?" All agreed. The Archbishop was right.

Part Two

VII

THE CONSECRATION OF
A PEOPLE
AND ITS CATHEDRAL

*The glory of this latter house shall be greater than of
the former, saith the Lord of hosts.*

Haggai 2:9

A consecrated Church demands a consecrated people.

STEPHEN VERNEY

AS LONG AGO AS THE SEVENTH CENTURY the diocese of Mercia was divided so that the southern part became Worcester and the "Arden" part became the See of "Coventry and Lichfield", stretching as far north-westerly as Chester. In 1836, four deaneries were transferred, by Act of Parliament, to the Worcester diocese, and "Lichfield" became the title of the former See. The See of Coventry thus passed out of existence until 1918 when, after long years of argument, often abortive, it was re-created.

Since then it has been fortunate in its Bishops.[1] At the age of seventy-three H.W. Yeatman-Biggs was translated from Worcester. It was doubtless due to him that the diocese took as its motto *Deo adjuvante resurgo*, which could roughly be translated *God being (my) helper I rise again*. The motto was appropriate for the newly-re-created See. It assumed an even greater appropriateness in the years after the Second World War, and in the building of the new Cathedral close to the ruins of the old. The Bishop's tomb stands on the north side among the ruins of the ancient buildings.

Yeatman-Biggs was followed by Charles Lisle Carr, who brought comparative youth and vigour to the upbuilding of the diocese during his nine-year episcopate. Bishop Mervyn G. Haigh brought special gifts when he took up his work in 1931. He had been Archbishop Randall Davidson's senior chaplain at Lambeth, and had ministered to him on his death-bed. He thus came to the diocese equipped with a knowledge of the Church of England and of the Anglican Communion which was invaluable. He was the youngest diocesan bishop in the Church of England. It was a matter of no great surprise when he

---

[1] I am greatly indebted to *Seen in a See* by the Rev. Edward J. Bastin for useful information about the See of Coventry.

went to be Bishop of Winchester in 1942, and a matter of regret to many and of loss to the Church when ill-health compelled him to retire ten years later. After Temple's death, so it was said, he was "the brains" of the Bench.

It was during Bishop Haigh's time at Coventry that the great blitz of the city took place and the Cathedral was destroyed. Overnight, the ill-fated night of 14th November 1940, "Coventry" became a word known throughout the world for the ferocity of the German attack. The whole city was ablaze. The Provost, R.T. Howard, has described how the Cathedral guard for the night, which consisted of himself, a layman aged sixty-five, and two young men in their early twenties, fought the fires in the great building. But supplies of water, sand and physical strength failing them, they had to give in.

> We learned afterwards that every [fire] engine was in use on some big fire, that many engines were trapped in narrow streets with a bomb crater at each end, and that engines coming in from other centres found the roads into the city blocked . . . All night long the city burned, and her Cathedral burned with her – emblem of the eternal truth that, when men suffer, God suffers with them. Yet the tower still stood, with its spire soaring to the sky – emblem of God's overruling majesty and love.[2]

Less than a year after that fearful night, on 26th September 1941, Winston Churchill visited the stricken city and Cathedral, and on 25th February 1942, Bishop Haigh and Provost Howard welcomed King George VI and Queen Elizabeth to see the ruins. Their visit brought cheer and courage to their people.

Built about 1373–1433, the old Cathedral had stood for long centuries and borne its witness to God. Now the tower and spire remained – indeed, during the night of the blitz its clock had continued to strike the hours. The outer walls of all the chapels and the sanctuary also remained; the walls of the five-sided apse were still standing, as was also the south porch. What of the future? The Provost was no man to sit and wring his hands. By the day following the blitz, he was looking to the future. *Deo adjuvante resurgo!*

---

[2] *Ruined and Rebuilt: The Story of Coventry Cathedral: 1939–62*, by R.T. Howard. Published by the Council of Coventry Cathedral 1962, pp. 11 and 14.

While some people were clamouring for reprisals against the Germans for that night in which more than five hundred people were killed, countless homes obliterated and nine churches, including the Cathedral, destroyed or damaged, the Provost's mind began to plan for the worship which must continue. A defiant prophecy from Haggai was hoisted to a prominent place in the ruins, declaring that the latter glory of the House would be greater than the former. Permanent provision must be made for the needs of generations yet to come.

Archdeacon J.H. Proctor, who was to come to the diocese in 1946 and to serve successively as Precentor, Canon Theologian and Archdeacon of Warwick, describes the scene in the years immediately following the blitz:

In a spiritual and practical sense, the life of the Cathedral never stopped – though in detail its nature was obviously vastly altered. Two ancient crypt chapels were opened for worship – not only on Sundays – of some hundred or more people. One of the crypts was turned into the first ever Chapel of Unity – and the ecumenical movement received a significant early kick-off here. In the ruins – once the debris was cleared away and tidying up was done – innumerable services were held. There was nothing unusual about a congregation of two thousand worshippers in the ruins. Microphones and loudspeakers were installed, and soon multitudes of people who otherwise had no connection with the spiritual life of the Cathedral, looked forward to attending these services. The occasions were diverse indeed – Battle of Britain Sunday, School leavers' services, National Days of Prayer, Services for Pensioners, Civic Services, and services for such Societies as the Independent Order of Oddfellows, all had their regular place. And – every Christmas Eve – there was a carol service with a vast attendance.

Religious drama also had an important part in the Cathedral activities. An outdoor stage was constructed, and year after year, programmes of plays were put on. In the Festival of Britain Year few theatres had more dramatic activity than the Cathedral – all in the open air, and I can hardly remember any being cancelled because of bad weather! The first performance of the Coventry Mysteries since the reign of Elizabeth I drew great audiences for

Cuthbert aged 6

Below: The Bardsley family, 1918: Joan, Dorothy (who was to become a special companion), Eric, Monica, Cuthbert, Mrs Bardsley, Hilda, Canon Norman Bardsley

38 years later – Cuthbert takes tea with his sister Dorothy (1956)

Rowing for New College, Oxford 1928 (behind Stroke)

(Front row, second from the right)

In his first car – a Clyno

The Reverend P. B. (Tubby) Clayton, 1933

Consecration as Bishop in Southwark Cathedral, with Bishop Maurice Key and Archbishop Geoffrey Fisher, 1947

The ruins of Coventry Cathedral devastated by a night Blitz, 14th November 1940

Laying the foundation stone for the new Cathedral with the Provost, The Very Reverend R. W. Howard, Her Majesty the Queen and The Duke of Edinburgh

The new cathedral; view of the altar and Sutherland tapestry

Below: Signing the official Deed of Consecration on the occasion of the Consecration of Coventry Cathedral in the presence of the Provost of Coventry, The Very Reverend Harold Williams and Canon Simon Phipps, later Bishop of Lincoln

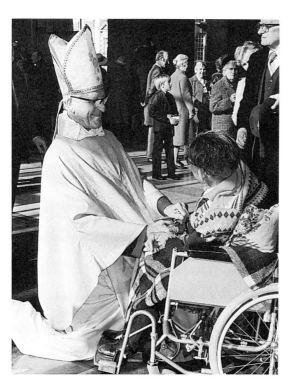

Above: A call to mission

1982: a service of thanksgiving to celebrate:

Ten years of marriage
Twenty years as Bishop of Coventry
Forty years as a Bishop
Fifty years as a priest
And a seventy-fifth birthday

With a group of miners: Bedworth Colliery

Below: Opening an exhibition of children's art in the diocese, "The Instant Communicator"

Engagement to Ellen Mitchell, 1972

The artist at work in the study at Bishop's House, Coventry

the many performances. Sometimes the actors were drawn from local drama groups, sometimes well-known "outside" companies came to do their entertaining. The plays were usually "religious" – e.g. *The Boy with a Cart, The Lady's not for Burning,* and so on, but also not specifically religious plays were included in the list.

In 1949, the first of many colourful pageants took place in the ruins. This was in celebration of the four hundredth anniversary of the Book of Common Prayer. The performers in this came from all over the diocese, and every rural deanery was closely involved.

Side by side with all this colourful, exciting and much publicized activity, other equally important things were going on. A normal – as far as it could be normal – congregational life was built up and became very strong and devoted. The choral tradition was maintained valiantly.

Then there were constant broadcast services, sometimes in the regular BBC programmes, and sometimes more specialized as, for instance, when schools broadcasts took place from the crypts. And of course there were the visitors! O my! The visitors! They came, day after day, in their thousands from all over the world. I once asked a collection of them to say the Lord's prayer in their own language, and discovered that twelve languages had been used in that one group! The fanfares were obviously sounding. The great "Pageant" was about to begin![3]

The main work of planning and construction was to take place under Bishop Haigh's successors. As we have seen, Haigh left for Winchester in 1942, and Neville Gorton became Bishop of the diocese early in 1943. His enthronement took place, under an open sky, in the ruins of the Cathedral on 20th February. It would be hard to think of conditions more bleak and grim than those under which he began his work.

Neville Gorton was a very different man from his predecessor – but that is how God enriches his Church with a wide variety of gifts. No administrator – he once offered the same parish to two men – he was a prophetic figure, full of love and humility. A Coventry Rector,

[3] In Bishop F.R. Barry's *Mervyn Haigh*, the writer gives a verbatim transcript of a conversation recorded by Bishop Haigh with the Provost of Coventry, H.C.N. Williams, in March 1961. It gives a lively picture of Coventry in the closing period of Haigh's episcopate and, incidentally, of the man himself (S.P.C.K. 1964, pp. 207ff.)

the Rev. F.W. Moyle, edited a book[4] in which some of his friends recorded their reminiscences of him as schoolmaster and headmaster, teacher and artist, man of God, Bishop, and so on. Very unconventional in thought and action, Gorton's first care was for his clergy, especially the lonely and the despondent in the closing years of the war and in the decade which followed those years. New housing estates were springing up designed for people who had been bombed out of their homes, and for immigrants flooding into the city. The building of churches, church halls and vicarages; the raising of clergy stipends; the work of education – these and a dozen other concerns cried out for attention as war gave place to an uneasy peace.

While this was going steadily forward Bishop Gorton was wholly at one with Provost Howard in beginning to plan for the building of the new Cathedral. He saw it as a building for Anglican worship of the highest order, an instrument of compassionate service for the city and diocese, and also a centre of Christian unity. Neville Gorton died on 30th November 1955. The foundation stone of the new Cathedral was laid by the Queen on 23rd March in the following year. Cuthbert Bardsley, yet to be enthroned, was present. Archdeacon Proctor writes:

"Foundation stone" is a misnomer, since the foundations had long before been well and truly laid, namely a hundred and eighty reinforced concrete piles driven deep into the earth . . . From the ruins of the old Cathedral the site of the new one broke like the forward and outward spreading decks of an aircraft carrier . . . The undercroft, itself a building of major proportions, had already been faced with the lovely pink stone which will eventually stretch upwards like a gorgeous rosy cliff pierced with towering windows . . .

The day of the laying of the stone was fine but cold. The Head Sacristan, Mr (later the Rev.) Clifford Robinson, has described the preamble, if "amble" is the right word – perhaps scamper would be better – to the service:

In the Order of Service specially prepared for this historic event the first two rubrics read:

[4] *Neville Gorton, Bishop of Coventry, 1943–55* (S.P.C.K. 1957)

> At 11.30 a.m. the Provost and Cathedral Chapter, led by the Verger, Cathedral Churchwardens and Cross of Nails, will conduct the LORD BISHOP and THE LORD ARCHBISHOP OF CANTERBURY preceded by the Cross of Canterbury into the ruins.

and

> At 11.37 a.m. the Cathedral bells will ring to announce the approach of the Queen, and they will continue ringing until she enters the Cathedral.

All should have been well. Robed and ready . . . those of us named in the first rubric waited on the North side of the Ruins, concealed by a tall wooden fence which surrounded the site of the new building.

All *would* have been well but to our astonishment, at 11.28 the bells rang out. Either Her Majesty's train driver had been exceeding the limit, or the Chief Constable's watch was fast; whatever the reason the Queen was nine minutes early . . .

As bearer of the Cross of Nails I had never run in a procession, but we all scampered that day, alongside the fence, around the base of the great tower and spire which had survived the fire sixteen years earlier, past Her Majesty as she stood there, patient and serene, looking for all the world as if the sight of full-robed trotting clerics and their escorts was a normal part of her daily routine.

Our mini-explosion into the Ruins proved so undignified that the BBC cameras were temporarily switched to some more respectable subject for the viewers of television to watch. Richard Dimbleby, a few hours later, asked me what had gone wrong, and why had we burst into view "like a cork coming out of a bottle".

Archdeacon Proctor, too, has his memories of that windy day:

> Copes and such-like things flew about their wearers. The Duke of Edinburgh, obstructed by a flying cope as he tried to shake hands with Percy Loveitt, a churchwarden, said: "I'll get to you as soon as this bloke's parachute comes down!"

Two hiccups were mercifully unknown to the thousands of worshippers and spectators. One was just before the Queen was

131

due to arrive. I thought it wise to go into the ruins and have a last look around to see that everything was in order, but my way was blocked by an enormous policeman, from a force outside of Coventry, brought in for the occasion. "You can't go in there", he said. "The Queen is coming and no unauthorized person is to be admitted." "Well," I said, "I'll tell you this, officer. If I don't go in now, the Queen need not bother to come because nothing, repeat nothing, can happen until I, and I alone, give the signal." Fortunately at that point the Chief Constable of Coventry saw that something was amiss, came over and rebuked the officer. I said, "Thank you. But don't tick him off. Security is his business and he's doing it well." So I did my searches and the Queen and Duke came and the great ceremony went ahead.

Another hiccup occurred after the service, when the Queen was leaving through the door of the old cathedral. Somehow Archbishop Fisher had lost his way and was still at the rear of the clerical procession when the Queen was far away about to leave. Fortunately Provost Howard had stuck close to the royal party and said an official, graceful and grateful farewell. But the Archbishop was not amused. "It's my place to do that", he said, and called the Provost to him and began to dress him down. I was about to plunge in and tell His Grace not to be childish, but Cuthbert, just behind me in the procession, pulled back on my cope and kept me in place! But my big job came later, as some of the eagle-eyed press had spotted the upset, and I had a hard job in persuading them that no good would be done to them, to the community or to anyone else if they wrote it up. Nothing appeared in the press – and what would have marred a great occasion passed into oblivion.

*   *   *

Cuthbert Bardsley's enthronement as "the Fifth Lord Bishop of the Revived See of Coventry" took place on Saturday, 5th May 1956. Thirteen years had passed since Neville Gorton had also been enthroned in the ruins of the old Cathedral. Its spire still stood firm, a symbol of undefeated hope. Beyond it, the ruins had been cleared of rubble and laid out with gravel aisles and paths and grass lawns. The floor was laid, the foundations out of sight. Soon the walls were to rise. All was ready for the great service of enthronement. The cherry trees were in bloom.

Two thousand people from all parts of the diocese and from parishes at Woolwich, Southwark and Croydon, where Cuthbert had previously served, were present. The Armed Forces were represented, among others, by General Sir John Crocker, former Adjutant-General, and Major-General R.E. Urquhart, shortly to become the Commanding Officer at Sandhurst. Among the visiting clergy were the Bishops of Worcester (Mervyn Charles-Edwards), Leicester (Ronald R. Williams), Aston (Michael Parker) and Singapore (Harold Baines), the Chaplain-General (A. Cole), the Chaplain-in-Chief R.A.F. (G. Druitt), the Provosts of Birmingham and Southwark, and the Archdeacon of Croydon. Lee Abbey was represented by its Warden and staff.

At 3 o'clock, the Bishop, his Chaplains, the Archdeacon of Canterbury, and the Chancellor and Registrar of the diocese, were escorted by officers of the Church Lads' Brigade to the West Door of the Cathedral. There the Bishop knocked three times on the door with his staff, and asked of the Provost admission to his place as Bishop in the Cathedral Church. The Provost, R.T. Howard, ordered the door to be opened. The Archdeacon of Canterbury, Alexander Sargent, presented the Archbishop's Mandate to be read, and the Provost welcomed the new Bishop. Then Cuthbert with his chaplains, the Revds Patrick Ashe, H. Manley and Jesse Carter, preceded by the Cathedral Churchwardens, the Cross of Nails and the Chapter, and attended by the Provost and the Archdeacon of Canterbury, entered the Cathedral and proceeded to the Chancel, the Chapter taking their places before the throne.

The Bishop took the Oath of Allegiance to the Queen, made the Declaration of Assent to the thirty-nine Articles of Religion and to the Book of Common Prayer, and of the Ordering of Bishops, Priests and Deacons. He then made the customary Declaration of Fidelity to the Cathedral Church and its Statutes. The Provost commended the Bishop to the prayers of the congregation, and then, taking him by the right hand, placed him in the throne.

(The "throne" was a simple oak chair taken from the West Crypt. On it, Archdeacon Proctor records, was "the maker's 'trade mark' carved on the leg, a delightful little mouse! This was, however, *not* an appropriate symbol for our new Bishop! Delightful, yes. But little, no.

And a mouse! Well, it is laughable to think of it!") The chair stood on a dais overlooking the rising walls of the new Cathedral, on the spot where the Bishop's throne had been before the destruction of the Cathedral in 1940.

The Archdeacon of Canterbury assigned to Cuthbert "this chair, which shall be thy Episcopal Seat until such times as the Cathedral be rebuilt, and I place thee therein, in the Name of our Lord Jesus Christ". The Provost addressed the congregation: "We present to you our Bishop, now duly inducted and enthroned as our Father in God, and we ask for him your loyalty, your affection, and your prayers." A fanfare rang out.

"Let it be my first act as your Bishop", Cuthbert said to the people, "to pray with you to God, that together we may open our hearts afresh to his Holy Spirit and ask his blessing upon ourselves and upon all men." All joined in singing the *Veni Creator*.

The Provost and Chapter and the Diocesan Clergy made their profession of obedience to the Bishop, who was then greeted by Free Church Ministers representing the Free Church Federal Council of Coventry. "May we have fellowship one with another through our common faith and service", Cuthbert replied.

In the address which followed, Cuthbert said:

I have come among you at a moment of acute tension in the life of our nation. The peace of the world is precarious. Racialism, nationalism, class-hatred may lead us over the precipice into the total destruction of mankind.

For the first time in history we are more clearly aware than ever before of the possibility of a cataclysmic finale.

We have reached the turning of the ways for Britain. We can either go forward through the discovery of a new moral seriousness into mature Christian leadership in the affairs of the world, or backwards through increasing laziness and apathy, sectional distrust, individual self-seeking and escape from responsibility to the place where we become a fourth-rate power of quarrelsome, querulous self-seekers, whose only object in life is to be cosy and cushy.

That road spells death. We must choose life and greatness or death through littleness.

Our present task in the diocese is to love the multitudes into the fellowship of the Church and to ensure that the fellowship is warm, welcoming, and worthwhile when they get there.

To achieve this mighty task we need new methods, new men, new money.

New methods, because we clergy can no longer sit around expecting that people will come to church. They won't come unless we get around. The home-visiting parson is still the church-filling parson. But in these days we must not merely visit the home. We must visit the club, the pub, the factory. We must not merely use the pulpit for our propaganda, we must use the press, the wireless, the television, the play, the cinema. . . .

We need **new men** – not so much new in quality, for it is my belief that the average C. of E. parson today is more alive, alert, on his toes than for a long time past. We want new men in the sense of more men – more priests, many, many more of the right sort. We need more lay men and women who are prepared to live out their faith, and, at times, speak about their faith in factory, in workshop, on bus and tube, in pub and club, with friends and foes.

We also need **new money**. Twenty years ago sixpence in the plate was enough. It's not enough today. Values have changed. You cannot buy a packet of cigarettes for sixpence. You cannot buy a pint of beer for sixpence. You cannot build an effective church with sixpence in the plate. We've got new schools to build, new churches in new housing areas, new literature for this new age. It all costs money. An effective Church is built upon effective almsgiving.

We need a new vision, a new sense of vocation, a new belief in ourselves. Above all, a new belief in Christ.

If every churchman really prayed for thirty minutes every day – wrestling with God on behalf of his church and nation – there would come a mighty spiritual awakening in this land within a year . . .

We shall not win men by sudden eruptions, such as commando campaigns or MRA plays or Billy Graham crusades – though these have their part. Fundamentally we shall win men from within by being identified with them where they are for a long period, in all their interests, taking an active part in borough council, trade union, and in complete identification with people in their groups, winning them into fullness of a personal faith in our Lord and his Church.

What of the future of our country? We have descended from our imperial heights into the valley of mediocrity, trailing clouds of glory in the murky muddiness of personal self-seeking. We cannot remain in that valley, for if we do we shall perish. We must climb out to other visions, other heights. We cannot all reach the headlines, but each of us has a vital part to play. Every one of us can stop being a spectator. If you can believe that the Church is a society of people who believe in God and seek to obey him, then do not be a disinterested spectator of the life of that society but a living part of it.

Your ultimate final decision is between yourself and God, before whom we must all eventually answer.

The future of our country is at stake – the future of the world is in jeopardy – the future of your immortal soul is in the balance. To drift is to drift into decay. To watch is to watch the sands of time running away. To leave it to others may well be to leave it undone.

I thank God for being alive at a moment like this; I thank God for the privilege of coming among you at such a moment as this. In Church and nation we have been given a great heritage. We dare not, we must not, throw it away. To everyone of us comes the challenge: "What think ye of Christ?" Every one of us sooner or later must give the reply.

Those who attended the Enthronement Service that May day could be in no doubt that the new chapter in the life of the diocese of Coventry was off to a vigorous start.

*　　　*　　　*

In a BBC television programme some four and a half years after Cuthbert Bardsley began work in the diocese, he was interviewed by Canon William Purcell. "What", he asked, "do you think is the chief duty of a bishop in the modern world?" Cuthbert replied in terms of pastor and prophet – the shepherd who looks after Christ's flock, and the prophet "who tries to relate the mind of God to the needs of a very needy world, and to proclaim God's message in terms that will be understandable to people who are bewildered by the world as they find it".

He was to pursue these two aims for twenty years in his own diocese, and far beyond it. Pastor and prophet – what greater task could there be? He went to it with a will.

He worked from a secure and happy base. His sister Dorothy, who had stood by him so gallantly through the blitz and supported him in the eleven years after the end of the war and before the move to Coventry, was still with him. It was her task to preside over a considerable household. She was an excellent hostess. The house and garden were ample for their needs (the garden has now been considerably reduced in size). There was a resident housekeeper, a chauffeur (Wentworth Jennings, known to all as Wenty), two gardeners, and a daily helper. There was a personal assistant and his secretary, and a personal secretary and her assistant. This team was gathered gradually as time went on, and the cost of a considerable part of it was met from Cuthbert's own resources. From the early days, the nucleus of that little group – the Bishop, his sister, the secretary, the gardener and the cook – would meet regularly for prayer.

Cuthbert's arrival at the house was not without incident. While the furniture was outside and he and his sister were unpacking in the hall, a small elderly figure arrived on a motor-cycle. Thinking he was the postman, Cuthbert said: "Is this the second post?" "No", said the visitor, "I am the vicar of Coventry." Cuthbert wondered whether, if he continued to drop bricks of that kind, he would be removed from office.

The new Bishop planned the rooms of his home in such a way that visitors, on entering the house, would find the Bishop's study on their right and, immediately on their left, his chapel. It was only a step or two across the hallway from the one to the other. It was thus possible, a conversation having reached its end, to take the caller across the hallway and pray with him before he left. And it became Cuthbert's habit not only to make this chapel the centre of his Eucharistic worship and the place where he said the daily Offices, but also the place into which he would step for a brief moment of prayer before he set out on a diocesan engagement, and to which he would return when his task was completed. This became an unbreakable habit. The chapel became, too, the place where Cuthbert exercised his healing ministry. Many found healing of body and peace of mind in this room, the focal point of all his work. Here was his prayer-desk, the carpet near it strewn with photos and letters to remind him in his work of intercessory prayer.

*   *   *

The city of Coventry, though still bearing the "honourable scars" of the war, was enjoying boom years. Unemployment figures were low. Workers poured in from places as far away as Scotland, Ireland and Wales, attracted by the high wages offered to them by industry. Indeed, it was said that Coventry had the highest paid male population of any city in Great Britain. There was great demand for cars, machine tools, and other products of the engineering industry.

Here Cuthbert's knowledge of industry in South London was to stand him in good stead. His contacts at board-room level and on the factory floor had been considerable. In Coventry he got to know Mr William (later Lord) Rootes, and persuaded him to preside over a lunch for leading industrialists. That opened the door to many of the main industries, and also led to major assistance in the big financial appeal which had to be launched for the Cathedral. He welcomed opportunities to visit the workers in the factories and in the working men's clubs, and in the big stores such as Woolworths and Owen Owens – one of these firms opened half an hour early in the morning so that he could meet the staff.

The diocese was, in Cuthbert's opinion, an ideal one, not too big, not too small, partly urban, partly country. It was possible for him to get to know all his clergy well. He recalled that Bertram Simpson, his former Bishop of Southwark, had, on going to his diocese, refused to sit on any committee until he had met personally every priest in his diocese. Cuthbert determined to follow his example, and to spend the first three months of his period in Coventry in visiting every deanery – there were some fourteen – and every clergyman in his own home – there were some two hundred and twenty men. The visit to each deanery lasted about four days. Cuthbert was soon on Christian name terms with the clergy and their families. Had he not paid these visits at this time, it might well have proved impossible to do so later on, when other claims on his time and energy were multiplied. Best of all, he enjoyed visits to separate parishes. He would be met on the outskirts of the parish by the vicar and a little group of parishioners. They would then go visiting – the old and the sick, the young in homes and

138

schools. He was interested, not only in the churchgoers, but in everyone in the parish. He constantly kept in mind that, however good the church attendance might be, there were many still unreached. He, the Bishop, and the vicar and his people cared about *them*. These visits, in all parts of the diocese, began to prepare the way for the great missions which later were to be a feature of Cuthbert's work in the diocese.

*   *   *

At the heart of the diocese was the Cathedral. From the day of his enthronement – indeed, from the day when he had attended the laying of the foundation stone – Cuthbert had been eager to press forward with the work of building. The planning had been fraught with difficulties. Many questions had to be answered before even the decision could be reached to build "on or near its present site". Early in 1942 Sir Giles Gilbert Scott was invited to design the new Cathedral. In 1944 and 1945 his designs were submitted to and approved by the Cathedral Council, only to find no favour with the Royal Fine Art Commission. The distinguished architect, who had been responsible, among many other great projects, for the design of Liverpool Cathedral, resigned. The Cathedral Council then appointed a commission of public men to advise on the problem. After six months of hard and detailed work, the Harlech Commission reported and the Diocesan Conference gave its "general approval", a competition was launched for the choice of an architect, the winner being Mr (later Sir) Basil Spence (August 1951). He was forty-three at the time of his appointment.

This is no place to go into the controversy which followed the publishing of his designs, and the story is told in some detail in Provost Howard's *Ruined and Rebuilt*.[5] To say that the debate was a heated one is to make a considerable understatement. There were difficulties in obtaining a building permit, for there was a severe housing shortage. At last, in April 1954, the Minister of Works, Sir David (later Lord) Eccles issued the licence. By the time of the Bishop's enthronement the main decisions about shape and structure had been taken, and, within nine months of the enthronement, the

---

[5] Published by the Council of Coventry Cathedral 1962, pp. 44ff.

walls began to rise. By the end of 1961 the nave was completed. By 1962 all would be ready for its consecration. Cuthbert – Geoffrey Fisher thought him "tailor-made for the job" – considered himself to be the most privileged man in the Church of England to be its bishop; and, surely, he was the first bishop in history to see such a cathedral conceived and brought to birth in a fraction of a lifetime, such is the miracle of pre-stressed concrete.

He felt himself privileged, also, in the men with whom he had to work. Chief among these was Basil Spence. Cuthbert himself and R.T. Howard, the Provost, found Spence to be a deeply religious man, a genius with a great ability to create in solid form the vision which came to him, itself the outcome of his prayers. He was, in the words of the Provost, a man "humble before the Source of his inspiration". His aim was to create a building that would speak to the twentieth-century man or woman, that would express the faith in contemporary terms; a building in which all the worshippers could see from all angles, unobscured by pillars, what was going on in the doing of the liturgy; a Cathedral into which the passer-by could look and catch a vision, could even stop and stare and share (hence the great West Doors made of glass), worship and world being integrated in one great building.

Then there was Graham Sutherland, the creator of the huge tapestry which was to take the place of an east window, a great "Christ in Glory". Begun in 1959, it took 30,000 hours to make, woven in the little town of Felletin in the heart of France not far from Aubusson. The Bishop found Sutherland easy to work with, a man open to suggestions, who created hundreds of drawings and paintings before he was satisfied with the final expression of what was in his mind – a Roman Catholic, "a very remarkable, dedicated man of God".

Cuthbert was impressed with the humility of John Piper, whose great Baptistry window, together with the Nave windows created by younger artists, added such wonderful splashes of colour to what without them might have been a sombre building. Basil Spence wished to alter the original design of the font, which was too ornate. He suggested that a big lump of stone should be quarried from near Bethlehem and brought to Coventry. This was done, and Piper's baptistry window adds a wonderful riot of colour when the morning sun shines down through it onto the font. A visitor does not see the nave windows until he reaches the altar. This was done deliberately, as Basil Spence explained to the Bishop:

> In Christian experience, we start with a splash of colour and light at our baptism. Then most of us have a long pilgrimage, sometimes hard, until we come to the great central place, the table, the altar. There we turn, and are confronted with angels and archangels and all the company of heaven, there at the foot of the cross. I deliberately did it that way, so that you should not see all that glory until you went right into the heart of the encounter.

Meeting John Piper one day, Cuthbert said to him: "Your baptistry window is the greatest feature of all the things in our cathedral which evoke joy and satisfaction." Piper replied: "Don't tell me that, no, Sir." He did not want to hear lest it should make him vain.

There were others like John Hutton who would incise his designs on glass in the presence of those who watched him work – one slip of his instrument and the whole panel would be wrecked – and the masons whose leader received a well-deserved award in the Queen's Birthday Honours. Cuthbert enjoyed his contacts with all these men as the building moved towards its completion in 1962. It was a good team.

*   *   *

"A cathedral", Sir Basil Spence maintained, "is only the frame for a mystery." It is a work of art, and Coventry Cathedral is a great work of art. But it is far more than that. It stands to proclaim the mystery of God's love and truth at work in men's lives, to reconcile them with God and with one another, to lift them from despair to hope. It is a house of *prayer*.

Clifford Robinson makes the point well:

> Many of us shared in the privilege of taking visitors around the new Cathedral and I remember none more vividly than [the visit] of a retired bishop, well-advanced in years, and every inch a man of holiness and love.
>
> It was late afternoon and together we walked through the nave beneath the honeycomb canopy of new timber, down the North

Aisle, enjoying the windows, seventy feet high, gazing for some time at the immense High Altar and just behind it the great gold Cross capturing images of the charred Cross of roof beams in the ruins – but also the sudden freedom of a bird in flight . . . Crucifixion and Resurrection caught in one glance.

Our walk took a long time, and as always, I had a secret feeling of pride in all of it. We stood at the West Screen before he left. "Splendid, isn't it!" I said, and immediately wished I had kept silent. "Hmm", grunted that good priest, whose name I never knew. "Yes, very nice. . . . It needs praying in!"

None realized this better than the Bishop. He realized also that, humanly speaking, everything depended on the men and women who formed the team at the heart of the work of the cathedral and of the diocese. This had been uppermost in his thoughts and prayers from the day of his arrival in Coventry, and he bent all his energies to the gathering of such a team.

He was fortunate in the man who occupied the post of Provost and who welcomed him as the new Bishop. R.T. Howard took up his work in 1933 and so had served the Cathedral for some seven years before its destruction. It was he who sought to fight the fires on the terrible night of 14th November 1940, who had planned the Cathedral's "resurrection", had nurtured the worship of the congregation during the remaining years of the war, had travailed with the pains and frustrations of postwar planning, had supervised the preservation of the ruins of the old Cathedral and the foundations and stone-laying of the new, had seen the rubble removed and the pavements laid down, had built up the nucleus of the future congregation. After the death of Bishop Neville Gorton, Provost Howard and Cuthbert Bardsley worked together very happily for some six years. With great grace and humility, Howard felt that he was too old to undertake all that would be involved in planning the consecration of the new Cathedral and the immense activity which would follow. He offered his resignation, and concluded his work in 1958. He put the Cathedral even further in his debt by writing its story from 1939 to 1962 in *Ruined and Rebuilt*, a story of which we have already made use in this biography. A simple plaque "In memory of Dick Howard, Provost of this Cathedral 1933–58 and his wife Marjorie" in the floor of the old Cathedral in front of the altar is a fitting tribute to their great service.

Who should follow him? The appointment was of crucial importance. The Bishop was looking for someone who would lecture to a
conference of his clergy which was to convene after Easter 1957.
Roger Lloyd, Canon of Winchester and historian, mentioned to him
the name of the Vicar of St Mary's Church, Southampton, the Rev.
H.C.N. Williams. Cuthbert had never met Williams, but, on the
strength of Lloyd's recommendation, invited him to be the lecturer.
"Your invitation terrifies me," Williams replied, "but I will do my
best." He did, and Cuthbert wrote in October – the Conference had
had to be held later in the year than had originally been planned – :
"From the bottom of my heart I thank you for the magnificent
contribution you gave to us. It was a word from God . . . I hope this
may be the beginning of a friendship which will be of value to the
Church." It was: on 12th December we find him writing to Williams
again, asking him to join the cathedral staff, to do "one of the most
worthwhile pieces of work in the Church of England". He could not
at that moment say precisely what that post would be, for Provost
Howard had not yet announced his retirement, but he assured
Williams that he wrote with the unanimous assent of the cathedral
staff.

The Bishop, Williams and Joseph Poole (soon to be Canon
Precentor) met, and at the end of April 1958 the press was told of
Williams' appointment as Provost. It was an appointment which was
to continue to his retirement twenty-three years later, in 1981.

To Cuthbert the choice of the new Provost was an inspired one.
"Bill" Williams had been brought up in South Africa, and in a
television interview in 1987 he was to tell how cramped he felt in
England after the open spaces of Africa – and not only in a physical
sense. England seemed to him like a club, and the Church of
England, as by law established, like a club within a club. He was
deeply "moved by the beauty of the ruins" of the bombed Cathedral.
He saw in them the opportunity to start again, untrammelled by the
shackles of the past. He wanted the new Cathedral to be "a laboratory
of experiment", a place anchored in reality, a place where people hurt
by life could find hope. In later days, he was to be very critical of the
building in its finished state. He himself did not like the tapestry,
feeling it was "like a poster". He quoted someone who said that the
Cathedral was marvellous, but one could not breathe in it (there was
no ventilation), one could not see in it, one could not hear in it.

Williams' predecessor had caused the words "Father, forgive" to be incised in capitals on the wall in the sanctuary of the ruins. It was the new Provost's aim to "give that vision a programme". A man of great imagination, of prophetic fervour, and greatly gifted as a preacher, he longed to make the Cathedral a place for the healing of the wounds of history. One word above all others will be associated with his work: "reconciliation". He was determined that as Coventry had been brought to its knees by war, so Coventry should stand for forgiveness and reconciliation after the war. Indeed, he arranged that, soon after the completion of the main building, a party of German young people should come over to be employed in rebuilding the vestries that their fathers had destroyed, and in building an international youth centre (later to be dedicated in memory of John Kennedy by Bishop Otto Dibelius).

If this was the Provost's first great passion, his second great desire was to make the Cathedral not only the mother church of the diocese, but also the very heart of the life of the city. His mind and heart were devoted to the relating of religion to society, to linking the great church to the life of the community. To that end, he was prepared to stump the diocese and make his purposes known. No one could have pursued these ends with greater zeal than did Provost Williams.

The relationship between Bishop and Provost down the years was a close one, and the terms of their constant correspondence are affectionate. But it was not always an easy relationship. As with many people of genius, the Provost was a sensitive man. He was watchful for anything which he felt might detract from the estimation of his Cathedral in the eyes of those who came into contact with it. He was jealous for its reputation. The Bishop, in whose own organization and diary arrangement there could at times be found flaws, resented the making of decisions by the cathedral authorities of which he was unaware until it was too late for him to have a full share in them. The constant correspondence between the two men shows the Bishop as a man determined to preserve his control over areas where he had a right to decide, a man deeply affectionate and anxious not to exacerbate difficult situations, ready to apologize when there were diary clashes or when there had been forgetfulness on his own part. He clearly hated any possible rift in relationships, and was anxious to obey the biblical injunction never to let the sun go down on his wrath.

On 21st June 1988, Bill Williams looked back over the three

decades which had passed since Cuthbert called his team together. In a personal letter to Cuthbert, Williams wrote:

My dear Cuthbert,

I have been writing a reflective history of my twenty-three years as Provost, and I have had cause, of course, to refer to diaries. June, thirty years ago, was the month in which you brought the original team together in Coventry. And in a very real sense it was the beginning of a fulfilled ministry. Writing this reflection has been so far an amazing experience. A phrase of Kierkegaard which I have for long loved is "Life must be lived forward, but understood backward". And looking back I realize to the full how much I owe to you for your trust, your love, your forgiveness, your encouragement.

I think you know that mountaineering is one of my favourite diversions . . . Climbing is to me an analogy of a purposeful life: one puffs and blows, rests and goes on, fights failures, and looks to fellow climbers for support. And at the top one can – as I always do – sing the *Te Deum* at the top of my voice and can almost see the Lord sparing a smile. Then one looks down at the way by which one has climbed, and it shows itself to be a clear pattern.

So I do both – with your great heart in mind: I sing the *Te Deum* for having been in your company and I look back with understanding of how much I owe to you.

I send you not only my thanks, but my sincere love. Please give my love too to Ellen.

Yours ever,
Bill

*   *   *

If the Provost was to pursue his great aims, the pursuit would necessitate absences from the Cathedral and, fairly frequently, from the city. It was all the more imperative that at the centre of the Cathedral's life and liturgy, there should be a man content to give himself wholly to that end. Such a man was found in the person of Joseph Weston Poole, who came to the Cathedral as Precentor in 1958 and served it with great devotion until his retirement in 1977.

A perfectionist, a lover of Cathedrals and of Cathedral worship and

145

music, Joseph Poole had been a Minor Canon of Canterbury Cathedral for thirteen years and its Precentor and Sacrist for twelve of them. After that he had a period of parochial experience. He was well qualified to take up his work at Coventry. No detail escaped his eye – to him the order of a procession and the carriage of those who took part in it *mattered* because it was part of the worshippers' offering to God. (He caused 1962 penny pieces to be inserted at intervals in the nave and choir aisles so that those processing through them should keep a straight line.) He went to immense trouble in drawing up the series of services which followed the consecration of the Cathedral, and Cuthbert recalls that he himself took part in at least eight rehearsals of the consecration itself. The result of such care and attention to detail was that the services took place in an atmosphere of peace – there was no fuss, no whispered discussion as to what happened next or who went where. Bishop and Canon Precentor were at one in their desire that Cathedral and city should be closely linked – liturgy and life were one, and must be seen to be one.

The Cathedral team was beginning to gather. 1958 was to see further appointments of great significance – those of Simon Wilton Phipps, Stephen Edmund Verney, and Edward Henry Patey being among the most important for the developing life of the Cathedral and for its witness in the city and beyond.

Simon Phipps first met Cuthbert when the latter conducted a Quiet Day at Westcott House when Phipps was a student there. Both men were old Etonians, but there was something deeper than that which drew them to one another. There was a passion and a spirituality about the older man which appealed to the younger. When, as a chaplain at Trinity College, Cambridge, Phipps arranged a shop-floor job at an aircraft factory during the Long Vacation of 1956, he probably renewed his friendship with Cuthbert, but at no great depth or intimacy – Phipps was engaged in getting experience in the industrial field. Now, at the age of thirty-six, he consulted Ted Wickham who was doing pioneering work in that field in Sheffield under the inspiration of its bishop, Leslie Hunter. When Phipps found that Cuthbert was very keen to open up and develop all possible contacts with industry in and around Coventry, he was happy to take up the post of Industrial Chaplain, a post which he combined with a curacy at the Cathedral for ten years and which, as a Canon, he only left in 1968 to become Bishop of Horsham. He showed great creativity in building up a force of young men who were prepared to work in this borderline world between the Church and industry, and to pioneer in an area where all too little had been done since the Industrial Revolution changed the face of Britain.

In Stephen Verney Cuthbert found a man after his own heart, "a humble, unassuming, dedicated man of God, a man of great depth and spirituality", as he described him. He combined his work as Diocesan Missioner with the work of being Vicar of Leamington Hastings from 1958 to 1964, when he was appointed Canon Residentiary. He held this last post until he was made Canon of St George's Chapel, Windsor in 1970.

Verney was a pastor in his own parish, but his influence radiated beyond the parish bounds out into the diocese. He proved to be a man against whose able mind Cuthbert could test his ideas – the Bishop often enjoyed the hospitality which Stephen and his wife Scilla offered him in their home, and the two men would go for walks together. It was from Stephen Verney that a phrase came which was to prove influential in the life of the Cathedral and the diocese – "a consecrated Cathedral demands a consecrated people". We shall see more of this shortly.

Verney responded freely to the feeling of warmth and appreciation which Cuthbert showed him, and realized that together they were engaged on a spiritual adventure. He wrote of the Bishop: "He had the amazing quality of seeing Christ in us, and enabling Christ to come to the birth in us. What more can I say?"

Edward Henry Patey was another who joined the team in 1958 and was to remain a member until he became Dean of Liverpool in 1964. He brought to his work parish experience; and the fact that he had been Chaplain for Youth to the Bishop of Durham for four years, and secretary to the Youth Department of the British Council of Churches for another four, enabled him to make his influence felt in the world of youth and education. He had an alert and original mind and proved to be a loyal colleague to Cuthbert; he was a man capable of hard work, efficient, loving, an asset to the group.

Williams, Poole, Phipps, Verney, Patey.

It was typical of Cuthbert [Edward Patey wrote] to take the plunge and appoint the five of us simultaneously, trusting that we would be able to work with him and together in preparing the new ministry of the Cathedral in the four years before the consecration, and bringing it into action when it was completed. I can see that he was prepared to take a considerable risk (or venture of faith?) in appointing us in this way. Certainly we were aware of the unique privilege which he had entrusted to us in an enterprise that was . . . to become well-known all over the world.

Perhaps Coventry Cathedral "took off" in the way it did [Simon Phipps wrote] as a result of a combination of the hot helium of Cuthbert's vision, plus the bags of solid sand from the theology which Edward Patey, Stephen Verney and I provided, plus Bill Williams' big sense of direction in his outreach to Germany and the USA . . . I think Cuthbert sometimes felt that he had opened a bit of a Pandora's box in appointing us all. As a result, there were sometimes some tensions. But we could *always* talk to him and get a real hearing. And to each of us he was a very solid, caring, interceding friend.

If ever there was a bunch of individualists, this was it. Of course there were differences, sometimes sharp ones. Of course there were conflicts of judgement. And Cuthbert often found himself ending a meeting with a prayer which included these lines:

> Drop thy still dews of quietness
> Till all our strivings cease!

The quality of the team can be assessed by the work they achieved as well as by the tasks to which some of them were appointed when their time at Coventry came to an end – Phipps to Horsham and then Lincoln, Verney to Windsor and then Repton, Patey to Liverpool. "To have worked at Coventry", Patey maintained, "at such an important period in the history of that diocese and under such dynamic episcopal leadership, was a rare privilege. If Cuthbert sometimes infuriated us with his unpredictability, our next meeting with him always banished any annoyance we might have felt. He was such a loving and lovable pastor and friend. He showered affection on his colleagues to which they were only too eager to respond."

*   *   *

A bishop coming new to his diocese, as Cuthbert did in 1956, is dependent on the knowledge and experience of men who have already been working in it and who know the ground. Eric Ancrum Buchan was one such. He knew every corner of the diocese. He was Vicar of St Mark with St Barnabas, Coventry, 1945–59, and an honorary Canon and Rural Dean when Cuthbert took up his work. He was later to become Archdeacon of Coventry. The Bishop describes him as "a financial wizard" and put him in charge of raising some £750,000, in those days a very large sum, for the work of the Cathedral and the diocese. In 1959 he appointed him Director of Christian Steward-ship. The major part of this work of fund-raising was done by a long series of meetings, mostly small, mostly consisting of men, which the Bishop would address and to whom Buchan would expound the principles of Stewardship.

Jesse Heighton Proctor had also been at work in the diocese well before Cuthbert arrived. At the time of Cuthbert's coming, he was Canon Theologian, Director of Ordination Candidates and Post-Ordination Studies. The Bishop was to appoint him Archdeacon of Warwick in 1958.

When Cuthbert Bardsley became Bishop of Coventry in 1956 [Proctor wrote], we immediately knew that a giant of a man had arrived. He was tall of stature . . . wide in interests, deep in feelings, outward looking in temperament (yet not without plenty of inward, forward and upward projection) and as ubiquitous as one man could possibly be. It was impossible to doubt that things were going to happen and that a continuous and relentless impetus would come from this man. The new Cathedral was rising, the city was at last looking forward instead of just licking its wounds, the outer reaches of a largely rural diocese were limbering up for the new age.

Bishop Newnham Davis, formerly of Antigua, was Assistant Bishop in the opening years of Cuthbert's episcopate. The arrival of Bishop John David McKie in 1960 brought added wisdom to the diocesan team and episcopal help to the diocesan Bishop. He had had experience as a chaplain in the war and as Bishop Coadjutor of Melbourne, Australia, and was to be a loved figure as Assistant Bishop of Coventry until his retirement in 1981.

With such a team as this, staff meetings, which were held weekly and were of some hours' duration, were lively occasions. To them were invited, as needed, heads of departments, ordinands, people responsible for special projects in hand. Fun was a regular ingredient – at times the solemn assembly took on a riotous dimension – and there was always lunch at the Bishop's house presided over by himself and his sister Dorothy (or, in later years, by his wife Ellen). Quite early in Cuthbert's episcopate, Archbishop Geoffrey Fisher, meeting the President of the Mothers' Union of the diocese at a garden party, asked: "How are you settling down with Cuthbert Bardsley?" At once, he corrected himself: "No, that's the wrong thing to say – you don't *settle down* with Cuthbert Bardsley."

The Bishop knew how to get loyal help from his staff. One of them writes:

> The pressure was generally pretty heavy, and he kept a remarkably serene attitude. I only once saw him lose his temper – with someone who had failed to see the urgency of a situation and who dragged his feet. The explosion was monumental! That man was never the same again! And the job was done. But, loss of patience was never a characteristic of Cuthbert – thank goodness!

Two other people were of great help to Cuthbert in these years of intense activity, as the consecration of the Cathedral drew steadily nearer. The first was Lewis J. Davey. After war service and many years in business, and after the death of his wife, he lost his zest for his professional work. Years before, he had formed a close friendship with Cuthbert in the days when the latter had been engaged in work with the Oxford Groups. Cuthbert led him to faith in Christ, and their friendship deepened.

One day, as Davey was travelling home by train from his work in the city, he looked around at his fellow-travellers. They were all cast in the same mould. Bowler hats, rolled umbrellas and briefcases were in the rack over their heads; each wore a neat suit, white shirt and select tie. "Oh God," he thought, "I am just like that. Get me out of this rut. Let me do something more vital before I die."

Davey went to Cuthbert's enthronement, and met him again in a brief encounter after the service. Some three months later he got a letter from the Bishop.

He needed help, especially over administration, which was always threatening to overwhelm him. He wanted a trained mind beside him to cope with the intricacies of ecclesiastical procedure, for which as a diocesan bishop, he was now responsible. There was a new Cathedral being built, the City of Coventry was expanding rapidly, new housing estates were being erected and new churches would have to be provided. There was not much money available for my salary, he could not offer much but toil and sweat, but would I come?

I knew at once that this was the answer to my prayer. Instead of trying to turn myself into a priest for which I had few qualifications, I could use my whole life's training and experience in the service of the Church, and at the right hand of the man to whom we as a family owed so much, a man who was primarily an evangelist, whose dominant aim was to do God's Will and bring people to a living experience of Christ. The Church that I knew had few such men, especially in positions of authority. I believed that by serving Cuthbert, even in the ordinary, routine, mundane jobs, I could, by helping to set him more free, make the Church a better instrument for the carrying out of God's will, and find my own fulfilment.

I went to Coventry and talked it over with Cuthbert. I have often said since, that when he wants something done, he wants it done not tomorrow, not today, but yesterday. So it was now. When could I come? I told him, 1st October.

The year was 1956.

His arrival at Cuthbert's house as the Bishop's Personal Assistant was not wholly reassuring. He was late.

Flooded roads had delayed me, so I stopped for a meal at Southam and telephoned to say I would be late. I was nearly exhausted when I arrived at last, to be warmly welcomed and introduced to Provost and Mrs Howard – a heartening experience, for two kinder or more truly Christian people I have never met.

When I recovered, assisted by a tot of the episcopal whisky (reserved for cases as extreme as mine), the Bishop told me he had a splendid idea. The next morning at 7.30 a.m. he was celebrating Holy Communion and having breakfast with all the Coventry clergy. It was a grand opportunity for me to go and meet them.

At this moment I think I had a glimmer of what lay behind a remark made to me by one of his curates at Woolwich who, when he heard of my appointment said, "My dear Lewis, you won't last six months. No one could ever stand his pace."

There I was the next day at 7.15 a.m. being driven bleary-eyed through the Coventry streets. In my slightly dazed condition I have only a dim recollection of the service and breakfast, except that I was made very welcome and I found that clergy en masse were not really very frightening.

Back to Bishop's House where the staff assembled for a short service and I was introduced. At that time the Board of Finance offices were also in Bishop's House, so the staff numbered in all about six or seven, including June, the Bishop's Secretary, who had been secretary to Bishop Gorton, who had died in office.

In the afternoon Cuthbert and I went for a walk. This seemed an excellent idea to me, but later I was to discover that this was a very rare occurrence and he must have sacrificed some very valuable time to do it.

The following day I began to look round to try to get my bearings. There was no precedent, nobody to guide or instruct me. The job was there for me to make in my own way, which had some advantages. The difficulty was, I soon found, to get even a few minutes with the Bishop. His days were packed, from the time he came to his Chapel at 7 a.m. for Quiet Time and prayer – with pen and paper to record those things which required action – until he returned from his evening engagement, usually between 10 and 11 p.m.

The mistake I made in the first few weeks was in thinking I must get him "organized". Accustomed as I was to the tidy pigeon-holed organization of an accountant's office – and I, as senior partner, had been largely responsible for this – the Bishop's way of life seemed to me haphazard and disorganized. I was wrong on two counts. First, he was a much better administrator than I realized, with a good memory on which he relied heavily (too heavily at times perhaps), and second, what looked to me like chaos was in fact, organized chaos. He had worked "on his own" since his appointment to Woolwich in 1940 and he had developed his own technique. This enabled him to work at his own speed, which was phenomenal. Every attempt I made to introduce "efficiency measures" only slowed him down. He bore this with remarkable patience, but after a few months I began to see that my job was to leave him free to be himself, to work and express himself in his own way, and to be there to ease the strains, to carry some of the burdens, to be a kind of human dustbin into which he could throw anything he wanted to be rid of, leaving me to do a Steptoe, sifting and sorting and salvaging. After a time this began to work well and as my understanding of episcopal affairs developed I was able to take increasing responsibility. It took me about three years before I really got the feel of the job. I learned by experience.

That was the beginning of thirteen years of growing appreciation one of the other – the Bishop of his Personal Assistant, Davey of the Bishop. Cuthbert, assisted by Patrick Ashe, presided over his marriage to Miss Josephine Mary Gorton (a distant relative of Bishop Neville Gorton) in 1966 – his first wife had died in 1954.

Davey attended all the main diocesan committees, thus relieving Cuthbert of much administrative work and yet keeping him in close touch with what was going on in the life of the diocese. He was an excellent link man.

Davey owed him much, for Cuthbert had virtually saved his brother-in-law's life by bringing him hope and faith at a time of deep despair. He appreciated the reality of Cuthbert's discipleship – "he really loved his Lord – no humbug; and he keeps his promises – totally dependable. And very generous."

Then there was Betty Priddis (now Mrs Simpson, wife of Canon P.W. Simpson, Rural Dean of Coventry South). She came to Cuthbert as his secretary in 1960 and has worked for his two successors, Bishops John Gibbs and Simon Barrington-Ward, with quiet distinction. Before becoming secretary to Cuthbert, she had served for a couple of years as secretary to the Bishop's Personal Assistant, and so had begun to enter into the complexities of a diocesan Bishop's household and diary. Tactful and efficient and aided by a sense of humour, she has a way of keeping her head amidst a whirl of activity, and is second to none in her respect for Cuthbert.

Lawrence Jackson who, as incumbent of Holy Trinity Church for eight years, lived opposite Cuthbert's house and was thus in an ideal situation to observe the goings-on across the road, has given a lively description of the Bishop setting off on his frequent journeys abroad:

The whole of his secretariat – Betty, Lewis Davey, Beryl, Joan, and "Wenty" the chauffeur-gardener, surrounded the car with suit-cases and briefcases galore, in a frenzy of activity. Only when Cuthbert's car disappeared "at the speed of knots" down the drive of Bishop's House did a corporate and individual sigh of relief come over the entourage. It goes without saying that all those close to Cuthbert were entirely devoted to him, and he, of course, always was the kindest of men.

The Consecration of a People

The Bishop had gathered his team. It was a strong group whose members brought to the diocese a great variety of gifts and expertise. They differed widely one from the other, but they were bound together by the ties of prayer and consultation. Sometimes, under the guidance of the Bishop, they would go off to a country house to spend a couple of days together in prayer, seeking the mind of God for his Church. And every Monday morning Cuthbert would celebrate the Eucharist, when each would acknowledge his need of the others and all acknowledge their need of God's forgiving and sustaining grace.

Meanwhile, the new Cathedral was steadily rising. Everyone was beginning to look forward to 1962 when the building would be complete and ready for its Dedication.

But was the *diocese* ready? That was a different matter. As we have seen, Stephen Verney had said that "a consecrated Cathedral demands a consecrated people". Cuthbert was entirely at one with him in this. Together, they set about the preparation of the *people*.

The story has been told by Stephen Verney in a small book whose importance is out of all proportion to its size. *Fire in Coventry*[6] has run into many impressions. The first half of the book tells the story of the preparation, the second half expounds its meaning. Here one can do little more than summarize.

It all began three years before the Consecration of the Cathedral, in Monks Kirby. You have never heard of that place? It is not the focal point of English history or life and activity. It is a village near Coventry; and there a small group of clergy (a Rural Deanery

[6] First published by Hodder & Stoughton in 1964

154

Chapter, to give the group its official name) used to meet regularly. No shiver of excitement runs down your spine as you envisage the gathering? That is not surprising. But God has a way of working from small beginnings.

One of the members of the Chapter group said: "We are faced with the Consecration of our Cathedral in just over three years. I believe this is going to be a great spiritual opportunity." What did he mean? The Queen would come. The Archbishops of Canterbury and York would take part. Trumpets would sound. But "a great *spiritual* opportunity"?

It was a very ordinary group of very ordinary clergy who met at Monks Kirby that February morning in 1959. They knew one another and were friends, but at no great depth. They were busy and very active but, if truth be told, like many other Christians had not over-much time for prayer. But as they met with Stephen Verney, himself a parish priest as well as the Diocesan Missioner, they began to see that in their regular meetings they had all too often given time to the discussion of financial matters and to the arrangement of routine duties, and all too seldom had allowed time to wait on God, to be silent before him, to be open to his will and responsive to his grace and his demands.

For some nine months they met, seeking to know the mind of God more clearly in the light of the coming Consecration of the Cathedral. They began to get to know one another, their weaknesses and fears and suspicions, and to know God in a new way, in prayer and Bible study. Then they wrote to the Bishop to tell him what was happening. He called his staff together with others responsible for the life of the diocese. They went away for three days to find out how best to prepare the diocese for the great event of 1962. The Bishop refused to "lay something on", as it were from above: the Holy Spirit would show the way forward if they were prepared to pray and to watch.

Stephen Verney, together with a few other clergy, visited the other Rural Deanery Chapters in the diocese one by one. The clergy met, beginning the day with Holy Communion, following it with silent waiting on God, listening to an exposition of the Bible, entering into discussion. Throughout the diocese the conviction grew that, at whatever cost to other activities and to their own leisure, these groups of clergy must go on meeting, as the Monks Kirby group had done, and wait on God unhurriedly. So the Spirit began to move in the diocese.

In September 1961, the Bishop took 180 of his clergy away to

Oxford for a residential conference. There were only eighteen months to go before the Consecration of the Cathedral – there was no time to be lost. Together, they heard Stephen Verney tell of the movement of the Spirit already at work in the diocese. They heard a gifted woman, Dr Kathleen Bliss, speak of the place of the laity in the life and work of the Church – after all, they are 99.5 per cent of its membership. A plan of action began to emerge.

It could best be described by thinking of a stone dropped into a pond, causing ripples to expand in ever-widening circles. Already the first ripple had happened – the clergy had been touched. The second should be groups of clergy and laity meeting regularly for the next six months – Edward Patey drew up study notes to guide them. The third should be the congregations of every parish church, meeting to hear what the clergy and laity groups had discovered, to listen to God in prayer and obedience, to listen to one another. The fourth ripple would consist of certain dramatic acts, such as the carrying of the Cross of Nails round the parishes (of which we shall see more shortly); and the re-affirmation of baptismal and ordination vows. What all this would lead to after the Consecration of the Cathedral the Bishop, Stephen Verney and their colleagues were prepared to leave to God. "The Spirit bloweth where it listeth."

So the preparation of the people went on – "a consecrated people" was being prepared for "a consecrated Cathedral". No doubt there were areas within the diocese where, for all the work of the Bishop and the Diocesan Missioner, little result was to be seen: God never forces his way through the door of an individual's life or the door of a parish church. But that the Spirit of God was at work there could be no doubt. Here formality in prayer gave place to reality; there suspicion to trust. Here "busy-ness" gave place to a re-arrangement of spiritual priorities – prayer, Sacrament, Bible study became central; there the parish priest learned to trust his people and they to see that the Church was not *his* but *theirs*. Here broken relationships were healed, and there broken bodies and minds; wholeness and holiness were seen as two sides of one coin. Here despondency began to give way to hope; there resurrection was experienced as a present-day reality. Here a congregation saw this item of the creed come alive – "I believe in the forgiveness of sins"; there another congregation glimpsed the truth of "I believe in the Holy Spirit, the Lord, the Life-giver".

Much of this movement of the Spirit was quiet, steady, undemonstrative – the tide often comes in noiselessly and is none the less cleansing and refreshing for that. But sometimes the movement of the Spirit took on more dramatic forms, and two of these must be mentioned here.

The first began in a heap of rubble. The bombing of the Cathedral on the terrible night of 14th November 1940 had left great masses of charred timbers and molten metal in the ruins. Among these were hundreds of nails which for centuries had helped to hold the structure of the Cathedral together. A priest picked up three of these fourteenth-century nails and fashioned them into a cross, a cross of much the same shape as that on which Jesus of Nazareth had been crucified. Provost Howard and those around him looked at that cross and had the vision to make the Cross of Nails a symbol of their determination to follow the way of love: the Cathedral's ministry should be above all else a ministry of Reconciliation. There was an essential simplicity about those three charred nails – they spoke of the reconciliation of the individual with himself; of the reconciliation of the individual with his God; of the reconciliation of conflicting elements within society, and – where better than Coventry to say this to the world? – the reconciliation of the nations with Germany in the aftermath of World War II.

The symbol "took on" in a way that that priest never imagined. In 1976, guided by the experience of the first years of the rebuilt Cathedral and by a touch of his own genius, Provost Williams published *The Discipline of the Community of the Cross of Nails*. At first, there were only individual members, but soon there were groups in various localities around the world, and these were gathered together in chapters within the Community. Membership of the Community committed those who entered it to a common discipline for Christian living, a common programme of work, prayer and study, and a Ministry of Reconciliation and Renewal in terms relevant to their own situation. Williams travelled indefatigably in the cause of that reconciliation of which the Cross of Nails spoke so eloquently. In their own persons Provost and Bishop forged links, supremely with Germany, which no subsequent international difficulties could weaken.

In addition to these crosses of three nails, now silver-plated and used increasingly throughout the diocese and beyond, was one great cross of charred wood. It consisted of two roof timbers rescued from the flames, and it stood on an altar in the ruins of the old Cathedral. Behind it, incised in capitals on the wall, the words stood out: "Father, forgive." Its very starkness accentuated its message. Reconciliation is costly. Death comes before new life.

That charred cross continues to speak with a strange power. Lewis Davey tells how he found a German woman standing before it. She was in tears. "Will you British never forgive and forget?", she said. Davey made her look again at that cross. "See what it says: not 'Father, forgive *them*', but simply 'Father, forgive'. We *all* stand in need of that forgiveness."

Canon Eric Buchan, Rural Dean of Coventry, suggested that the cross of nails should be carried round the diocese, from parish to parish. Over forty days and forty nights, there should be a pilgrimage. Each parish where the cross rested should be a link in a chain of prayer, and while that particular parish prayed for the diocese and for its Cathedral so soon to be consecrated, the whole diocese would pray for that parish. On the eve of the consecration, the cross would come back home and be set on the altar of the new Cathedral – a symbol of sacrificial love and a sign of the unity of the diocese as the family of God.

And so it was. As one parish handed the cross over to another, these words were used:

> Receive this Cross of Nails, brought to you with the love and the prayers of your fellows from the ruined sanctuary of our Cathedral of St Michael. Cherish this cross, as a token of the merciful forgiveness of God, declared to us in the Passion of our Saviour Jesus Christ. Watch about this cross, in prayer for one another and for us, for Cuthbert our Bishop, and for all in this Diocese of Coventry who love and serve the Lord Jesus.

Canon Buchan's vision was an inspiration. The story of the effect of this dramatic act on parishes and individuals forms one of the most inspiring chapters in Stephen Verney's *Fire in Coventry*. The preparation of the people was proceeding apace.

*　　　*　　　*

The second movement of the Spirit found its centre in the Bishop himself. As he looked forward to the consecration of the Cathedral in which, of necessity, he would be the central figure, he longed, perhaps more deeply than anyone else, that the *people* should be a consecrated people. As he prayed, a conviction deepened in him that he himself should lead a mission to the diocese. He shared this conviction with his Diocesan Missioner, Stephen Verney, in March 1961. A month later he put it to his Diocesan Conference: "We are thinking in terms of the consecration of a people. It is my hope and belief that these mission services will lead many to put their whole trust unreservedly in the Lord Jesus Christ, and to accept him as their Lord and Saviour." During the summer and autumn, plans went ahead, and the ten days of 4th–14th April 1962, just a few weeks prior to the Consecration of the Cathedral, were set aside for the event.

It was a bold concept, showing the Bishop at his best as an initiator and a leader. Not every diocesan Bishop would have the daring to plan such a mission, and himself to be the central figure every night. But once Cuthbert was sure of God's guidance, he was prepared to take risks and to face the discouragements of those who were all too ready to raise objections, to procrastinate, or even to oppose.

In Captain Tom Reeman of the Church Army, Cuthbert found a man ideally suited to train some two hundred counsellors from various parts of the diocese. The Bishop himself toured the diocese, meeting clergy and people, calling for prayer, kindling enthusiasm. Every Rural Deanery was visited by Stephen Verney and the Bishop, each visit itself becoming a mini-mission.

The parish church of All Saints, Leamington, which could seat some fifteen hundred to two thousand people, was filled night after night, mostly with regular churchgoers from all over the diocese, but also with some "fringers". After opening hymns, Stephen Verney would speak briefly about prayer. Another hymn, and Cuthbert would deal with the basics of the Christian faith and call for individual response. Many lives were changed, and new hope seeped back into the parishes and far beyond. A new kind of joy broke through, a new openness to God and to one another. "Come, and let yourself be built, as living stones, into a spiritual temple; become a holy priest-hood . . . " – Peter's words were beginning to take on a new meaning throughout the diocese (1 Peter 2:5).

The last service took place on the Eve of Palm Sunday. The Vicar of Leamington, the Rev. Anthony Rouse, said of the mission:

It has been a great and inspiring occasion for us in Leamington Parish Church ... I do not believe there is any diocese in the Church of England with a Bishop who over ten nights could gather together by the Ministry of the Word some twenty thousand people.

The Diocesan Missioner, Stephen Verney, described the last service as "coming to an extraordinary climax". The Bishop himself warned that "just because hundreds of people had consecrated or re-consecrated themselves to the Lord, it did not always mean that it would last". Seed had been sown; if it was to grow and flourish, it must be properly watered and exposed to the sun.

The consecration of the people had begun. The great building was to be consecrated in little more than a month's time.

The Consecration of the Cathedral

Cuthbert had been in office as Bishop of Coventry for six years by the time that his Cathedral was ready for consecration. They had been years of great activity, in which he had come to know his clergy and their families with a considerable intimacy; he had visited their churches and their homes, and shared in their joys and sorrows. In the county, too, he was a known and loved figure, at home in boardroom and on factory floor, in the big houses of the "management" and in the farms and humbler dwellings of ordinary men and women. Warwickshire was aware that they had a Bishop in their midst, a man of stature in more senses than the physical.

A close friend of Cuthbert's has pointed out that the Bishop had "an inbuilt feeling for theatre". He would have made a fine actor, had he entered that profession. We have seen that he wrote some good sacred plays, and – to pass from the sublime to the ridiculous – he was the central figure every Christmas in after-dinner charades in his home. Arrayed in gold cope and mitre, he was fitted to play his part on the day of the Cathedral's consecration.

Who will ever forget his stentorian tones as he began the Consecration:

"Be here, be here, to bless the prayers and sacraments of thy Church;

160

be here, be here, to bless thy people's ministries;
be here, be here, to bless thy people, as we supplicate thy mercy"

But to say that he had natural gifts for such an occasion is not to forget
that he prepared himself with immense care. Had he not done so, the
service might have been just a memorable piece of theatre. That it was
far more than this, that it was in fact a superb act of worship, was in
large part due to his own performance. Two things must be noted in
this connection:

First, he was himself above all else a man of prayer. His own life
centred in prayer; and he relied heavily on the prayers of others. He
constantly enlisted the aid of Religious Communities in the diocese
and elsewhere. He started a fellowship of prayer at the Cathedral, by
means of which some three hundred and fifty people pledged
themselves to pray for half an hour every week on their knees in the
Cathedral. The great building, in his estimate, was not to be just a
show-piece of architecture and the arts; it was to be a house of God, a
place where visitors would *see* Christians at their work of prayer. The
Cathedral, to use his words, must be "filled with prayer, saturated
with prayer". When the great day came, his Personal Assistant, who
was sitting with him in the Bishop's room beneath the Cathedral,
noted how "in spite of the heavy responsibility he was carrying, he
appeared to be perfectly calm. When the time came, he committed all
to God and strode confidently to his place outside, to utter the words
'Open the doors' ".

Secondly, he paid the greatest possible attention to the details of
the service. Here his closest ally was the Precentor, Joseph Poole.
Together, assisted by the others who were to take their part in the
drama of the Consecration, they had gone over and over each section
of the service; nothing had been too small to engage their attention.
So it was that, on the day itself, each knew his part so well that there
was a freedom from anxiety which showed itself in a joy which almost
savoured of spontaneity. The Consecration was a *Te Deum*.

The two great services of Consecration of the Cathedral, held on
25th and 26th May 1962, were prefaced by a deeply significant event
on the evening of the 24th. The Cross of Nails had completed its
hundred-mile journey to every parish in the diocese, and was now
ready to be borne on its final stage by the Bishop himself from St
John's Church, Fleet Street, to the ruins of the Cathedral. As the

procession went into the ruins, there was difficulty in getting through the crowds. It seemed as though the whole city had come together to watch this strange phenomenon. People looked on from every window. Some stood on the roofs of the houses. Others occupied the stands which had been erected for the Consecration on the morrow. Arrived at the entrance to the Cathedral, the Bishop handed the cross over to the Provost who was to carry it through the length of the ruins, down the steps, through the porch and glass screen and into the new Cathedral. There he was to take it up to the high altar, to be placed in the middle of the huge cross – at its centre was a large space resembling a great heart and it was in that space that the Cross of Nails was to be placed.

For forty days the Cross of Nails had been the focal point of continual prayer in the churches of the diocese. Now the crowd joined in singing "When I survey the wondrous cross". "Receive this Cross of Nails", the Bishop said to the Provost, "at the end of its long pilgrimage round the diocese, surrounded with the love and prayers of many thousands of people in every parish. Cherish this cross . . . watch about this cross . . ." It seemed to bring with it into the Cathedral the prayers of the whole diocese. The Cross of Nails was the cross triumphant. Christ reigned from the tree.

A vigil of prayer was maintained throughout the night in the Wyley Chapel in the ruins.

The Church Times, in its issue of 25th May, devoted its "Portrait of Personalities" to the Bishop of Coventry, "the right man in the right place at the right time". Its leading article, "Salute to Coventry", began:

> This is a royal day for Coventry. It is more. The whole Church rejoices with that diocese; indeed, the whole world must be encouraged by what has been achieved in a few short years in that busy city, where the new Cathedral, actually begun in 1954, now stands like a firm rock to crown Coventry's recovery from its wartime ordeal.
>
> During the war, Coventry had a unifying effect on the nation, when it seemed to stand alone against evil forces. When peace came, and the rebuilding of the ruined Cathedral gained impetus, it was soon apparent that in a special way Coventry would stand for that spirit of reconciliation which is at the heart of the Christian

Gospel. The will to victory had harboured no bitterness. Forgiveness and reconciliation have been the driving powers of the builders. Germany and other nations have contributed and helped. Any great building nowadays is a gesture of confidence and hope for the future, but Coventry Cathedral, because it rises from ruin, is a vivid reminder of the rejuvenating power of the Gospel of Christ, by which all things are made new.

A royal day it was. Her Majesty the Queen, who had been present at the laying of the foundation stone in 1956, was present again, together with the Duke of Edinburgh, Princess Margaret and the Earl of Snowdon, and the Archbishops of Canterbury and York. The Prime Minister, Anthony Eden, attended, as did diplomats from fifty-seven nations, more, so it was said, than had attended any single event since the Coronation. Among the Germans present were members of the Christian Action for Reconciliation, young men and women who had helped to turn the old ruined vestries into an International Centre of Christian Reconciliation – no one could forget the message "Father, forgive". The visiting choirs of the cathedrals of Birmingham, Gloucester, Leicester, Lichfield, Oxford, Peterborough and Worcester joined that of Coventry in leading the singing, while at the organ were Sir John Dykes-Bower and Sir William McKie, the brother of the Assistant Bishop of Coventry.

The Anglican Communion was represented by a number of Bishops from across the world. Sir Basil Spence was present to see the consummation of his years of work and prayer, and so were representatives of all strata of the national and civic life. But for no one could the day have been more deeply moving than for Dick Howard, Provost Emeritus, whose determination to build something glorious out of the ruins was born before the terrible heat of the bombed rafters had cooled.

The visitation of the Bishop to various parts of the Cathedral, to bless font and pulpit and altar, was marked with great precision and dignity, reminding one who was present of Francis Thompson's words about the Hound of Heaven – "With unperturbèd pace ... majestic instancy ..."

The sermon was preached by the Archbishop of Canterbury, Dr Michael Ramsey, who took as his text the words of the prophet Haggai: "The glory of this latter house shall be greater than of the former, saith the Lord of hosts, and in this place I will give peace". He spoke of the "glory which is here today . . . a house in which all the arts and the craftsmanship of our time have united: stone, wood, glass, metal. The designer, the builder, the painter, the sculptor: a generation has made its offering of beauty in the service of God." But the greatest glory is "in the flesh and blood of human lives". In the round of life and duty God would build himself a house: "its walls the souls and bodies of Christian people, its glory Christ himself, our crucified and risen Lord."

The service of 25th May was only the first part of the Consecration of the Cathedral. When its doors were at last closed that night, no service of Holy Communion had been held in it. The first was to take place next morning. In the presence of Princess Margaret and her husband, and to the accompaniment of trumpets and great music, but perhaps with a more relaxed feeling than had been possible on the previous day, "the most comfortable sacrament of the body and blood of Christ" was celebrated. The preacher was the Archbishop of York, who took as his text the words from the book of the Revelation: "He that sat upon the throne said, 'Behold, I make all things new'." He began by referring to "this lovely thing risen out of chaos" and ended with these words:

"Lift up your hearts" the Bishop will say to us in a few moments. What a day for dedication! – the past behind us, forgiven and blotted out; the future before us, big with opportunities to serve our Lord and his needy ones; the present ours to look up and say, with full hearts and dedicated wills: "We are not worthy . . . But thou art the same Lord whose property is always to have mercy . . . Here we offer and present unto thee ourselves, our souls and bodies . . ."

In *Fire in Coventry*, Canon Verney, who had done so much in preparing for these two great days, wrote:

It is not my place to describe in this book 25th May 1962, the day we had prepared for so eagerly . . . But without doubt the greatest moment of all came the next morning, when the Consecration of the Cathedral was completed by the celebrating within it of the Holy Communion. Then the Bishop stood at the heart of his diocese, and taking a little loaf of bread in his hands, he repeated the words: "Who, in the same night that he was betrayed, took bread, and when he had given thanks, he brake it, and gave it to his disciples . . ." As the prayer ended, the trumpets sounded, and there followed a profound silence.[7]

The services of these two great days were over. If, as the building rose, there had ever been a danger that it might be seen as a majestic piece of architecture, a museum of art and craft, that and nothing more, it could be so no longer. From now on, it was to be, above all else, a place of worship, adoration, praise and prayer, set aside for the glory of Almighty God, for the blessing of his people in Coventry and through them for the blessing of the world. No one was more insistent on this than the Bishop. "It must be a power-house of prayer – constant, regular, sacrificial prayer", he declared. It was "seeking to express the Christian faith in a modern, contemporary idiom", a Cathedral closely related to everyday life, "with a right-of-way through it" – he always rejoiced in the great West Doors through whose glass the city could see the altar and the Church could see the world.

Deo adjuvante, resurgo – "God being my helper, I rise." Coventry's prophetic motto had found its fulfilment.

*   *   *

It might have been thought that after two such tremendous days there would have been a sense of anticlimax in Coventry and in the diocese. No such thing happened. For nearly five years plans had been maturing for a great Consecration Festival of the Cathedral. The Rev. Clifford E. Ross (Vicar of Claverdon, and later Hon. Canon of Coventry) had been released from his parish to organize it. He was supported by a strong committee of businessmen. Cuthbert described the purpose of the Festival when he wrote in his Foreword to the *Programme Book*:

This Festival is an attempt by all sections of society to express their gratitude to God for the building of the new Cathedral: they are doing so through music, drama, pageant, lectures, dancing,

---

[7] *Fire in Coventry*, p. 49

exhibitions and sporting events. In these three weeks every part of
the diocese of Coventry will have the opportunity of expressing its
thankfulness for this great event . . . I feel I must express a special
word of gratitude to the Berlin Philharmonic Orchestra, whose two
concerts are their way of expressing the hope that together the
nations of the world may find their way through to a mutual
understanding and lasting peace.

What a galaxy of talent visited Coventry and other centres such as
Kenilworth, Leamington Spa and Warwick, through the three weeks
of the Festival! Here are the names of some who took part: John
Barbirolli, Arthur Bliss, Thomas Beecham, Malcolm Sargent,
Benjamin Britten, Peter Pears, Michael Tippett, Yehudi Menuhin,
Clifford Curzon, Frederick Ashton, Peggy Ashcroft, Ninette de
Valois, David Willcocks, George Solti – one could go on. And the
London Symphony Orchestra, and the Royal Ballet, and the Covent
Garden Opera . . . Among them all the Bishop moved, entering into
all facets of the Festival, delighting in its gaiety, sharing in its
friendships, leading here, encouraging there.

During these three weeks, no less than twenty-nine services were
held, if we include the two services of Consecration on 25th and 26th
May. Four of them were televised on the national and international
networks. All of them had splendidly produced Orders of Service,
most if not all of them showing evidence of the Precentor's skill. Let
Stephen Verney describe that memorable period:

We experienced an extraordinary outburst of worship and happi-
ness as the whole diocese celebrated a festival from end to end.
Great services were held in the new Cathedral, offering up to God
every part of our daily lives. There were services for Industry and
Agriculture, for Schools, for Local Government, the Armed
Forces, Youth, Old Age Pensioners and the Medical Services, to
mention only a few. There was a service of International Reconciliation, when young people of many nations asked the burning
questions that confront the world today, and when churchmen
from many countries and denominations moved together into the
Chancel, and kneeling before the great tapestry of Christ reigning
in glory, prayed for his forgiveness and for the coming of his
kingdom.

Many of these acts of worship were made by artists. There was the first performance of Benjamin Britten's *War Requiem*, that work of unbelievable power and beauty and insight, where the futility of war is set against the eternal mercy of God. Sung under the compassionate gaze of the Christ who looks down from Graham Sutherland's tapestry, it summed up and expressed the whole meaning of the Cathedral with a poignancy that was almost intolerable. After the service Sir Basil Spence, the architect, and Benjamin Britten, the composer, met, and, both deeply moved, thanked one another for the music and the Cathedral. Through the inspiration of those two men and the travail of all their fellow artists who had built and adorned the Cathedral and sung and played the music, God's truth had come to the birth and been spoken that night, and we who had seen and heard "rejoiced with an exceeding great joy". Many of the artists who performed in the Cathedral during those weeks were caught up into the worship: Yehudi Menuhin, standing alone in the chancel, seemed almost to shine and become transfigured and to be one with his violin and with the music which poured out of him; Cedric Connor, going up to sing, whispered, "Pray for me", and then sang with such electrifying power of Jesus rescuing a darkie from hell that two thousand people gripped their chairs in terror and relief, and he himself returned to his seat trembling and pouring with sweat.[8]

No wonder that the eyes of the world were on Coventry during the spring of 1962!

[8] *Fire in Coventry*, pp. 49–50

167

VIII

THE COVENTRY YEARS:
IN THE DIOCESE

Be to the flock of Christ a shepherd, not a wolf; feed them, devour them not. Hold up the weak, heal the sick, bind up the broken, bring again the outcasts, seek the lost.

The Book of Common Prayer
The Consecration of Bishops

WHEN ON ALL SAINTS' DAY 1947 Archbishop Geoffrey Fisher consecrated Cuthbert as a bishop in the Church of God, he sent him to
his work in Croydon and in the Forces with these unforgettable
words:

> Be to the flock of Christ a shepherd, not a wolf; feed them, devour
> them not. Hold up the weak, heal the sick, bind up the broken,
> bring again the outcast, seek the lost. Be so merciful, that you be
> not too remiss; so minister discipline, that you forget not mercy . . .

Cuthbert returned to these words frequently in his praying and
thinking – the ideals set out in them were high: how did the actuality
of his performance as a bishop correspond to them? In the day-to-day
round of duties, he sought to be a true shepherd – in the celebration of
the Sacraments, the preaching of the Word of God, the visiting of the
sick and the ministry of healing, the confirmation of young and old,
the institution of clergy to their incumbencies, the ordination of new
deacons and priests. The daily round of a bishop in his diocese
brought him deep satisfaction – for that, primarily, he knew he had
been consecrated. "A great door and effectual" had been opened for
him, and he entered it with enthusiasm.

But it was not easy to get his priorities right and to keep them right.
He kept a careful watch on the discipline of his prayer-life. He gave
absolute priority to the meeting of human personal need. There were
instances when he abandoned the chair at a meeting and went at once
when word was brought to him that some crisis or accident had
occurred which demanded his pastoral care. Prayer and people
mattered above all else. *But* the burden of administration and the
never-ceasing inflow of letters, how was he to deal with this? He knew
that administration was one of the gifts of the Spirit, according to St

Paul (Romans 12:7), but he did not find it easy always to remember that. He acknowledged that he was not an administrator, and often he would lean heavily on his diocesan experts when the agenda was long and the items complicated. He had a bigger secretarial staff than most other diocesan bishops (their salaries were often found from his own resources). But the in-tray by his desk was much more heavily weighted than were those of many other diocesan bishops. As the years went by, he found himself increasingly in demand, and the tension between diocesan calls and those from outside the diocese became ever greater. "Cuthbert Coventry" was wanted over the length and breadth of the British Isles and far beyond them. When was he to say "Yes" and when "No" to the ceaseless stream of invitations – to be president of this and patron of that, to preach here and to conduct a mission there, to chair the council of this venerable institution or take the initiative in launching a new one? There was to be no end to this tension before he retired in 1976. He insisted on having holidays, when he would find relief from his work in painting and in travel in the English Lake District and abroad. But those who worked most closely to him would notice with concern the lines of tiredness which marked his face at the end of a fifteen-hour day, and the recurrence from time to time of trouble from a stomach ulcer. Even his fine constitution sometimes protested at the demands which he made on it.

It was not his fault that the calls kept coming in. He had a dynamic personality, a charm which made him welcome in any company, a faith which he longed to communicate, a power in preaching given to few. It is easy for an outsider to think that perhaps he said "Yes" too often; but it is hard for a man with vision, who sees a need and welcomes the opportunity to meet it, to deal with his diary on the basis of a "nicely calculated less or more". A certain abandonment, a certain element of risk is part and parcel of a prophet's response to the calls made on him. Cuthbert's mind often went back to the picture of Tubby Clayton and his self-giving at All Hallows on Tower Hill . . . The example of that rotund little man could not be forgotten.

Lewis Davey, the Bishop's Personal Assistant, has given us the outline of a far from untypical day in his life:

The Bishop's day had started at 7.00 a.m. with a service of Holy Communion in a Coventry city church. Back for breakfast at 8.00

a.m., he started work on his correspondence at 9.00 and worked, with interruptions for interviews and telephone calls, until 12.45 p.m., when he had to keep an important luncheon appointment. From 2.00 to 5.30 p.m. he had a series of meetings, some of them requiring decisions of far-reaching importance. A news item broke that afternoon and the press were on for a statement from the Bishop, which he gave. From 5.30 to 6.00 p.m. he signed his post – over thirty letters. At 6.30 p.m. we were due to have a meal with his Archdeacon and Legal Secretary prior to an Institution Service for a new Vicar in the north of the diocese. When we left Bishop's House he looked all-in. My own day could not compare with his, yet I was exhausted and feared for him, wondering how he would get through the evening. I drove the car and he closed his eyes for about twenty minutes – his first relaxation for twelve hours. Over the meal he maintained a lively interest in a conversation which ranged over many aspects of diocesan affairs. Just before 7.30 p.m. we drove to the church. "How do you feel?" I asked him. "Pretty weary, but I'll be all right", he said. As he processed with others into the church I looked anxiously at him; he certainly looked tired but his step was firm. The time came for his address; how would he make out? I need not have worried. He gave one of the most dynamic sermons I had ever heard, challenging yet full of encouragement, faith and hope. From 9.00 to 10.00 p.m. he was in the church hall, drinking tea and going round shaking hands and chatting with every person in the room. Not one was overlooked, though there were about a hundred and fifty people there. Everything about him suggested a gay carefree personality, enjoying himself hugely (as he was) without a trace of tiredness. When he got into his car he had been going non-stop for fifteen hours, yet his cheerful goodbyes sounded as if he were on holiday. Only I saw the sudden slump as he sat back in the seat; only I knew how terribly tired he was.

This kind of day was not exceptional, indeed it is typical, and I have seen successions of such days over a whole week, or even longer, with perhaps one half-day break in that time.

*   *   *

Cuthbert was a man of the mountains rather than a man of the plains.

He was an initiator rather than one who attended to details. He was a man of big ideas: others could work them out. His paintings reflect his character – there are the bold strokes, the strong lines, but clearly he can hardly delay to fill in the background: there are other ideas waiting to be captured and put on canvas.

"Let there be a garden party", he would say to a somewhat startled staff. And there was one: his had been the bright initial idea, theirs would be most of the detailed work which would give flesh to it. It generally worked – men need the inspiration which springs from vision. But the fulfilment of the vision needs a team of people prepared for sweat and tears if not for blood. Cuthbert had such a team, devoted to him. And often the tears were tears of laughter as the big idea took shape, and the garden party (or whatever) was voted a huge success. Hard work and gales of laughter were never far apart when Cuthbert was around.

"Let there be a diocesan newspaper." The edict went out early in 1957. And there was one; the first edition appeared in November of that year. Lewis Davey was the Business Manager, and his brother-in-law, Leslie Bartlett, advertisement manager and photographer throughout the eleven years of the paper's existence. Five people acted as editors during that time, including the Rev. G. Southeard who had been a journalist before ordination and who bore the initial brunt of the new venture, Lewis Davey, the Rev. H. George and Mr J.D. Ross. The one who served longest was Mrs Margaret Stoneman. She resigned her editorship in 1967 to return to her career in local government, this time as Chairman of Coventry Education Committee.

Her description of her first meeting with the Bishop in 1961 gives a good impression of the "incarnation" of a courageous idea launched and carried on almost on a shoe-string:

I met him first in the Autumn of 1961 when he sent for me after I had written a series of articles in the Coventry Cathedral Review, of which I was the Joint Editor. He asked me to become Assistant Editor of *Shire and Spire* with a view to taking over the Editorship. I worked on the paper for four and a half years almost single-handed, with a part-time secretary. Because we had no money to pay professional writers, I had to do all the articles myself – interviewing national figures – Sir Bernard Lovell, Sir John Maud, the Archbishop of Canterbury in his shirt sleeves eating his breakfast at Bishop's House before the Consecration! – and many more. This was one of the most worthwhile and creative periods of my life. I saw the Bishop about the paper about every fortnight to tell him what I intended doing but he never interfered except to offer suggestions. I was in daily contact with Lewis Davey, his personal assistant, and his secretary Betty Priddis, now Simpson. I had a free hand which was very challenging but sometimes frightening with a blank front page! Some features like the Bishop's Diary and letter were regular features, but the rest had to be thought up from scratch every month. I interviewed practically everyone connected with the Consecration and the Festival. We ran a sports page and a column for youth and tried to be up to the minute.

Why did the Bishop want to launch this paper? He made his mind clear to its readers in the first edition:

What is it and what is it trying to do? It is a monthly newspaper published by the Church for all willing to hear what the Church is doing and what the Church is saying about matters of national importance. The criticism is sometimes made that the Church too often "sits on the fence". There will be no "sitting on the fence" in this newspaper. *Shire and Spire* will have a mind of its own. We shall not steer clear of controversial issues nor hesitate to give a judgement popular or unpopular. This newspaper is not a parish magazine, nor is it a rival to a parish magazine . . .

Cuthbert himself wrote regularly for the paper – he valued this means of communication with people inside the life of the Church and outside it. In the fifth birthday issue he wrote:

One enterprise that is very close to my heart is this newspaper. It was launched and has been developed mainly by voluntary support from hundreds of people who recognize its value as a means of communication with those who are outside the organization of the church.

The paper started life as eight pages, then became twelve, and was for a very short time sixteen pages. The original price was 3d, then 4d. After April 1968 it was issued free of charge. In September 1967 it made church history and became a controlled circulation newspaper, and was delivered free of charge to all church magazine subscribers throughout the diocese. Because of this the circulation rose from 25,000 to 90,000.

In the summer of 1968 Lewis Davey retired from his position with *Shire and Spire* under the weight of other work. He had given valuable assistance in building up and maintaining the paper, and had contributed trenchant articles. In December that year *Shire and Spire* expired!

It had been a pioneer venture – another example of the Bishop's initiative and of his success in calling into action and holding together a team of workers. On the demise of the paper he wrote:

> This is the end of an eleven year battle. We are compelled to bow to the inevitable and go out of business. This paper has been . . . the Bishop's paper – there is nothing quite like it in existence . . . We have had no financial backing . . . the original team worked without financial remuneration . . . we have had no money to pay professional writers. It leads me to the conclusion that *Shire and Spire* is ahead of its time. Over the years it has meant so much to me and added strength to my arm in attempts to weld this diocese into a coherent unit. . . . It is a bitter disappointment to me . . . no diocese can carry out its corporate task without an instrument of communication.

Shire and Spire could not survive as a free circulation paper at a time when costs were rising so steeply that even national dailies were in trouble. That was a natural explanation. Would it be truer to say that a people had failed to catch their Bishop's vision and had been unwilling to pay the cost? "I feel as if I had lost my right arm", the Bishop said to a friend.

*   *   *

In 1966 the Bishop celebrated the first ten years of his episcopate in Coventry. Though he could not know this, he was at the half-way mark of his work there. Much had been achieved: much remained to be done. At the Diocesan Conference held in Leamington Spa on 5th November, Lord March presented Cuthbert with a painting by Peter Coker and expressed the gratitude of the diocese for his leadership. The Conference "almost unanimously" voted the funds to support three priests in non-parochial ministries – a chaplain to immigrants, a chaplain to the new University of Warwick, and a youth chaplain. These appointments gladdened the Bishop's heart, for they indicated that the Church in the diocese was looking *outwards*, not simply catering for the needs of its own members.

In his presidential address that day, he said that he looked forward to 1968 when Coventry would celebrate its Golden Jubilee as a separate diocese. He specially mentioned an evangelistic mission planned for that year, centred in the See city but reaching out to the whole area. He was not thinking of a mission like that which had preceded the consecration of the Cathedral in 1962, but of something quite new and on a different scale.

Evangelism, in the broad sense of the Church's task of proclaiming to the world God's redeeming love in Christ, had always been uppermost in Cuthbert's mind and was to remain so throughout his ministry. In maintaining this stance, he had incurred the criticism of many, including some of his fellow Bishops, when he associated himself with Billy Graham's Greater London Crusade in the summer of 1966. He was critical of some features of the Crusade, but he went to the Wembley Stadium on 2nd July and, at the end of the gathering of nearly a hundred thousand people, called on them to "thank God for raising up a man who has shown us . . . how great are our capacities as a nation to respond to the challenge to live and work for God and the service of others". Then he gave the blessing.

Writing in *Shire and Spire* a few days later he said: "However critical we may be of Billy Graham and his campaign, we can, in all humility, learn lessons from it." He touched on some of them: there was a wistful hunger for faith in the nation; there was evidence of a desire for preaching with authority and with a positive content; there was evidence that youth is not as pagan as some critics would like to assert; there was evidence that many people who long for faith are acutely critical of the Church; there was evidence of the life-changing power of prayer; there was evidence of the compelling attraction of the Person of Jesus Christ.

176

For the mission which the Bishop announced to his Diocesan Conference in 1966, there would be no invitation to any one missioner drawn in from outside to conduct it in 1968. Cuthbert himself would be the missioner, the chief shepherd of the diocese exercising his care, his oversight (his *episcope*) of the people in his spiritual charge. He would, of course, be assisted by others, and the preparations would be long and detailed. But the central figure would be the bishop – not indeed because of any egocentricity on his part, but because he was persuaded he had a responsibility to discharge and no one could carry it for him.

Writing in *Shire and Spire* in May 1967, and seeking to answer the question "Why should a 'Call to Mission' be held next year?", Cuthbert noted "a widespread malaise" in the nation "which in the final resort is attributable to loss of faith", and in the Church, in spite of many good signs, "the fact that many clergy have lost heart – and in some cases have lost faith and their sense of vocation, while many of the laity feel uncertain, insecure and frustrated." "A Mission", he wrote, "provides an opportunity for the re-examination of our faith, for a re-assessment of the Good News of the Gospel . . . a focus, a concentration upon first-priority matters."

Interviewed in March 1968 when there were only some six months to go before the beginning of the mission, and asked what was his charge as the wheels started moving faster, Cuthbert replied:

My charge is as follows: Open your imagination to realize the immense potentialities for good of this "Call to Mission" which may bring hope through renewed faith, not only to the people of this Diocese but to the whole Church. Open your hearts afresh to the love of God, so that your gratitude may be deepened. Open your pockets so that you may give generously and sacrificially to defray the expenses of the "Call to Mission." Open your mouth so that you may begin to speak with real conviction about your faith, give your reason for the faith that is in you, to your neighbours and your friends. Open your hands so that you may give personal service more deeply and more consistently, remembering that witness by mouth and service by hand go together. Finally, open your mind so that God may speak to you through prayer and through the reading of the Bible, opening your minds afresh, not only to the opportunities of this hour in which you live, but to the limitless love of God revealed in Jesus Christ.

Two years' hard work went into the preparation for the Mission. A committee under the guidance of the Diocesan Missioner, Canon Geoffrey Rogers, produced a booklet entitled *Prayer: Five studies in Preparation for the "Call to Mission" 1968*. As the organizing secretary of the whole venture, the Bishop appointed a young priest of twenty-seven years, Peter J. Larkin, Curate of Rugby. The circumstances of his appointment cast a light on Cuthbert at work. Larkin describes them:

In November I had a summons to attend Bishop's House concerning some important work which the Bishop wished me to do. He was ever dramatic in his summonses. I was actually packed up ready to go to a Conference at Swanwick – I think we literally had our coats on. But the first response to the phone-call from the Bishop's secretary (not knowing it was the Bishop's house) was an evasive one from my wife as it was my day off. The reply was "It is the Bishop who wants to speak to him." He had arranged a lunch party that very day for several people who would be involved in setting up the Mission to the Diocese, and he was insistent that I be present. I was to delay my plans for going away with my family and please would I be at the house at 12 o'clock. I was. Three hours later the vast vision of the Call to the whole diocese had been presented to approximately twelve people and each one had been appointed to his or her task. This was typical of Cuthbert Bardsley. He could see the big questions and was ready to produce the big answers. Never was there a hint of any doubt or pride, but just to go all out by every means to reach the people of Warwickshire for Christ.

Something of the spirit and method of the preparation can be gained from Larkin's description:

The real impetus for the Mission came from the Bishop. He was the visionary, his were the big ideas, his was the leadership. Other people often had ideas but it was Cuthbert's which for the most part got through to reality. He was never proud or arrogant about this – it was just that he knew what he wanted and he felt he knew what

God wanted. He was the overriding and enabling power under God, but the bones of his new creation were provided by Geoffrey Rogers. He grounded it all in theology, in biblical exposition and in teaching material. My task was to see that it all got done. If Cuthbert was the spirit and Geoffrey was the brains, I was the brawn. But none of us was alone in these areas, for there were small groups galore working on every aspect of the preparation and the planning. The most memorable were the days together when those in the main leadership positions for this vast Mission met together, mostly at Honiley Rectory, the home of Geoffrey Rogers. We would sit for hours around pots of Persian stew – the spicy aromas going up as it were as incense with our prayers – these were times of waiting on God for his guidance. Frequently there would be questions as to who should do this, what should be done in this situation, how should we deal with this or that problem. I remember the Bishop saying "We must have the best, we must have the best", and so the very best people were pulled in – the best equipment – the best venue or whatever it might be. For instance, Keith de Berry was known to be excellent at training counsellors. "I will 'phone up Keith tonight" was the Bishop's response. Douglas Webster was widely acclaimed for his understanding of mission. "Then he must come and address us" would be the Bishop's immediate answer.

A Mission Headquarters was set up in Priory Row near the Cathedral, under the guidance of Sister Peggy Boynes of the Church Army. There the General Council, the Mission Executive, the Public Relations Committee, the clergy seconded for the work, and all the rest met for prayer, discussion and planning. From this centre, the Bishop, Geoffrey Rogers, Stephen Verney, Kingsley Walker and others would go out to the clergy chapters and to the Rural Deaneries to mobilize prayer, and set in motion study courses for use by parish groups and by individuals. At this centre, plans would be made for practical matters such as transport and the training of a big body of counsellors – some seven hundred people attended the latter course, and some four hundred offered and were accepted for counselling work.

There were cynics who scorned the idea of evangelistic outreach. There was criticism in plenty. Canon Geoffrey Rogers records:

Nine months before the Mission one of the churchwardens of a village church out in the "deep south" of the diocese 'phoned to say that his vicar would have nothing to do with the Bishop's project. We replied that no vicar could prevent his lay people from co-operating with the Bishop in an activity of the whole diocese. I went to the parish to meet any who would co-operate. The vicar was not there! But seventy-five members of the parish were, eager to follow their Bishop into this Call to Mission.

And the students from Lanchester College of Technology asked, tongue in cheek, in their newspaper *Hosanna*:

> While not wishing to be the sort of newspaper which goes out to make news, can anyone tell us the legal position about suing the Bishop of Coventry for disturbing the peace? To wit, overamplified performances of maudlin ditties in the Old Cathedral which could be heard all over the City Centre.

After the Mission, too, there was criticism. The Rev. Trevor Beeson, writing in *New Christian*, described his reactions on "trying to discover what the Bishop and his diocese were up to". He found "Coventry's Old Wine" to be inadequate "as part of the Church's mission in a secular society". He went so far as to say that his visits to Coventry had left him "with a firm conviction that the use of the word 'mission' in this context is misleading and dangerous". "This approach," he said, "really will not do." A fortnight later, Canon Lawrence Jackson, Vicar of Holy Trinity Church, replied, in a letter to *New Christian*:

> However regrettable it may seem to Mr Beeson, I must tell him that the approach which he scorns already has done, and is doing, under God, great things in the city and diocese of Coventry.

He went on to write of a new-found vigour and enthusiasm in the diocese, of imaginative plans for follow-up to the mission, and of lives touched by its message. A month after the mission, one of the senior clergy wrote in his parish letter:

I am more grateful to the Bishop and his Call to Mission than I can say. For me it has been a second dedication of my life to our Lord; it is bliss.

Even within the central team there were, as one would expect, differences of opinion and of approach, but the differences often proved fruitful. Peter Larkin says:

It was clear that the Bishop expected a lot from his helpers. He knew the Lord expected a lot of him and he sought to give it. Yes, his demands were high but his enthusiasm was irresistible. What a magnificent inspirer of men and women he was! Did we ever flag? Yes sometimes; but the Bishop would always come in with a highly challenging but friendly and invigorating remark to encourage us to be bold and strong in the work of the Lord. Sometimes it worked in the other way. Once in a while the Bishop would be diverted by some new idea or different set of dates for a meeting, or different venue, or something relatively minor like that; and I found myself having to say "But, Bishop, you can't change it, it is already advertised. It is in the Diocesan news sheet and the posters have already been sent out."

Lewis Davey put his whole weight behind the Call to Mission and acted as its treasurer. When all expenses were paid – and they were very considerable – some £6000 was left over and used for the Church's missionary work and for the hungry and homeless. Publicity, under the skilled charge of Mr John S. Haynes, was of a high order. Radio, television, press, printing, cartoons – all were involved. (John Haynes, who before the Call to Mission had done little about his religion, after the Mission was found on Lawrence Jackson's doorstep. "I've gone and got converted", said he. "I went to tell the Bishop and he said: 'Well done; alleluia. Now go and tell someone else.' So, I've come." John Haynes became a Reader. Now he is Incumbent of Radford Semele, Leamington Spa.)

The central "Call to Mission" occupied the period 17th to 27th September 1968. But it was preceded by two events of importance, both of which showed that evangelism was being thought of in no narrow way. Rather, it was looking out to the world through the compassionate eyes of Christ.

The first of these events was an exhibition held in the Cathedral in January. Entitled "Task 6" it showed something of the outreach of the Church's medical, educational and evangelistic work in the six continents of the world. Over ten thousand people visited it.

The second was a conference called "People and Cities" held in July. Owing much to the leadership of Canon Stephen Verney, and planned on an international scale, it sought to face the crisis and the challenge of Megalopolis – "extra-human in dimension and inhuman in content", as Dr Doxiades of Athens put it.

At last all was ready for the Call to Mission itself, under the over-all title of *Learn to Live*. Night by night the people met in the Cathedral (with closed-circuit television relaying the proceedings to the neighbouring church of Holy Trinity, to the Lanchester College of Technology and to the Methodist Central Hall). Lawrence Jackson acted as compère, leading the congregation with reverence and humour, in an opening half-hour of singing. The general programme was that there would be two speakers before the Bishop entered, one of them a well-known figure from varying spheres of the nation's life – these included Quintin Hogg, Andrew Cruikshank, Lord Carron, Colin Cowdrey, the Archbishop of York – the other a man or woman from within the diocese, often little known, often speaking with trepidation but with a testimony none the less powerful for that. Then the Bishop gave the main address – *Learning to Live* – with yourself, with others, with suffering, through death, with freedom, with purpose, with power, in Christ, for others, for God. And there was an evening specially designed for youth, when Derek Nimmo and Cliff Richard spoke before the Bishop's address. (When they had done so, the heavens opened and rain came in a deluge. Many thought the crowds would dissolve before Cuthbert spoke. Not a soul moved.)

The series began with the Archbishop of York lighting seven huge torches fuelled by gas. (The Archbishop was heard to remark that in all his experience he had never before seen a rubric bidding the Archbishop to turn on the gas.) The torches were set up in the Cathedral precincts, to symbolize the prayer which would rise to God throughout the mission. Then hundreds of young people carried hand torches to the last great service which was held in Stoneleigh Abbey. It was an open-air Eucharist. Canon Joseph Poole, chairman of the Coventry Diocesan Church Choirs Association, was in charge of the singing. The Band of the Welsh Guards played.

Canon Jackson was responsible for the orderly conduct of this act of worship. Let him describe what happened:

For weeks and weeks before the great Eucharist at Stoneleigh, in the Grand Ring of the Royal Agricultural Society, all had been prepared to receive many thousands of folk from all over Warwickshire, to this great Service, which was to be broadcast "live" on BBC Television. The day in question was Sunday, 29th September – Michaelmas Day; this was the exact fiftieth Anniversary of the Diocese.

In all the weeks of preparation, planning for the parking of buses and motor cars had been arranged between "National Car Parks" and the Warwickshire Police, but we had forgotten the weather! During week after week it poured with rain, and the fields around Stoneleigh were sodden and eventually impassable. One week before the great Eucharist, we had a meeting in a double-decker bus on the long drive to Lord Leigh's Stoneleigh Abbey. The parking of vehicles was seen to be so critical, that Lord Leigh generously agreed to allow us to lop the long avenue of his famous lime trees to accommodate double-decker buses on his tarmac drive.

The rain continued to pour down every day, and all through the night preceding our Open-Air Eucharist. I went to see Cuthbert, our Bishop, in a great panic, after I had helped to throw down tons of sawdust on Stoneleigh Showground, to soak up the standing water. Cuthbert, as always, was serene and trusting, and merely rebuked me in a kindly way, saying "The Good Lord both rules and overrules".

After raining all night, the sun climbed up into the sky for the first time for many weeks, on Michaelmas Day, 1968. Soon thousands of folk were converging on the Showground, and buses and motor cars were efficiently parked according to the new plan laid down by the Police and N.C.P. only a week earlier. The Eucharist was a splendid Act of Worship in sunshine, under blue skies. I was the last to leave Stoneleigh, having seen the last coach pull away as the skies were darkening once more. I left in driving rain, wondering at what I will always describe as "The Miracle of Stoneleigh". The rain poured down continually for another three weeks or more, without any abatement.

Fifteen thousand people attended that Eucharist, served by the clergy and representing the whole Christian family of the diocese. It was more than a thanksgiving for fifty years of past diocesan life. It was a dedication to future work and service.[1]

*   *   *

From the moment of his arrival in the diocese, the Bishop was determined to build and maintain sound ecumenical relationships with clergy and laity of other denominations. With this in mind he gathered together a group of clergy, Roman Catholics, Baptists, Methodists, members of the United Reformed Church, to meet regularly for prayer, for planning evangelistic advance, for joint study of social problems.

This group met, usually in his study. The meetings were frank, constructively critical, often hilarious. The clergy became friends. That friendship enabled them to enter into joint pastoral work in the University of Warwick, in the building and siting of new churches, in joint work for the needy, in the joint manning of clubs for the homeless, for old people, and so on. Nothing was undertaken separately that could not be tackled better together.

These friendships deepened and matured over the years. On a number of occasions Cuthbert was invited to preach in different churches – the Baptist Tabernacle, the Methodist Central Hall – to take part in services of welcome to new ministers, and to receive gifts. This atmosphere of deep brotherly friendship was manifest throughout the city and to the furthest ends of Warwickshire. It owed not a little to the friendly spirit of the Bishop and to the prayer which preceded all the meetings of those concerned.

*   *   *

Cuthbert himself was essentially a town man. Brought up in Lancaster, having spent his ministry in London, Woolwich, Southwark and Croydon, he was in his element in a city such as Coventry. It pleased him that his Cathedral was set right in the heart of a flourishing city,

---

[1] The story of the Mission is told fully in *I Believe in Mission*, by Cuthbert Bardsley (A.R. Mowbray, 1970).

its services open to the eyes and ears of the people as they went about their daily work. He cared deeply about its welfare and was glad to associate himself, publicly and privately, with its affairs.

Regularly and over a long period, privately and unknown to the general public, the Bishop would gather in his study representatives of every facet of Coventry's life and work – leaders of both parties in the City Council, representatives of industry, trades unions, education and commerce. There would be detailed discussion of the city's needs and of opportunities to promote its welfare. The members of the group would then move across the hallway into Cuthbert's chapel, there to wait on God in silence and in "free prayer". These meetings continued up to the time of his retirement.

Then there were weekends when Cuthbert would arrange conferences at Ettington Park Hotel, near Shipston on Stour, for different groups of people. The first was a conference for landowners and farmers. There was one for industrialists, another for trades union leaders, and yet another for members of the professions. Discussions were lively as the members examined the basis of the Christian faith and sought to see its bearing on their life and conduct.

This fruitful venture was run on ecumenical lines, the Bishop organizing the course in close co-operation with the leading Methodist minister in Coventry, the Rev. Lincoln Minshull. These conferences continued over a period of several years, and Cuthbert regarded them as being among the most important things that happened during his twenty years at Coventry.

His enthusiasm for the Coventry City Football Club knew no bounds. He was proud to be its President. He advised fellow supporters not to sit in front of him at a match, for it was likely that he would become so excited by the game that flailing arms might well damage people in the next row.

*   *   *

The University of Warwick was the scene of much activity on the Bishop's part. Indeed, it could be said that he was one of its founding fathers.

He was present at the first meeting in the Lord Mayor's parlour, when its site and its name had to be decided. Should it be called the

University of Coventry? Or the University of Warwickshire? There was a strong difference of opinion. "Why not the University of Warwick?", said Cuthbert. And so it was.

The University received its Royal Charter in 1965. Its first Vice-Chancellor was John (now Lord) Butterworth. He had been Fellow, Bursar and Sub-Warden of Cuthbert's College at Oxford – New College. Vice-Chancellor and Bishop worked closely together, and their co-operation was fruitful in the establishment of the Chaplaincy Centre. It was opened jointly by Cuthbert and the Roman Catholic Archbishop of Birmingham at Easter 1975. The first Anglican Chaplain was the Rev. Richard Cain (1967–73); the second the Rev. Donald Humphries (1974–79). The latter served on the committee for Evangelism under the chairmanship of Alan C. Warren, the Diocesan Missioner (later Provost of Leicester). The Anglican Chaplains worked closely with the Roman Catholic Chaplain (Father Louis McKaye) and with the United Reformed Chaplain, the Rev. Peter Poulter.

Cuthbert was a regular visitor to the Chaplaincy, and preached there once a year. Thanks partly to his generosity, it was possible to appoint pastoral assistants who lived in the Chaplain's house and ministered to a student population which by the 1970s had risen to five thousand. Donald Humphries bears witness to his sense of being loved by his Bishop, and to the latter's deep concern for his work among the students.

The Bishop served on the Council from its inception until his retirement in 1976, when the Chancellor, Lord Radcliffe, who had known him since he was a boy of seven, conferred on him the degree of Doctor of Letters, *honoris causa*. The connection between University and diocese was made the clearer in that the annual conferment of degrees took place in Coventry Cathedral.

*   *   *

Speak of industrial mission and at once a picture of factories and smoking chimneys springs to mind. Woolwich, Southwark and then Coventry had never allowed that picture to be far from the Bishop's thinking. But, of course, one of Britain's greatest industries is agriculture, and Coventry, for all its proximity to Birmingham and the industrial Midlands, was very largely a country diocese. Within a few miles of the city of Coventry was Stoneleigh and there, from 1962 onwards, was held the annual Royal Agricultural Show of England.

Cuthbert was quick to see that the Church must be at the heart of this great industry and worthily represented at the Show. With the whole-hearted support of himself and of his neighbour-bishop of Birmingham (Leonard Wilson), the annual service held on the eve of the opening of the Show became a major event with 2,500 to 3,500 people in the congregation. Cuthbert often conducted the service himself but made sure that it was run on a firmly ecumenical basis.

The Church stand was inadequate to represent the concern of the Church for this great industry. Cuthbert was delighted when, in July 1972, Her Majesty the Queen opened and he himself blessed the Arthur Rank Centre which had been funded by the Rank Foundation and by Colt Buildings. Its *raison-d'être* was to provide an ecumenical base for promoting interest in the Church in rural areas, to foster understanding between the farming and non-farming communities, and to examine Christian attitudes to modern farming and to the environment. Cuthbert did much to ensure that it became the national centre for such concern, and that its interests reached out far beyond these islands. At the opening and blessing he was accompanied by his future wife, Ellen.

The appointment of the Rev. Peter Buckler as chaplain to the National Agricultural Centre at Stoneleigh in 1971, and as Warden of the Arthur Rank Centre in 1974, did much to ensure that the objects of the Foundation were vigorously pursued, and with the coming of the Rev. Anthony Russell (now Bishop of Dorchester) in 1973 the future development of the work was assured. As a Canon Theologian of Coventry Cathedral since 1977, and as an occasional lecturer in the sociology of religion in Birmingham and Oxford, he has won an international reputation as a writer and speaker on ecological and agricultural matters.

Coventry had given a lead which other dioceses were glad to follow.

IX

MARRIAGE

He that findeth a wife findeth a good thing.

Proverbs 18:22

THE MOST IMPORTANT SINGLE EVENT in Cuthbert Bardsley's personal life was his marriage to Ellen Mitchell. This was no sudden decision. Ellen had been an increasingly close friend of his sister Dorothy for many years. Indeed as Dorothy (who was nine years older than Cuthbert) became more frail and forgetful she turned increasingly to Ellen for support and friendship. On one occasion she said, "I wish you were here always". Ellen used to take her for drives into the country and help her with her letters. She and Cuthbert's sister had many common links. Both were from the north-west. Both their roots were firmly in Lancashire. Both had been outgoing in the service of the Girls' Friendly Society; Ellen in fields of public service and other local and county council work. Both delighted in the theatre, music and reading. Both enjoyed foreign travel, including two pilgrimages to the Holy Land led by Cuthbert.

When Cuthbert found himself deeply in love with Ellen Mitchell, he was, naturally enough, perplexed as to how best to break the news to Dorothy, who had shared his work so closely and for so many years. Let him tell the story in his own words:

> On the morning after I had proposed to Ellen, I was at home wondering how to put it across. Dorothy came into my study and said: "You know, Cuthbert, if ever you want to get married, you must not hesitate." I said: "Well, my darling, I am engaged and I hope you will understand." And she said: "Oh, yes, of course", living with them until her death in January 1983.

Ellen Edith Mitchell was born in Newchurch in Rossendale, Lancashire. She was a grand-daughter of two mill owners in business for over a hundred years in the Rossendale valley, between hills and moorland. Her paternal grandfather became bankrupt before the First World War, largely because he bought a fifth mill which proved to be one too many, whereas her mother's family business went into voluntary liquidation in recent years.

Another link with Cuthbert's early life was that Ellen's mother's large family home, like his own, was on a hill and also resounded with happy laughter as the eight children brought their friends into it, encouraged by their hospitable and much loved mother, Ellen Shepherd.

The home of her grand-daughter Ellen (an only child) was also full of laughter. During the last war the sweet voice of Elizabeth, her valiant mother, was often heard about the house singing "Onward Christian Soldiers" and "Rule Britannia".

Ellen's father, Walter Mitchell, was educated at a Quaker school on the Oxfordshire/Warwickshire borders, and later on the Rhine at a school run by Moravian Brethren. He was always a member of the Church of England – outgoing, with an infectious laugh – intelligent and well read – and a good linguist. His war service consisted in the production of vital raw materials for the three Armed Services. Ellen remembers one of his old workmen saying: "If your father had been alive now we should still have been in work." In those days in the north the trust placed in good employers by employees was implicit.

Ellen was educated in Yorkshire at Duncombe Park, Helmsley and Queen Ethelburga's School, Harrogate. On leaving school she lived at home for fifteen years looking after her mother, who was in poor health and often in great pain; and during the war doing all-night air raid precaution duty. Her mother died in 1945.

On her father's remarriage three years later Ellen moved south to Stratford-upon-Avon, where she became secretary to the owner of the Arden Hotel. It was a fascinating place to work in, as so many of the world's outstanding actors, actresses and musicians who were working at the theatre across the road lived there. International scholars, painters and writers stayed in the hotel year by year.

A recurring work in Ellen's life had been secretary of the parochial church council both at St Thomas's, St Anne's-on-Sea and St James's, Alveston. She served on the Ruri-Decanal Conference and the Diocesan Conference in the Dioceses of Blackburn and Coventry, and she was also elected to the General Synod. She did a considerable amount of Conservative work, starting as a ward secretary and becoming vice-chairman of the Women's Auxiliary of the Constituency of Stratford-on-Avon and South Warwickshire. She was also a Warwickshire County Councillor, serving on Welfare, Planning, Fire Brigade, Museum and Weights and Measures committees, being Vice-Chairman of the last. It was her delight to be a member of the Cathedral Chain of Prayer and to work on the great diocesan missions.

Ellen was a very caring person with strongly held views, practical, down-to-earth, with a good memory, a good organizer and a mind for detail. She had just those gifts which could best supplement Cuthbert's own. But far more important than this, she came as a shaft of light into his life, radiating love and laughter wherever she went.

How Cuthbert and Ellen, during their engagement, succeeded in keeping their rendezvous week by week without raising a suspicion within the Diocese or County of what was afoot, remains a mystery impossible to solve. When at length in May 1972 the news broke, there was general delight. "When would the marriage take place?" "Some time in August", was the reply – not, it must be admitted, wholly satisfactory for the press and public. True to his word, but succeeding in holding the date, time and place from the enquiring media, Cuthbert and Ellen were married on the morning of 1st August in the presence of some dozen people in Packington Church in the private estate of Packington Hall. In the absence of the vicar (Bishop John McKie, the assistant bishop), Cuthbert's old friend Bishop John Daly, a former bishop in Korea, conducted the service, assisted by the Rev. George Burgess, vicar of Alveston, Ellen's home parish. Cuthbert's brother-in-law, Sir Thomas Harley, suitably clad for a wedding but with an ancient macintosh and slouch cap superimposed, with cameras strung around his neck, arrived well before the service. "I'm from the *Daily* . . .", he said to the astonished clergy. "I hear that an elderly bishop is going to be married this morning and my paper wants to give it headline coverage." This news was passed on to the horrified bridegroom, who had gone out of his way to avoid publicity!

The service was accompanied by beautiful music played on an organ frequently used by Handel. The newly married couple went back to Bishop's House after the service, for a small reception and luncheon, and were surprised to hear the announcement of their wedding service on the 1 o'clock Midland news. From Coventry they disappeared into the blue, returning some five weeks later ("the longest and loveliest holiday I ever had", said Cuthbert) from honeymoon in Wengen and Cyprus.

Cuthbert had no regrets about the events on 1st August 1972. Ellen was to prove his ideal partner in work and leisure, in diocese and in retirement, in sickness and in health; and if at times he regrets he did not marry her earlier, he is never much of a man to look back. Indeed he said to a television interviewer who remarked that in view of their age they might not have a very long married life: "But there's always eternity."

Ellen thinks that it would have been very difficult for Cuthbert to fulfil his busy travelling ministry if he had not been a bachelor. She was able to share to the full his last four years in Coventry, before they moved to their retirement home.

X

BEYOND THE DIOCESE

With unflagging energy, in ardour of spirit,
serve the Lord.

Romans 12:11

A BISHOP'S FIRST CONCERN is his diocese. That is why he takes its name in his signature. That is why he wears a ring – not for self-glorification but as a constant reminder that he is "married" to his diocese. But he is more than a diocesan bishop or a suffragan bishop. He is a bishop in *the Church of God*. His vision and his care must reach out beyond the bounds of his diocese – to the over-all welfare of the Church which he shares with other members of the episcopate.

This chapter describes some of Cuthbert Bardsley's activities which reflected interests that ranged beyond his diocese, though most of them were exercised also within it. For example, the Church's ministry of healing was exercised through his hands within the confines of his diocese, but it took him further afield, as indeed it still does. His passion for evangelism found its primary outlet within the diocese of Coventry, but it also took him on journeys to many other parts of the world. In the Anglican Fellowship of Prayer, it worked somewhat in reverse: the work which he did under its banner was done mostly in the United States of America, but he brought back its inspiration to England and especially to his own diocese.

If in Chapter 8 we watched him at work within his diocese, in this chapter we watch him reaching out to the world. That applies to his work at Lee Abbey in Devon, for that became, partly under his influence, a place by which the worldwide Church was enriched. That applies also to his speeches in the House of Lords, where *world* issues were high on the list of the subjects which engaged his attention.

The Ministry of Healing

My interest in the Church's ministry of healing (Cuthbert has recorded) began when I was Rector of Woolwich. One day a beloved lady church-worker came to me in great distress, having been told she was suffering from terminal cancer with six weeks to live. At that time I had no connection whatever with the Church's healing ministry; I had never laid hands on anybody and didn't feel any call to do so. But at that juncture I could not just say "My dear, I am so sorry"; so I suggested that we should ask two priests, who were concerned with the ministry of healing, to come. We held a small service in the Lady Chapel of my church, and for the first time I was invited to lay hands on the head of a sick person. Well, as it happened, she lived for seven years, seven healthy and wonderful years.

As I returned to my house I made one of those pledges to God which are dangerous unless one is prepared to carry them out. I said, "Lord, if you want me to go further into this, I am ready." The good Lord took me at my word, and within a week I received a letter from the wife of an old friend saying that, in addition to the angina which he had had for some years, he was suffering from a terminal illness; would I go up north to give him the ministry of healing? On the way I remember arguing with God: "This is a bit much to start with! If it had been a mild case of influenza, yes, but this is asking a great deal!" Nevertheless, I went to his bedside in hospital, where I found that he was a very sick man. I asked if he would be willing for me to give him his communion the next day and at the end of it to lay hands on him and anoint him with oil, following the injunction in the Epistle of St James (5:14). He said he would like this, so I did it, and when it was over I remember him saying: "Thank you for coming. Now I am ready for whatever God has in store for me. If I am to live, please God I shall live closer to his will, but if I am to die, I shall die in peace."

To me that has always been the right reaction. There is nothing magic in the Church's healing ministry. It is just invoking the will of God to help a person to face whatever is to be his future, whether to live, or to die in peace, and to bring him all the resources of God so that doctor, clergy and praying laity can work together for total healing, healing of mind and body and above all of soul.

For Cuthbert this was the beginning of a part of his ministry which has since been for him of great importance. He had begun it at Woolwich; he continued it at Southwark. A retired diocesan bishop tells how my sister developed an inoperable cancer in 1948 when she was not yet forty . . . I knew that she greatly admired Cuthbert's broadcasts etc. . . . so I told him of her illness, knowing that there was no one else among my friends who had the kind of approach which my sister would find most strengthening. He was splendid in the loving care he devoted to visiting her in St Thomas' and I believe that he, for his part, gained much from her simple faith. I shall always be grateful for that.

When he came to his consecration as a Bishop in the Church of God, Archbishop Fisher charged him: ". . . Hold up the weak, heal the sick, bind up the broken . . ." "Heal the sick" – the phrase was coming to have increasing meaning for him. He saw that God cared for the *whole* of a human being, cared for him or her as an entity of body, mind and spirit. To that whole entity he was called to minister.

All members of the Church are called to share in that ministry. But there is no doubt that to some the gift of healing is given as it is not to others, just as the gift of teaching or administration is given to some in a measure not given to others. Cuthbert had this gift of healing. He recognized it for what it was, literally a gift from God, and as such he exercised it. Perhaps he realized the danger of pride, and for this reason said little about the undoubted cases of physical healing which occurred after he had laid his hands on people in his chapel or in their homes. One might mention the recovery in Brompton Hospital of a man who had had three heart attacks, or that of a boy who emerged from a coma of two months' duration – both after prayer and the laying on of Cuthbert's hands. He preferred to emphasize the healing of the whole person which so often comes with the laying on of hands and with the prayers of the community. Physical healing may or may not result. Integration of being, peace with God and one's fellows, quiet confidence about the future – this is *shalom*, this is wholeness.

In 1953 the Archbishops of Canterbury and York appointed a *Commission on Divine Healing.* Its first meeting took place at Lambeth Palace on 27th October, under the Chairmanship of the Bishop of Durham. Cuthbert was not a member of the Commission, but on 7th and 8th July 1954, as Bishop of Croydon, he gave evidence to it. That evidence was very similar in content to that which he was to give in a letter to a friend many years later (11th December 1987). In that letter he expressed his anxiety about some aspects of so-called healing work and summed up, positively, his own approach to the subject:

1. There are very different kinds of "healer". The best are those who humbly acknowledge that God alone can heal and that he *will* heal in his own way at his own time.

The less good are those who claim to have healing powers in themselves and do not refer to God. This is dangerous and arrogant.

2. I dislike intensely the title "faith" healer because it gives the impression that healing is dependent on our faith. That is not so.

3. I prefer the title "The Church's Ministry of Healing" which seeks to bring God's healing to the *total* man – his soul, his mind, his body.

And the body is the least important of the three. God wants to heal the *soul* to remove fear, distrust and anxiety and to help the sick person to trust in God absolutely.

He also wants to heal the *mind*, the person, from all that afflicts the mind – resentment, jealousy, vindictiveness, and to bring peace of mind.

He also wants to heal the *body*, which often begins to be healed when the soul and mind are cleansed.

All this is the Church's Ministry of Healing brought through prayer, with counselling, the laying on of hands and anointing with Holy Oil. In all this the Church humbly acknowledges that God is the healer and that he will heal in his own way, at his own time.

Summary: I distrust many so-called "healers" just as I distrust large often emotional healing services and meetings. I prefer the one-by-one quiet encounters with sick people, in which we do not demand a particular kind of healing but leave to the Lord to heal as he will and when he will.

It is important to surround the healing ministry in a volume of prayer. To this end, I have always sought to have the backing of a group of praying people who bring one's healing ministry to God in prayer. At Woolwich there was a large book located just inside the church entrance – the church was always open – so that people could come in through the day and insert requests for prayer in the book. Their names and the bare outlines of the needs of the sick were then taken by a prayer group into the crypt of the church where, once a week, the members of the group met for prayer, not least for me in my healing ministry.

Cuthbert's attitude to death was integral to his approach to the healing ministry. He frequently spoke of it as "the great adventure, moving from one room to another in God's great household of life". The assurance of life, abundant life after death, given us in the resurrection of Jesus Christ, had taken the sting out of death and made it a door of hope. On one occasion, he was called to visit the home of a teenage boy who was dying. He said to him: "I hear you are going to die. How absolutely thrilling . . ." As in quiet confidence he spelt out for the boy the meaning of the Christian approach to death, the atmosphere in the home was completely changed – from gloom to expectancy. The power of the Lord of Life penetrated this world-order and reached out and beyond into the life to come. In that conviction, Cuthbert exercised a continuous healing ministry.

On another occasion, on 4th March 1976, he was giving the address at the funeral of his Personal Assistant's wife, José Davey. After speaking of Christ's resurrection and of his appearances to some of his friends, he went on:

José has not gone from us, far away out of sight . . . she has gone into life – into a deeper awareness of what life is all about. She is in peace, for she was in peace for many days before her death – particularly in the never-to-be-forgotten Holy Communion service held in the hospital ward where she was sick. Jesus was present in that service and was preparing her for her adventurous journey through death into life. Yes, José has not gone away – she has gone *into* life and she is very much with us, and will be with us in the days that lie ahead. We must never cling to her or try to bring her back. She will be wonderfully there to greet us when our turn comes to go through the great adventure of dying.

Cuthbert's concern for a renewal of its ministry of healing within the Church brought him into contact with a woman with a like concern. His friendship with her and with her work was to occupy a large part of his time and energy over a long period of years. Her name was Dorothy Kerin. Born in 1889, in her teens she suffered from tuberculosis and associated complications. When she was twenty-two her doctor abandoned hope of her recovery: her death, he was sure, was imminent. On 18th February 1912, she had been pulseless for eight minutes; then she stood up and walked steadily across the room, healed. The news of this event aroused great interest in the press, and she left home to escape their attentions and to stay with friends. There she received certain visions, as a result of which she was convinced that she had been brought back from the brink of death for a special purpose – to heal the sick, comfort the sorrowing and give faith to the faithless. She was to enter a long period of suffering, a sense of desolation, and she received the wounds of the stigmata. In 1929, she opened her first Home of Healing, and further houses were later added. She gained the support of Bishop Lloyd of St Albans.

In 1948, Burrswood was opened. It was a large house in Groombridge, in the county of Kent on the Sussex border and in the diocese of Rochester, set in extensive grounds. Cuthbert Bardsley, when Bishop of Croydon, paid his first official visit as Bishop Warden in 1954. He was to become chairman of the board of trustees and Visitor to the Community, working closely with the diocesan bishop. A period of building ensued, culminating in the erection of the Church of Christ the Healer within the grounds. On 29th September 1959 the foundation stone was laid, and on 14th May 1960 Cuthbert dedicated the church, in the presence of the Bishop of Lewes (J.H.L. Morrell) and the Dean of Guernsey (E.L. Fossard).

Dorothy Kerin travelled widely, spreading the message of the Church's healing ministry. Between the years 1959 and 1961, she visited Sweden, France, Switzerland, Ireland and the USA. But the centre of her work was at Burrswood, where she gathered round her a community of people dedicated to the task of helping those in distress, deepening the spiritual life of those who felt themselves to be lost, and often, but by no means always, bringing physical relief and health to the sick in body. She was a woman whose life was rooted in prayer; and the Chapel was at the heart of the life of the community.

Dorothy Kerin died in 1963. The funeral took place on 31st January, and Cuthbert gave the address at a Memorial Service at St Martin-in-the-Fields on 18th February. In the course of the sermon he said:

We have met here today with very sad hearts. Every one of us in one way or another has known and loved and been grateful for the life and work of Dorothy Kerin. For fifty years she was a burning and a shining light. I never knew her in her earlier days, but by the time I did come to know her, her face was expressive of the spiritual life that burned like a flame within her. She lived in the supernatural; like Moses, she was a friend of God. She communed with him, and lived her life under his orders. Seldom if ever have I known anybody who more consistently sought the Will of God or who more loyally obeyed it. She would never move forward in strategy, without first seeking to discover whether it was God's Will.

Having to her satisfaction discovered his Will, nothing and nobody could stand in her way. Prayerfully and triumphantly she literally surged forward – obstacles seemed to fall away, vast difficulties were overcome – money seemed to drop from Heaven, people and property arrived at the right moment. It all seemed to happen so easily that one tended to forget the sacrifice and rigid discipline that lay behind her quiet serene face. Morning by morning she got up at five to spend one hour in prayer, and then to write a vast number of letters. This early vigil of prayer seemed to support her throughout a nonstop day of devoted activity.

With Dorothy Kerin's death the work did not cease. "The Dorothy Kerin Trust" was set up that year to continue "the work of spiritual and medical healing" and to "receive gifts and subscriptions for both promoting and furthering the said work". It "is empowered to receive (without distinction of race, colour or nationality) patients at the nursing home at Burrswood; to arrange for services according to the rites of the Church of England at the Church of Burrswood, known as the Church of Christ the Healer . . . and for that purpose to pay or contribute to the payment of the stipend of a Clerk in Holy Orders duly authorized to conduct such services by the Bishop of Rochester". Dr Edward F. Aubert succeeded Dorothy Kerin in the leadership of the community and its work, and he in turn was succeeded by other wardens, all of them determined that the work should never cease but rather spread. The founding of the nursing home at Burrswood and the building of the Church of Christ the Healer are symbols of the partnership of religion and medicine. It is a holy partnership of which the Church must be increasingly made aware, and the Community is dedicated both to the immediate task of the alleviation of suffering and to the longterm education of others in regard to this essential facet of the Church's work.

Cuthbert's interest in Burrswood has never flagged. As with the community of Lee Abbey in North Devon, so with the community of Burrswood in Kent, he saw the powerful working of the Holy Spirit through men and women dedicated to their tasks. That being so, he thought it worthwhile, at the expense of much personal energy, to give liberally of his time to such work in the wider world beyond his diocese. When he first consented to become Warden of Burrswood in 1954, Dorothy Kerin wrote to the Friends and Members of the Fellowship:

> We all know how full his life is and are therefore doubly grateful. The Bishop has warned me that he will not be able to take a very active part in the life and work of the Fellowship, but we shall have the support of his prayers, his understanding, his sympathy . . .

The warning proved to be ill-founded. Cuthbert could never do things by halves. When the Trustees met, as they regularly did at least three times a year, he would not simply preside over the meeting and then disappear. He would stay for three days, moving about the place, talking to members of the community about their individual problems and needs. He might as likely be found in the kitchen as in the council room. He invariably celebrated the Eucharist on the morning of his departure. Knowing the strains that are part and parcel of community living, he arranged for Father Geoffrey Curtis, C.R., to come to Burrswood every two months for a day, when he would be available to meet members of the community.

A measure of Cuthbert's concern may be seen in the fact that he continued to serve Burrswood for no less than seventeen years after Dorothy Kerin died – from 1963 until 1980.

The association of his name with the work had given confidence at a time when spiritual healing was less well understood than it is today and, indeed, in some quarters was regarded with suspicion. As early as 1940, Archbishop Lang had consented to be Patron of the Burrswood International Fellowship; that also helped. The appointment of Bishop Morris Maddocks (since 1983 Adviser on the

Ministry of Health and Healing to the Archbishops of Canterbury and York) as Cuthbert's successor as Bishop Visitor at Burrswood assured the movement of continuing wise oversight.[1]

Evangelism

Cuthbert Bardsley's deep concern was that evangelism should be at the centre of the Church's thinking and strategy. He was not the first to be concerned about this matter. To go back no further than 1944, Archbishop Temple announced that he and Archbishop Garbett had appointed a commission on evangelism under the chairmanship of the Bishop of Rochester, Dr Christopher Chavasse. Its report, *Towards the Conversion of England*, issued in 1945, became a best-seller and included this now well-known definition of the aim of evangelism:

> So to present Jesus Christ in the power of the Holy Spirit, that men shall come to put their trust in God through him, to accept him as their Saviour and serve him as their King in the fellowship of his Church.

Perhaps the most important recommendation of the Commission was the setting up of a Council on evangelism. This the Church Assembly refused to do. That, no doubt, was a matter of great disappointment to Bishop Chavasse and to most of the members of his commission – perhaps it was indicative of the importance, or lack of it, which the Assembly gave to evangelism, or perhaps it indicated its mistrust in the usefulness of Councils as such. None the less, the report had raised interest in evangelism which hitherto had been lacking. One of the most interesting indications was the Mission to London which its

---

[1] The story of Burrswood has been fully told in Miss Johanna Ernest's *The Life of Dorothy Kerin* (published by the Dorothy Kerin Trust 1983). Sir Alister Hardy, in a Foreword to the book, described it as "a most valuable addition to the literature of spiritual experience". I am much indebted to Miss Ernest for her help in conversation and for the gift of many papers about Dorothy Kerin, the centenary of whose birth will be celebrated in November 1989.

Bishop, William Wand, launched in 1952 after three years of careful preparation. Cuthbert Bardsley shared in this, one of his activities being to address a thousand men at a lunch-time meeting in the Guildhall.

The years went by and Cuthbert's anxiety about the place of evangelism on the Church's agenda continued. In 1967 he brought the matter to the attention of the Archbishop of Canterbury, Michael Ramsey, and gained his approval, with the support of the Archbishop of York, for the setting up of an unofficial body to be known as the Archbishops' Council on Evangelism. Cuthbert was to be its chairman. It was to be financed not by central funds but mainly by private donations. Its members, about twenty in number, were both clerical and lay, drawn from various walks of life.

In the November 1972 meeting of the General Synod, Cuthbert drew the attention of its members to the work which the Council was doing:

> The Council comprises twenty-four clergy and laity, including four bishops, and we are responsible to the two Archbishops. We have very close links with Church House, with the Methodist Church, with the British Council of Churches, and with the Board for Mission and Unity. Our purpose is to measure, evaluate and send out news of evangelistic enterprises, and to ensure that training facilities in evangelism are available. It is also to give encouragement to specific experiments in evangelism. We have a whole-time research and development officer,[2] who has recently written a first-class book on this subject and who has the help of an almost whole-time assistant. Many demands are made to the Council for advice on evangelistic methods which are of value particularly in this day and age. They come from deanery synods and from diocesan synods.
>
> We have initiated a series of experimental local level schools of evangelism which have been held in different parts of the country. We are also very much engaged in a deep research programme to study why certain evangelistic approaches as it were pay off and others do not at this moment in time. We issue a bulletin called *ACE*, which goes out to several thousand people throughout the country.

[2] The Rev. John F. Poulton

Two years later, he addressed the General Synod again. "For a number of years", he said,

> it has been my privilege to be Chairman of the Archbishops' Council on Evangelism. During these years the members of the Council have striven to keep evangelism in the forefront of the mind of the Church. It has not been easy always, indeed at times the word "evangelism" has become something of a dirty word in the minds of many. This has partly been due, perhaps, to the kind of evangelist who has given the impression of high pressure salesmanship and also partly due to a misunderstanding of what evangelism is all about.

He went on to quote with approval the words of Visser 't Hooft:

> I do not believe that evangelism is adequately described as answering the questions which men are asking, however deep those questions may be. For evangelism is in the first place the transmission of God's question to man. And that question is and remains whether we are willing to accept Jesus Christ as the one and only Lord of Life.

He continued:

> In all debates and at all levels the issue of mission ought to be to the fore. It seems to me that for far too long we have been too much concerned with maintenance of structures, thinking of the Church as a building or an organization, rather than with renewing of our life and mission and thinking of the Church as a missionary force.

He went on to speak about

> the ever closer relationship between the Archbishops' Council on Evangelism and the Board for Mission and Unity, and also between the Archbishops' Council and the Missionary Societies.
> First, then, the relationship between ACE and BMU. This has been getting closer and closer during recent years. As a Council we have been directly responsible to the Archbishops but with our closer relationship with BMU we shall, through BMU, be also responsible to the Synod. A considerable proportion of the mem-

bers of ACE will be members of the BMU. The whole-time executive secretary of ACE – the Rev. John Poulton, to whom high tribute ought to be paid for his magnificent work throughout the country in recent years – has been constantly in touch with the officers of BMU. Many of our plans have been laid in consultation with BMU.

Next I think the General Synod would like to hear of the ever-growing relationship between ACE and the Missionary Societies. Indeed, one Missionary Society, conscious as they all are of the need for home evangelism if we are going to make a mission impact on the world in general, has contributed money to pay for one whole-time officer of ACE. How right these Missionary Societies are in recognizing that if the Church is going to continue to make an adequate evangelistic impact upon the world that impact must also be made on our own country.

This brings me to another point that I wish to make. For far too long church people in this country have failed to recognize that this country is a mission field. Vast numbers of people in Britain today have little knowledge of the Gospel and a very faint and possibly diminishing understanding of the Church. They turn to it at high moments and holy days, but for the rest they ignore it because they regard it as unimportant. This is partially the fault of the Church. We have not sufficiently accepted our responsibility for living out and proclaiming the Gospel in such a way that people respond to it in commitment and obedience. The Gospel is the same today as it has ever been but the expression of the Gospel changes from generation to generation, and what interests me is to try to discover what shape and form evangelism is taking today. Part of the work of ACE has been analysis of evangelistic efforts to discover what are effective in this day and what are not.

He concluded:

But there are one or two aspects of effective communication in this particular day and age which must not be forgotten. First, there is the essential necessity for ecumenical evangelism. I no longer go into any evangelistic enterprise unless I find out first that it is ecumenical. Secondly it must be a ministry of humility and service. People will not listen to what we have to say unless they see us in a humble ministry of serving. And it must be an open ministry: people must see us willing to open our homes, open our pockets, open our friendships, and open our hearts. Above all, it must be a sacrificial ministry in which we who seek to communicate have gone far enough for fun and are prepared to give all we have and all we are all the time, with no letting up, no retirement, no compromise.

It is probably more difficult today to evangelize than it has been for many years past. We are living at a time and in a nation in which people are affluent and, at least outwardly, happy, albeit frustrated and increasingly worried. It is into this difficult, frustrated, insecure generation that you and I are called to fulfil the command to go into all the world and proclaim the good news of the love of God in Jesus Christ in such a way that people will respond and commit themselves to him.

Cuthbert never ceased to be an evangelist. He was not content to preach about evangelism or to preside over committees dealing with it. He engaged in it inside the diocese and beyond.

Within the diocese of Coventry he conducted missions, now at Stratford-on-Avon, home of Shakespeare and haunt of visitors, now at the other end of his area of work in industrial Nuneaton, and so on.

Beyond these shores he was invited by the then bishop of Toronto, George Snell, to conduct a mission in the city and diocese of Toronto in 1970. Canon Lawrence Jackson, Canon Geoffrey Rogers and the Rev. Alan Boddington had prepared the way over a period of three weeks; they had visited every congregation in the diocese, so that when Cuthbert arrived to conduct the ten-day mission in St Paul's Church, Bloor Street, the largest church in Canada, there was an air of expectancy. Night after night the church was filled to overflowing.

Canon Jackson compèred the meetings as he had done in Coventry Cathedral. He also kept a careful eye on the Missioner, to see that Cuthbert got back to his hotel when the service and greetings were over and into a dry shirt to relax. If Jackson then laced the Bishop's *Canada Dry* with something a little stronger than that particular national drink, who are we to comment?

People came long distances, in some cases over a hundred miles, to take part in the mission. Many came into a much deeper understanding of the meaning of commitment to Our Lord. Many came into a much more vigorous churchmanship. The Mission made a deep impact on the life of the diocese.

It cannot often have happened in recent church history that an English diocesan bishop was invited to lead a mission of this nature and size to a diocese in another part of the Anglican Communion. At the end of it Cuthbert and the other missioners returned to Coventry tired but happy and stimulated.

There have been people who thought that Cuthbert Bardsley should not have been called to the episcopate, but should have remained a full-time evangelist journeying about the world like an Anglican Billy Graham. That would have been to deprive the Church of a bishop who ensured that his episcopal ministry was truly evangelistic, who loved and cared for his laity and clergy, and who taught them that they must never be content with the comparatively few faithful who frequented their parish churches. He insisted that they must be outward looking and outward moving, ever caring for the great unchurched masses who seldom crossed the threshold of their parish churches.

Among his evangelistic activities mention must be made of his visits year after year to the famous Church of St Aldate's in Oxford. In 1952 Keith de Berry discussed with Cuthbert a letter he had received asking him to become Rector of St Aldate's. Should he go? He remembers the Bishop shooting out his arm and pointing a firm finger: "You must go." Keith replied: "Only if you promise to preach for me once a year." Cuthbert promised, little realizing that Keith would remain at St Aldate's for twenty-three years. The church was always packed, with people sitting on the steps and window ledges.

Men and women from the city and the university stayed on at the end of the services to make a solemn contract with God. Cuthbert made it difficult for them, in order to reduce the chance of frothy emotionalism. He asked them to wait in their seats until everyone had left the church. Then, when the church was quiet, he would call them to come forward to the Lady Chapel and speak to them briefly about the importance of what they were about to do. He talked about the love of God and the forgiveness of sins, and then led them in a prayer of dedication.

In later years Cuthbert has frequently met people who in deep gratitude have said that they became committed Christians after coming to a service at St Aldate's. He recalls an occasion when, having given pastoral advice to a group of thirty to forty youngsters, a man who had been sitting at the back of the church came forward to meet the Bishop. He said:

> A year ago I gave my life to Jesus as a result of your sermon. I have never regretted doing this. Indeed, life has been very different and far more satisfying since then. But I think you should know that, twelve months ago and shortly before your visit, I came to this church in great unhappiness and perplexity. I listened to a deeply moving sermon on the subject of the Atonement. I longed to yield my life to the Lord. But when the sermon was over we sang a hymn and I left the church. I was angry and frustrated that no opportunity had been provided for me to make my commitment to Our Lord. The following Sunday you came, and you gave me the opportunity to make a surrender of my life to Our Lord. Thank you.

The services in St Aldate's Church were followed by a lunch in the neighbouring parish hall. Here Cuthbert would speak and answer questions, and often would move over to the rectory study where he would help young men and women in their commitment to God. Keith de Berry himself, together with a remarkable team of fellow priests, took great care in following up the contacts made during Cuthbert's visits.

Cuthbert believes that "conversion" has become a suspect word in our generation; too seldom do sermons call for a verdict; too seldom do clergy provide opportunities for personal response to the call of our Lord for surrender and obedience. He recalls a saying of Father Talbot, Superior of Mirfield: "Too often we build a large edifice of sanctification on an inadequate foundation."

*　　　*　　　*

It is not to be wondered at that, in a ministry involving so much activity and such wide travel, Cuthbert did not write many books. Those that did come from his pen reflect his deep concern for evangelism. We have mentioned his plays, in which his evangelistic passion and his sense of drama came together in a happy alliance. *Victim Victorious* and *A Sword shall Pierce*, both Passion plays, concentrate on the central acts of our redemption.

Bishop's Move, which Mowbray published in 1952, was written while Cuthbert was Bishop of Croydon. The characters "are entirely imaginary", and the book clearly reflects his experiences in the Forces. The chapter titles make it obvious that the writer's aim is to give some straightforward teaching on the basics of Christian belief under the guise of an imaginary story.

Sundry Times Sundry Places came out ten years later when Cuthbert was Bishop of Coventry. It consists of twenty-seven addresses given in a wide variety of places and under varying circumstances. It reflects the experiences of a diocesan bishop in his day-to-day work and in his outreach beyond his diocese.

Him We Declare (1967) was written in conjunction with Canon William Purcell. In this book the two men share with their readers what the "Christ encounter" has meant to them – a phrase which, they acknowledge, "is easy to use, much more difficult to define. What do we mean by it?" They seek an answer to that question by telling of the impact made on them by people who "have been with Jesus" and whose characters, in different ways, show the results of their encounter. Purcell had met and written the biography of Geoffrey Studdert Kennedy ("Woodbine Willie"), "a poet, a prophet, a passionate seeker after truth". He told something of his extraordinary work among soldiers and others. Purcell had met Phyllis Webber who lived her life in an invalid chair; Douglas Hyde, converted from active membership of the Communist Party to membership of the Roman Catholic Church; Father Potter of Peckham, former boxer, private detective, and then one who exercised a ministry among unfortunates in general, and boys in trouble in particular. Cuthbert Bardsley wrote of the influence on him of B.K. Cunningham, his Principal at Westcott House; of Tubby Clayton, his Vicar at All Hallows by the Tower; of Father Algy Robertson (Society of St Francis) and Father Geoffrey Curtis (Community of the Resurrection); and "the tenderest and the most sacred of all these memories is that of an obscure little man whose influence persists for the one reason, that he was the living embodiment of that rarest of all qualities – holiness. This was Father William of Glasshampton."

From the point of view of this biography, the most interesting chapter in *Him We Declare* is chapter 4: "This Happened to Me". In it, Cuthbert tells of the influence on him of his father and his work

("Anglican piety at its best"); of his father's death; of his experience at Oxford; of the death of his sister; he touches on his experiences at Woolwich and at Southwark and in the Forces. Near the end of the chapter he writes:

> That there are dangers of considerable misunderstanding in speaking of it at all is obvious enough, of which the chief is of seeming to seek to put on record some personal achievement. Nothing could be further from either the truth or the intention. I am not aware, here or elsewhere, of having succeeded in anything: only of having tried hard. The truth is that, to be personal . . . I am fully conscious that neither in this situation, nor in any of the others of major test in which life has placed me could I ever have survived without the enabling power of Christ . . . This . . . is of the essence of my faith and my life.

I Believe in Mission (1970) is a record of the Coventry Mission of 1968. It includes the addresses of the main visiting speakers. It also includes, in addition to the addresses which he himself gave, an introductory chapter, "Background to a Mission", and a concluding chapter, "The Continuing Task", both by Cuthbert. In these two chapters, he was able to look back and to estimate the strengths and weaknesses of a great operation, and to look forward to the never-ending task of evangelism to which the Church is committed by its Lord.

*   *   *

Cuthbert enjoyed mixing with and working among *men*. We have only to think of his work in industry (management and shop-floor), among the Armed Forces, or in the Church of England's Men's Society, to see evidence of this. Perhaps it was this, at least in part, which led him to become a Mason in the early days of his episcopate. The fact that many members of Croydon Parish Church were Masons also had something to do with it.

No doubt he hoped that in Masonic circles he might be a positive Christian influence. In the Masonic "hierarchy", he rose to be Grand

Chaplain to the United Grand Lodge of England. There seems to be evidence that in his later years his interest and involvement considerably declined.

Anglican Fellowship of Prayer

Prayer has been central to all Cuthbert's life and work – and still is. In his home at Coventry, there was only a step between chapel and study. In his cathedral, he saw to it that there should be a band of people constantly at the work of prayer. "The world will be saved by only one thing and that is worship", William Temple had said. Cuthbert agreed.

It is, therefore, a matter of no surprise that, when he heard of a movement in America whose sole purpose was to alert the Church to the centrality of prayer, its meaning, its purpose, its power, his sympathy was readily enlisted.

The Anglican Fellowship of Prayer began through the agency of Helen Shoemaker, wife of the Rev. Samuel Shoemaker, at one time Rector of Calvary Church, Pittsburg. She devoted herself to helping the women of the Church to learn to pray, by conducting schools of prayer and prayer study groups. To this end, she travelled widely in the American Church. She found a deep interest, among a wide variety of people, in the message which she brought.

As her work developed she became convinced that, though there were many local schools of prayer, Quiet Days and Retreats, there was need of a great annual occasion to which those concerned with this emphasis on prayer might look for help, inspiration and direction. She went to the Bishop of Pittsburg, Bishop Austin Pardue, and found him sympathetic. He suggested that a quiet, unheralded experiment be undertaken in Pittsburg. So it was that in 1958 the first Prayer Groups Conference was held, and Cuthbert Bardsley was invited to conduct it. He agreed. The following year Dr John Coburn, then Dean of the Episcopal Theological Seminary in Cambridge, Massachusetts, was the conductor; in 1960, Bishop Marmion of South-Western Virginia; in 1961, Cuthbert again. Each year the numbers grew. A need was being met, clergy and laity were being given the help that they needed, the springs of prayer were being renewed.

So deep was Cuthbert's interest in this movement that he is regarded as one of its founders and, according to the present Executive Director, the Rev. Harry Griffith, has been the most popular speaker at its conferences. "There would be no A.F.P. without Cuthbert", writes Mrs Shoemaker. We find him back at Calvary Church, Pittsburg, in 1963, telling those who attended the conference about the consecration of his own cathedral in the previous year, and especially about the consecration of the people. In 1966, he led the diocese of Ohio in their Sesquicentennial celebrations, when Provost Williams brought over the Coventry Cross of Nails, which was then carried, with twenty-four-hour prayer vigils in each place, to a hundred and forty churches in the diocese. In 1974, he was in Albany Cathedral, New York, where nearly two thousand people packed the church. In 1977 he was in Christ Church, Detroit, when the theme of the conference was Prayer and Evangelism. In the words of Donald M. Hulstrand, Bishop of Springfield and at that time Executive Director of A.F.P., he

> had the audacity to send the affluent Episcopalians . . . out into the streets of Detroit two by two to do the work of evangelism. They came back rejoicing that they actually survived this new experience. Now they could have the nerve to do it in their own communities.

The work of the Fellowship spread to Canada and further afield. World leaders like Bishop Chandu Ray of Pakistan and Bishop Festo Kivengere of Uganda were deeply interested, and took their part in extending its influence in other parts of the Anglican Communion. The Fellowship made its presence felt at the Anglican Congress held in Toronto in 1963 and at the Lambeth Conferences of 1968 and 1978.

That Cuthbert was willing to devote so much of his time, thought and energy to the work of the Fellowship during the busiest years of his episcopate was indicative of the fact that he knew that a Church bereft of prayer might be a great organization but it would be devoid of power. The Church must hear that message and take to heart that lesson.

The Church of England Men's Society

When in 1956 Cuthbert Bardsley was invited to become National Chairman of the Church of England Men's Society, he accepted with enthusiasm though with some concern as to its future. He enjoyed work among men – his parochial experience and his work with the Armed Services had given him ample opportunity to exercise his gifts among them. Now he was to lead a Society which comprised some thirty-five thousand men in Britain and some ten thousand overseas.

Some people saw little future for C.E.M.S. inasmuch as it was a Society working among men only. They may have been right in the long view: the day of mixed fellowships of men and women lay ahead. Cynics – realists perhaps – would say that the Church which preached much about the sacred unity of the family actually succeeded in *dividing* the family with its Men's Society, its Mothers' Union, and its multiplicity of youth organizations. The advocates of work among men only, on the other hand, could point to the success of movements such as the British Legion, Rotary, and so on; Cuthbert noted this and took courage.

Every year in some major city hundreds of representatives would come to the annual conference of the C.E.M.S., and Cuthbert would rejoice in taking part in a great procession of men wending its way to a central church or cathedral. Such conferences and services presented opportunities for speaking out on the Church's attitude to social problems in the light of the Christian Gospel, and the Bishop was quick to seize them. To take but one example: addressing the men at their conference in Wigan, he spoke of the improvement in social conditions in this country over the last half century, but went on to lift the sights of his audience to a *world* where malnutrition, bad housing and illiteracy still abounded. He asked his listeners to size the situation up, to prod their leaders into action, to stimulate

> our best Christian leaders to go to the East and give their brains and talents to the work of education, housing and industrial development. [If no costly action is taken] we shall feel very uncomfortable when we stand before the judgement seat of Christ. . . . We men of the Church have two dynamics, not one. We have the dynamic of obvious need, and we have the dynamic of the Cross. Forward, then, in the power of this two-fold dynamic, to proclaim our

witness to the resurrection of the Lord Jesus and to distribute to every man according to his need.[3]

There can be no doubt that when the delegates went back from these Conferences to their own parishes, they took with them a vision and an enthusiasm which were infectious.

Abroad, the main work of C.E.M.S. was in Australia. In 1959 Cuthbert went to Australia for three months, speaking at big meetings in Perth, Adelaide, Melbourne, Sydney, Canberra, and in Tasmania. This gave him the opportunity to see the life of the Church in that vast country, and to stimulate the men of the Church in their witness to the Faith and in their service to the world.

In Germany, there was work among men similar to that of C.E.M.S. in England, and when the annual Conference was held in Coventry the Germans sent over a large contingent of men, thus strengthening the work of reconciliation which the Bishop and Provost Williams had begun and were keen to foster.

Among the headquarters staff of C.E.M.S. Cuthbert worked with men of the calibre of Charles Birtles, Ian Pettitt, Ivan Bailey, and David Woodhouse (now Archdeacon of Warrington). The latter tells of his challenging preaching ("he was much given to 'points' which could number over ten!"), his infectious enthusiasm, his personal piety which was both catholic and evangelical and was centred in devotion to the Person of Our Lord.

National Chairman and General Secretary worked closely together. "The drill", wrote David Woodhouse, "was usually to talk in the study" after dinner "in time for viewing the 10 o'clock TV news ... One was expected to retire after that." It was Cuthbert who brought his visitor a cup of tea next morning; and "there was always a Christmas present ... I must have been fairly well down the list, so goodness knows how long a list it was. The gifts were usually from Harrods."

It was a source of sorrow to Cuthbert when, many years after he had given up office, C.E.M.S. ceased to be (1984). Had the Society, in his years as National Chairman, been at fault in leaning too heavily on his dynamic personality? Had they sometimes avoided looking at their corporate identity, purpose and effectiveness as a body? Had their

---

[3] *Sundry Times Sundry Places*, pp. 47–50

dependency on strong personalities such as Cuthbert's for heightening great occasions sometimes acted as a substitute for addressing issues? It is easy to be wise after the event. The Bishop, however, realized that for many decades the Society had played a very considerable part in the life of the Church, and its influence in the parishes and beyond them would continue to be felt. New times called for new methods.

Mr D. W. Yates, who was National Vice-Chairman of C.E.M.S. 1970–85, recalls Cuthbert's part in the Society's work during its most vigorous years:

One reflects with affection, joy and sadness, on those halcyon days of the Men's Society. With affection for the way he became one's friend and counsellor; with joy for the memories of those great rallies at which only Cuthbert Bardsley could have aroused and brought all men alive in the service of their Lord; and with sadness that it is all passed like a ship in the night. But many lives were changed in the process and many today are better men for that experience, and through their witness have brought others to Christ.

One recalls the great rally of 1958 in the Albert Hall. The building was filled to capacity with men. There was a choir of two hundred Welshmen on the platform sitting near the great organ. Cuthbert Bardsley was the preacher. The whole occasion sent a chill down one's spine.

Again, in Coventry at the time of the consecration of the new Cathedral: the annual conference of the Men's Society was held in the city, but there was no building large enough to house the well over two thousand delegates who attended. So we hired a large cruciform tent and erected it on the playing field of a local factory. We then had the task of transporting those men to the Cathedral for the Service of Thanksgiving. That new building was filled to bursting point – again Cuthbert Bardsley was the preacher – again what an occasion!

This experience was repeated in many towns up and down the country from Durham to Exeter – from Lincoln to St Asaph's. The venue depended on where the Church of England Men's Society chose to hold its annual conference. One recalls the processions of witness which were always a feature of these conferences. We finally became disillusioned as to their effect. Once, in Birmingham, whilst processing down New Street, a lady was heard to ask: "What are this lot protesting about?"; and again, in Cleethorpes, our procession was routed all round the back streets, finishing up in a disused car park. This was the beginning of the end and our final procession was in Nottingham in 1972.

It was in 1974 that we finally had to say "farewell" to the man we all loved and respected, and the occasion was marked, again in Coventry, when the Church of England Men's Society had its annual conference there. How fitting that our farewells should be made in his beloved Coventry Cathedral – again a full house of men and a stirring occasion. There were speeches and a presentation. One thing he asked for were some roses called "Iceberg". On this occasion he was accompanied by his wife. In a very busy life he had at last found time to get married. The farewell and the applause were far from icy. The mighty organ played "For he's a jolly good fellow" and every man-jack in the Cathedral joined in the singing. And that is how every member of that once great society will remember him.

On Cuthbert Bardsley's resignation as National Chairman, the C.E.M.S. decided, in lieu of a farewell present to him, to raise enough money to set up a trust. Its object was to encourage young people to offer new and positive thinking and service to the field of Church work. An annual prize, to the value of £100, was to be awarded for the best essay on a subject chosen by a panel of examiners appointed by the trustees. Applicants (laity, ordinands or clergy) must be under forty years of age. The competition continues to attract a good number of entrants.

The Council for Commonwealth Settlement

The Bishop's visit to Australia in 1959 gave him the opportunity to see at first hand something of the work of the Council for Commonwealth Settlement. The Chairman of the Council was Sir Harry Batterbee. Cuthbert was Vice-Chairman from 1958 (following the death of Bishop George Bell) till 1972.

On his return from Australia Cuthbert reported on what he had found on his tour. He had noted that Australians were very worried at the decrease in the number of immigrants from England as compared with the number of those pouring in from Europe and elsewhere. The number of Roman Catholics was increasing as compared with those of the Church of England. The Council's workers were few. He pleaded for the building or buying of a large number of houses in Australian cities, into which families of immigrants could temporarily move – hostels were a poor second best. He was anxious that the C.E.M.S. should appoint a man to meet immigrants off the ships and give them a welcome on behalf of the Church. Here was an opportunity for co-operation between two movements in which he was deeply involved, the Church of England Men's Society and the Council for Commonwealth Settlement. And in England bishops and clergy needed to be alerted to the work of the Council, and to the recruiting of the right kind of people to emigrate to Australia.

In 1972 the Council was absorbed into the Committee on International Affairs and Migration under the Board for Social Responsibility. Of this Committee Cuthbert became Vice-Chairman.

The House of Lords

Cuthbert Bardsley took a considerable part in the work of the House of Lords. Apart from reading prayers (a customary duty of those Lords Spiritual who have a seat in the House), he made a number of important speeches. His maiden speech, delivered on 4th March 1963, was made in the course of a debate on a campaign against hunger and malnutrition. He quoted from a speech in which the American, Dean Acheson, had said that Great Britain had lost an Empire but had not yet found a mission. "It would be a dangerous moment for our people", said the Bishop, "if that mission were not discovered." He believed that part of that mission was to be found in our contribution to the world problem of famine relief. "This can be one of our finest hours if, having trained many countries for self-government and freedom, we now train them and other nations for industrial self-development." He pleaded for a new kind of missionary, young men at the outset of their careers – he mentioned Voluntary Service Overseas, "a splendid alternative to National Service" – and for the short-term seconding of older, senior, more experienced men to give leadership for two or three, or more, years. He concluded:

> My Lords, this Chamber has witnessed many great occasions when the leaders of this country have been called upon to initiate some great humanitarian project that has brought enlightenment, freedom and development to vast numbers of people. I venture to say that never has this country been called upon to take its share in a project more far-reaching, more wholly according to the will of God, or more beneficial in its permanent effects for good in the lives of millions of world citizens. Here is something that may not immediately improve our own material well-being – although I believe that in the long run it will. The glaring and terrifying fact is that vast numbers of people are living, if not in actual hunger, at least at a level of constant under-nourishment. This ought to make us pause and think at any time, but most emphatically at a time in world history when the standard of living in the West has never been so high. Surely we owe it to our less fortunate brethren to ensure that this unequal state of affairs shall be put right as soon and as effectively as possible.
>
> The challenge to our generation is to make it possible for some of our best manpower, brains and equipment to be put at the disposal of these backward nations, so that they may be helped to advance to that level of well-being which is consistent with God's will for mankind. In this immense project the Church has an important part to play, and, as a Churchman, I am proud to have been given the privilege of making my maiden speech on this all-important subject.

This matter of relief for the Third World was no passing interest in Cuthbert's thinking. In the last major speech which he made in the House of Lords, on 5th November 1974, he returned to the subject of Britain's aid to Asian and Commonwealth countries. He urged Government intervention to ensure a balanced agriculture to divert some of the arable crops, which would otherwise go to domestic consumption, to the needy countries of the Third World.

Naturally enough, most of the subjects to which he called the attention of the members of the House of Lords had to do with matters nearer home, matters which faced him in the day-to-day work of his diocese. Immigration and race relations, care for the mentally afflicted, unemployment (five points here for the attention of their Lordships), youth (four points with an extra two thrown in for good measure), the aircraft industry ("five thousand men and women work in the Coventry factory of Hawker Siddeley Aviation, Limited" – he knew these factories from the inside), automation in industry and commerce, the police service, the BBC, part-time employment of married women, the education bill – all these speeches, and others besides, reflect the mind of a bishop who knew a good deal about the people whom he served and who cared about their welfare *as people*. The whole man, the whole woman, whatever the colour of their skin or their place in society, came under his purview.

Lee Abbey

Future Church historians who record the history of the Church of England in the latter half of the twentieth century are likely to see the work of the Lee Abbey community as one of its influential growth points in that period.[4]

In the years of the blitz Cuthbert Bardsley, then Vicar of Woolwich, shared with his congregation the vision of a house in North Devon being used as the home base of a Christian community. He was one of a group of remarkable men who included Roger de Pemberton (of the Pathfinder Trust), Jack Winslow (poet and one-time member of a community in South India), Geoffrey Rogers (who had helped Cuthbert in a mission in Woolwich and who later became his Diocesan Missioner in Coventry), and Leslie Sutton, a gifted layman. They met in the vicarage of Roger de Pemberton in Rochester. In an act of daring faith – for they had no money in the bank – they bought the somewhat derelict house together with its ample acres overlooking the sea, for the then large sum of £28,000.

It was intended to house a community of preponderantly lay men and women, though there would be an ordained warden and ordained

---

[4] It is a matter of surprise that Paul Welsby, in his *History of the Church of England 1945–1980* (O.U.P. 1984) makes no mention of Lee Abbey nor of its Northern counterpart, Scargill House. Perhaps the passage of time will make it easier for historians to get a better perspective of events. Lee Abbey's story has been told in *Growing in Faith*, by Richard More (Hodder and Stoughton, 1982).

chaplains. From the first, Cuthbert exercised a major influence over this significant development in the life of the Church. In doing so, he ensured that Lee Abbey remained faithful to two of its objects – to be thoroughly evangelistic in its outreach, and to have a deep loyalty to the Church while transcending the age-old party positions and labels. Though essentially a Church of England foundation, it would be ecumenical in its outreach.

For nineteen years he was Chairman of the Council and gave to its affairs a high place in the priorities of his diary. He served in this capacity during his last two years as Provost of Southwark, handing it over to Geoffrey Rogers for the next two years and, on the latter becoming Warden of Lee Abbey in 1950, resumed the chairmanship and held it until January 1968 when he was made a Vice-President. Gordon Strutt, Bishop of Stockport, took it over from him.

During those formative years, a remarkable development took place. There was much sacrificial giving – of money and of talents. The community that was needed for meeting and helping the guests, for running the house, for managing the estate, for developing the farm, grew as time went by, until now it numbers around seventy. Mostly young, the members live a disciplined life, with a simple structure of worship and work, sharing their money and their gifts and, amid the tensions which are inseparable from community living, grow in Christian character and spread their love and joy. Through them, and through the visitors who are touched by their witness, new life seeps back into the parishes.

Lee Abbey's founder and first Warden was Roger de Pemberton. Geoffrey Rogers succeeded him. Others have included Kenneth H. Pillar (now Bishop of Hertford), Geoffrey Paul (later Bishop of Bradford), and John F. Perry (now Bishop of Southampton).

During Cuthbert's chairmanship, Scargill House, north of Skipton in Yorkshire, was founded as a community centre to do especially for the North of England what Lee Abbey was doing primarily for the South. Like Lee Abbey the community was predominantly lay, and, though the activities of Scargill necessarily differed frequently from those of its sister foundation, the connection between them has been close from the beginning. Cuthbert shared in the vision which gave birth to Scargill; indeed, he conducted its official dedication, which took place on 27th June 1959.

After much thought and prayer, an International Students Club was established in London in 1964, and since that year has been doing much to provide for the needs, spiritual and material, of some of the great numbers of students from overseas who will be the leaders of tomorrow in their various nations.

1966 saw the twenty-first anniversary of Lee Abbey. To mark it, there was a Eucharist in St Martin-in-the-Fields, at which Cuthbert was celebrant and preacher. This was followed by a great Rally in the Albert Hall.

In his sermon at St Martin's, the Bishop preached on the words of St Paul: "reaching forth unto those things that lie ahead, I press on towards the goal" (Philippians 3:13–14). After thanking God for the growth of the tiny seed "into a great tree, the fruits of which have brought personal discovery of the saving love and power of Jesus Christ to tens of thousands of people all over the world", Cuthbert bade his hearers look to the future:

> What is God saying to us of Lee Abbey today? I believe that God is saying *first*, that nothing less than a major reformation is needed in Britain today, and *second*, that if that is to happen, the Church must get her priorities right, and evangelism must be restored to its rightful place in the scale of the Church's values. And *third*, if that is to happen, we must be far more deeply converted than most of us are at this moment. And *fourth*, if that is to happen, we must be brought once again, face to face with a living, loving, saving Lord – the Lord of Calvary.

Cuthbert enjoyed taking the chair at the annual "London Meetings", at which the growing number of Lee Abbey friends would gather on a weekday evening, often in the Central Hall, Westminster. But perhaps some of his most influential work was done through the love and wisdom he showed in his dealings with individual members of the community. This patient pastoral work did not a little in building up the life of the young men and women in Devon and sending them back to communicate their new life in Christ to their own parishes. Successive wardens found him affectionate, loyal, approachable and intensely human – it was clear, as one of them put it, "that all this came from the hidden springs of the Spirit which nourished him day by day".

XI

FAREWELL TO COVENTRY

I thank him who has made me equal to the task,
Christ Jesus our Lord; I thank him for judging me
worthy of this trust and appointing me to his service.

1 Timothy 1:12

CUTHBERT PLANNED HIS DEPARTURE from Coventry with a nice precision: he had been enthroned on 5th May 1956; he would finish his work on 5th May 1976. He informed the diocese in good time, and was able to announce the name of his successor, Canon John Gibbs, Principal of Keswick Hall Church of England College of Education, well before he left.

Something of what it meant to him to pull up his roots after so long in his diocese can be seen in the last monthly news letter which he wrote in the Diocese of Coventry *Diary*:

When we are young, we tend never to think about the end of the journey. We never imagine that there will come a moment when we shall retire and we hardly ever give a thought to death.

Suddenly, during these past few weeks, I have been made to realize that the end of my full-time active ministry is in sight and that shortly I shall be leaving the diocese which I have loved and sought to serve for the past twenty years.

I leave you with mixed feelings. One side of me longs for the freedom from administration and the burden of a post of thirty to forty letters a day, the endless round of committees, the continuous personal problems which a bishop has to try to untangle. The other side of me grieves deeply at the inevitable loss of many friendships. When a bishop leaves a diocese, he must leave and only very seldom return, so this letter and the message in the coming farewell services must, inevitably, be "Goodbye".

Goodbye

There are two ways of expressing goodbye – the first is the word "goodbye" and the second is the word "adieu". Goodbye means "God be with you": no doubt God *will* be with you, but you must

226

remain close to Him. God the Holy Spirit is mightily with you all at the moment. During these last few weeks as I have moved around my diocese saying farewell, I have been deeply impressed, as has my wife, by the quality of life and the vitality of fellowship that have been manifest in the parishes we have visited. Constantly my wife has remarked to me, "That Church is alive". Yes, I think I can say without exaggeration that the Church is indeed alive, alive under God, alive to the needs of the community round about. This does not mean that it is perfect, far from it, there are many weaknesses about which I am only too conscious, but there is a great spirit of love.

We have passed through the barren, lean years of the sixties, when evangelism was a suspect word, when our Christian faith was being challenged on all sides. Many people were all too ready to believe that God was dead. We have come through that lean period purified and enriched. I believe that we are moving out of the trough towards the crest of a new wave of the power of the Holy Spirit. The young people of today are critical of the Church, but very moved by the Person of Jesus. Many – old and young – are being caught up by the enthusiasm and guidance of the Holy Spirit. The charismatic movement, with all its dangers, is very much to be reckoned with. We are moving slowly and painfully into a deeper awareness of what it means to be united in the Spirit, what it means to be humble lovers, to climb down from our status pedestals, to cease to be patronizing to our humble fellow seekers after truth. Yes, there is much to encourage. God is mightily at work and so my first message is "Goodbye – God be with you".

Adieu

My second message is "adieu" which means "to God". I commit you all to him, knowing that he will overrule all the deficiencies of my leadership, knowing that he will supply all your needs and wants. The resources of the Deity are limitless.

If we will but put our trust totally in him, he will supply our financial needs. There will be enough money to train men for the ministry; there will be enough money for the new churches for expanding populations; there will be enough money for the Missionary Church overseas . . . and so I could go on. There will not be enough money for our greed, but there will be enough money for our need.

Secondly, he will supply all our spiritual and material require-
ments. If we put our trust in him, he will work in the hearts of men
to offer themselves for the Ministry; he will work in the hearts of
laity to offer themselves unreservedly in the task of witness, service
and leadership. Why be downcast with an all-powerful and all-
loving God at our side? If failure comes, it will be entirely due to our
lack of trust in God. Admittedly he will require all we have and are,
but he will supply all our spiritual needs. The Spirit of God will
refresh us. He will remove from us all tiredness and lethargy. He
will enkindle within us enthusiasm and send us on our way
rejoicing.

However difficult may be the surrounding state of the nation and
of the world, God rules and overrules. And so I say to you "adieu".
I hand you over to God, knowing that he will guide and provide.

I thank God for all that you have meant to me, for your
friendship, your love, your loyalty and your co-operation.

God bless you, one and all.

Cuthbert determined, during the closing months of his episcopate, to
visit as many parish churches, schools, factories, institutes and civic
bodies as time and strength would allow. He found the expressions of
gratitude almost overwhelming. Letters expressing appreciation
poured in, as did invitations to farewell dinners and parties. The
Warwickshire County Council gave the Bishop and Mrs Bardsley a
Reception. The Archbishop of Birmingham and some of his clergy
gave them a memorable private dinner party, itself a witness to the
warmth of relationship which had been established between the
Roman Catholic Church and the Anglican in the Midlands area.
Their gift of a silver tea service included a tray with the inscription:
"To the Bishop of Coventry, the Rt Rev. Cuthbert Bardsley, with
gratitude and appreciation from the Roman Catholic laity of
Coventry." The Bishop and his wife attended an evening service in
the United Reformed Church in the centre of the city, and were the
recipients of a valued gift from the congregation.

At the last meeting of the Diocesan Synod the Archdeacon of
Warwick, as Chairman of the House of Clergy, and Mr J.A.D. Owen
(now Dean of the Court of Arches) as Chairman of the House of
Laity, paid tributes to the Bishop, and the following motion was
recorded:

That the Coventry Diocesan Synod gives thanks to Almighty God for the episcopate of the Right Reverend Cuthbert Killick Bardsley for the outstanding service of work and love which he has unstintingly given to the Diocese and its people. As he and his wife move into retirement it desires to record its gratitude to them and its affection and good wishes for their future.

*   *   *

It is likely that there were three events which brought the Bishop and his wife almost more pleasure than any others. The first centred in their home; the second and third in the Cathedral.

A few days before his departure, the Bishop invited all the clergy of the Diocese to come to Bishop's House. Each was to choose one of his paintings and half a dozen books, thereby helping to clear his large stock of paintings – done in oil on hardboard – and his extensive library. It was a sunny morning, and by 9 a.m. the Bishop was busy putting his pictures on display all along the drive of the house and in the garden, and propped up against the wall of the house itself. Inside, book cases had been opened up. Books were all over tables and chests. The clergy were delighted to have in their homes a permanent memory of their Bishop.

There were two Farewell services in the Cathedral. The first was the Bishop's Family Farewell, organized by the Rev. J.B. Eardley, Adviser for Children's Work in the diocese, in conjunction with the Provost. It was for the ordinary people and especially for the young, a family occasion to which people came whom Cuthbert had baptized, confirmed, married, touched in their times of joy and sorrow and sickness. There were fifteen deanery banners. There was a Scout band which provided a fanfare as the Bishop and Mrs Bardsley entered the West Door. The Precentor, Joseph Poole, true to form, asked Ellen, if she had "a garment of heraldic colour", to wear it on that occasion. She obliged with a bright red coat. As they entered, the Provost called out: "Right Reverend Father in God, welcome to your cathedral. Your friends are here to greet you." And the people in their turn shouted back in response: "Welcome to your cathedral. Your friends are here to greet you."

It was a joyful act of worship, with a Celebration of the Bishop's Episcopate, songs by the Cross of Nails Group, an address by

Cuthbert who was loving it all, and a blessing of him and Ellen by the Provost. He added the words of St Patrick, themselves a prayer of blessing:

> Christ be with you, Christ within you,
> Christ behind you, Christ before you,
> Christ beside you, Christ to win you,
> Christ to comfort and restore you.

And the people, following the Provost's example, called out together those words of benediction.

The service over, the Scout band went to the foot of St Michael's Steps; the banners passed through the nave and lined the steps from St Michael's Porch to Priory Street; the congregation followed and, at the end of the great throng, came the Provost with Cuthbert and Ellen escorted by twelve children. Their costumes were those of the countries which the Bishop had visited in the course of his Episcopate. All the children in the Cathedral had been provided with coloured handkerchiefs. As Cuthbert and Ellen reached the West Door, there was a great flutter of waving handkerchiefs, the band played, everyone cheered, waved and clapped. Then came the surprise of the day: at the foot of St Michael's Steps, all unknown to the central figures, stood a magnificent white vintage Rolls-Royce, waiting to carry them home to the Bishop's House. Cuthbert's and Ellen's hearts were full.

But this was not the end. On the following day, the Cathedral was once again packed to capacity, this time for a service more formal though no less full of thanksgiving than that of the day before. This was the Bishop's Farewell Eucharist, at which he was preacher and celebrant. The clergy were there in great numbers; the civic dignitaries and Her Majesty's Lieutenants for the West Midlands and for Warwickshire were in their appointed places. The Lesson was read by Mr D.W. Yates, Chairman of the Church of England Men's Society in the diocese – a fitting personal reminder of Cuthbert's leadership of that movement. The Epistle and Gospel were read by the Archdeacon of Warwick, the Ven. Edward Taylor and Bishop J.D. McKie respectively. Before the sermon, gifts were presented by the Provost, by Mr C.M.T. Smith Ryland, Her Majesty's Lieutenant for Warwickshire, and by the Archdeacon of Coventry, E.A. Buchan.

In his address, the Bishop referred to the sermon which he had preached on the occasion of his enthronement exactly twenty years previously. He had spoken of the crisis which faced the nation and the choice between life and greatness or death through littleness. He went on:

Twenty years have passed and the choice still confronts this country.

Twenty years ago, though not young, I was still a comparatively young man, and like all young men I had a vision for the Church. My vision was that the Church should love the multitudes into the fellowship of the Church and ensure that the fellowship of the Church was warm, welcoming and worthwhile when they got there. I then went on to say that to achieve this mighty task, we needed new methods, new men and new money.

Has that vision been implemented? Yes, I think that in some ways it has. During the past twenty years we have seen many new and worthwhile methods. We have seen new and more virile forms of services; new and interesting translations of the Bible; the formation of new and worthwhile team ministries and group ministries; a great emphasis upon the training of the laity, who have become more knowledgeable of their Faith and more capable of expressing their Faith in personal witness; many worthwhile programmes of in-service training for the clergy which have renewed their Faith and helped them to communicate that Faith; a most impressive conference to consider the place of the Church in the increasingly urban setting of our nation – "People and Cities" was its title; several thoroughly worthwhile and effective Missions which have brought many into a new and deeper awareness of the claims of the Lord Jesus Christ upon their lives; a new Rule of Life called "The Discipline" which has radiated out from our Cathedral Church of St Michael to the world; and we have seen a form of this adapted for the use of many in this Diocese.

So I could go on and on. We have found many new and worthwhile methods of presenting the faith.

In my vision, twenty years ago, I called for new men – more priests of the right sort – more lay men and women, prepared to live out their faith and speak about their faith. Well, I have been much impressed by the quality of men offering themselves for the ministry. Though the numbers have not been as high as I had hoped twenty years ago, the quality has been good, and we have seen new kinds of patterns of ministry, such as the non-stipendiary ministry, the extra-parochial ministry, etc. And certainly today we have many more lay people who are prepared to live out their faith sacrificially and to speak about it courageously.

In my vision, twenty years ago, I said that we needed new money, and this most certainly we have got. I thank God for the magnificent way in which, despite inflation, the laity of this Diocese have risen to the challenge and raised their quotas vastly in order to maintain the ongoing, outgoing work of the Church. Perhaps one of the greatest encouragements for me as I leave this Diocese is the knowledge that this year 98 per cent of all the parishes have paid their quota in full.

I then went on . . . to speak about the nation, and I said that we needed a new vision – a new belief in ourselves based upon a new belief in Christ. Has this come about? I am afraid that here the answer is, to a certain extent, no. We are still doing far too much grumbling, too much self-depreciation, too much washing of our dirty linen in public. A loss of belief in ourselves, our democratic way of life and our nation. We need an entirely new morale, a new sense of our vocation as a country in the affairs of Europe and of the world. We need a realization of the many gifts we have to offer; a new confidence in our ability to offer them, based upon a new and vigorous faith in the God who has sustained us, guarded and guided us and blessed us throughout the long centuries.

A few months ago our two Archbishops issued a Call to the Nation to find new faith for new people in a new and better and more just society.

Although twenty years have gone by, I have never lost my vision, the vision of a young man; that despite the dangers of our age, despite the threat of cataclysm, despite the tensions in our own national life, God still rules and overrules. But now I am older and more mature; twenty years have gone by; I am fast becoming an old man. Well, it is the prerogative of old men to dream dreams.

There is nothing wrong in dreams, provided we don't cling to the past or live in the past. God has honoured the past of this nation; God has honoured the past of this Diocese; but it would be folly and dangerous to live in the past.

232

In my dream I realize three things more clearly now than I did twenty years ago.

First: that nothing worthwhile is achieved without suffering.

Second: that it is not by human activity but by divine action that progress is made.

Third: that hope is not man-made but God-given – that without hope we are lost, but that with hope we shall never perish.

After elaborating these three points, Cuthbert ended:

So I leave you today far from despondent, but on the contrary full of hope. I leave you with no sense that my visions of twenty years ago have failed to mature. On the contrary, I believe that God has honoured those visions and has brought many of them to birth. As I leave this Diocese, I hope that . . . you will share my dreams . . .

Your young men shall see visions; your old men shall dream dreams.

After the Bishop had blessed the congregation, he turned to face the altar. Slowly raising the great Cathedral crozier (made from a narwhal tusk), he placed it on the altar, to symbolize the laying down of his office. As he came down into the body of the church, he was joined by Mrs Bardsley, who walked along with him to the West Door. The spontaneity of the people's applause indicated their deep affection for the Bishop and his wife.

*　　　*　　　*

Shortly after his retirement, Cuthbert paid three return visits to Coventry. The first was to receive a red Sunbeam Alpine car, made (of course) in the diocese. It was a gift from his clergy.

The second was to receive the Coventry Award of Merit, given by the City to people who have been outstanding in their service. At the same time the award was made to the poet Philip Larkin, born in Coventry, and to Jack Jones the Trades Union leader. The ceremony took place in the context of a Civic Dinner in St Mary's Hall, Coventry.

The third visit was to the University of Warwick, to receive the honorary degree of Doctor of Letters, in recognition of Cuthbert's services to the University since its inception.

Part Three

XII

RETIREMENT: MAN AND MISSION

God's glory is in living men, and full life for men is in the vision of God.

Irenaeus

FOR ANY BISHOP WHO LOVES HIS WORK, retirement is at once a bereavement and a release. It is a bereavement, for he has been "married" to his diocese and he has loved it and cherished it. And it is a release from the heavy load of diocesan and central work laid on him, and from the stream of correspondence which never ceases so long as he is in office.

Cuthbert Bardsley was sixty-nine years old when he retired. He was weary, but by no means of a mind to discontinue his ministry. That would continue so long as he had strength to fulfil it. How could it be otherwise? A priest's ministry does not end when his salary ceases. Retirement should be spelt with a "y" – a new set of tyres and he would be off again, but at a more measured and leisurely pace.

That, of course, is to speak metaphorically. For he was to continue to drive a car for many years. Stories of his driving furiously go back at least to his Southwark days – how many lights could he shoot as they were turning red, with his sister in the back shrieking, "Bert, *do* be careful; *do* go more slowly!"? (Dorothy was the first person who ever called him "Bert".) Archdeacon Proctor bears witness that "Jehu had nothing on him. Sadly on one occasion he wrapped his car round a lamp-post when very tired – with painful consequences to his body. He was not a dangerous driver – simply a busy man who had to get there on time." He recalls an occasion when he was to drive the Bishop and the other Archdeacon (Leonard Stanford) to a ceremony in Coventry. The wives of the Archdeacons were invited and so was Cuthbert's sister. The two wives were to make their own way to the venue; Dorothy was to travel with the two Archdeacons and the Bishop. Eventually, along came Cuthbert – but alone. "Off we go", he said. "What about Dorothy?" said the Archdeacon, who was driving. "Goodness me," said Cuthbert, "I've completely forgotten her. Hold on." As he went into the house to fetch her, one Archdeacon said to the other: "Heaven help us if we were to forget *our* ladies like that!" Life was never dull in Coventry.

In retirement, the speed of life did lessen. With the lessening of the speed came opportunities to cultivate interests which often had to be neglected when the Bishop was in office. Painting had always been his supreme relaxation and, by the sheer discipline of trying to take a day off each week, he had managed to produce a great many pictures. Now he was able to engage that particular gift at greater leisure.

His biographer is no artist, and is therefore incompetent to comment on the works which Cuthbert produced, except to say that they were like the artist himself – big, colourful, bold; and there was no lack of paint. He and Ellen were staying with the Rev. Nigel Abbott and his wife in their house which overlooked Oban harbour and from which he was able to paint the Isle of Mull. "Can I have lots of newspaper?", Ellen requested; "Cuthbert is painting and we are never sure where the paint is going to land." As Cuthbert's successor said in the presidential address of his first diocesan Synod: "Bishop Bardsley has no doubt left his mark on the diocese!" Geoffrey Rogers once told Cuthbert that he put more paint on one of his pictures than he, Geoffrey, did on all the pictures he painted in a year. He used a palette knife with abandon. Woe betide a fellow painter sitting near him, unless he used protective clothing!

The Mediterranean countries provided him with just the opportunities which he loved, and he would come back armed with many trophies of scenes which he had captured. The brilliance of sky and sea was there for the taking – no matter if, as he himself said, he started a picture thinking it was to be a Rembrandt and after half an hour realized that it was just a Bardsley. He attacked it, however intimidating it was, with speed and panache.

Cuthbert sees painting as a way into an understanding of God, the author and source of all beauty. As he drives his car, he will notice a scene which later on he will convert into a picture. This may on occasion cause some concern to Ellen who is with him, for the car tends to lurch as he mentally notes "morning – October" or "afternoon – December". But the *noticing* faculty is developed, and the results will be seen later on. His chauffeur said, "Before I worked with you, Bishop, all greens were one to me". After all, his favourite painter is Rembrandt, and who better than he *noticed* the marvel of an old person's face, reflecting in its multiplicity of lines the inner beauty of a lifetime of experience?

But retirement for Cuthbert was not all painting – far from it. The fires of evangelism and the desire to reach the outsider continued to burn in him. "Grey Walls", the Bardsleys' retirement home in Cirencester, was to be the base from which Cuthbert would go out on missions of various kinds. For example, shortly after his retirement he received an invitation to conduct a mission to Cheltenham. He refused to accept the invitation unless all types of churchmanship were included in those who invited him. This being guaranteed, he promised to go. He conducted a mission for ten nights. The big church of St Matthew was the venue, and on the last night those responsible took the Town Hall. Every seat was occupied, and there was an overflow meeting of several hundreds outside. The work was worthwhile.

There was a mission at Northleach parish church which proved the beginning of a remarkable spiritual development allied with Lee Abbey – the Cotswolds were beginning to feel the pulsing of new life. And there was a mission to the industrial town of Stroud – industry had never been far from his thought and concern.

There were continued visits to America – Long Island, Denver (Colorado) and many other areas, and to Canada. These were partly on behalf of the Anglican Fellowship of Prayer (see pp. 213f), and partly in response to calls from bishops and other church leaders who were eager to enlist Cuthbert's help in the task of evangelism.

Cuthbert never lost his interest in Lee Abbey. The last time he visited it was in October 1982 when he was the guest speaker at their Harvest Houseparty. His themes were: "The Lord who was involved; the Lord who forgives and heals; the Lord who gave all and demands all; the Lord who expects."

He rarely returned to his old diocese of Coventry during his retirement, but he made an exception in that same year for a very special service which proved to be full of joy. It was a Eucharist in the Cathedral, "to mark the seventy-fifth anniversary of the birth, the fiftieth anniversary of the ordination, the thirty-fifth anniversary of the episcopal consecration and the tenth anniversary of the marriage of Cuthbert Killick Norman Bardsley, C.B.E., D.D., formerly Lord Bishop of Coventry." The preacher was Cuthbert himself. As the Epistoler read of the gifts which God gave to his Church for its unity and upbuilding, and the Gospeller read of the Lord's washing of his disciples' feet, a host of friends united in thanking God for one who, in his vocation and ministry, had served him in holiness and truth.

He paid another return visit to the Cathedral in May 1987, to join in the celebration of the twenty-fifth anniversary of its consecration. Six of the original team subsequently gathered during the summer, but Cuthbert was in hospital seriously ill after a major operation. He was, however, with them in spirit. He dictated a message to Ellen for her to convey by phone to Betty Simpson, his one-time secretary: Would she send a message to the previous Provost, Bill Williams, a word of loving greeting, and of gratitude to God that they had been privileged to share in the beginning of the resurgence of the Cathedral. He ended by sending them his blessing.

The fortieth anniversary of his consecration as a bishop on 1st November 1947 was celebrated very quietly in St Mark's Hospital, City Road, London.

His illness was prolonged and difficult, lasting for some four months. Cuthbert's surgeon, looking back on it, regards his recovery as "something of a miracle, something quite exceptional", the turning point occurring at the time when Cuthbert received the laying on of hands. The service took place in his room in hospital, in the presence of Ellen, the hospital chaplain, the Rural Dean of Islington, and the surgeon himself. Cuthbert, who had so often anointed others, now himself was at the receiving end of this means of grace.

His surgeon bears witness to Cuthbert's patience and gratitude, and to his refusal to grumble or complain during a long period of weakness and discomfort. He sensed that, as people came to visit the Bishop, *he* ministered to *them*.

The time in hospital was followed by a stay at Burrswood before returning home to Cirencester. When at last he was able to preach again, as he did on the first Sunday after Easter (for the first time in eight months), Cuthbert felt that his feet were firmly on the road towards recovery.

As he grew older, the big missions ceased and Cuthbert turned his attention to quieter undertakings. He relished the opportunities which came to him in considerable numbers to conduct Quiet Days and retreats for clergy, to sit alongside them, and together to make himself and them more available to God, more open to his grace, more responsive to his demands.

He became national president of the Retired Clergy Association. He worked in close liaison with Sam Woodhouse, formerly Archdeacon of London, and with Kenneth Lightfoot, deputy secretary of the London Diocesan Fund. The number of members of the R.C.A. rose rapidly. The Association did much to help clergy to realize that new ways of work were open to them, that they need not be lonely or feel that they were cast on one side just because they had retired. The closing years of their lives could prove to be years of spiritual maturing and of use to others.

For five years Cuthbert was an extra chaplain to the Community of St Mary at Wantage. He regularly heard the confessions of the sisters and ministered to them in a variety of ways. The three months which he had spent in Mirfield before going to Woolwich had taught him the value of the life and work of the Religious Communities, and he admired their adherence to the rules of poverty, chastity and obedience. He welcomed this work at the nunnery. His work with individuals concerned for progress in the spiritual life was done with great care, as his letters to them show. Always positive and encouraging, they were written with an insight born of prayer and wide experience of human need and frailty.

Once a month, for a considerable number of years, he celebrated the Holy Communion in a home for elderly people. He was delighted to be present when a lovely old house, Harnhill Manor, four miles from Cirencester, was opened in 1985, as a Christian healing centre, in the presence of the Bishop of Gloucester and of Bishop Morris Maddocks. This came about largely because of the impact which Lee Abbey had made on a number of clergy and laity during the visits of their members to the Cotswolds. The house, with its priest-warden and his wife, has a small resident staff, and is open for Quiet Days, for training in the ministry of healing, for people who need counselling, and so on. Cuthbert, who himself had throughout his years as a bishop given a central place in his ministry to the work of healing, rejoiced to see this work taking place so near his home, and to have a share in it. It was like a little Burrswood (see Chapter X, p. 201ff).

For a number of years he was National President of *Message*, a Christian telephone service founded by Norah Coggan and operating in many of the cities and towns of Britain.

*   *   *

So much for Cuthbert Bardsley's activities from 1976 onwards. Now we must look a little more closely at the man behind those activities.

Whether a man's biography should be written while he is still alive is open to debate. Certainly it is impossible to accord him his rightful place in history until many years have passed after his death; correct perspective can only be gained from a distance down the road. But it is possible to venture some assessment of his character while he is still living. This can be reached by putting together a great number of factors. Among them must be included the writer's personal knowledge of the man concerned; the evidence of a broad cross-section of people who have known him under a wide variety of circumstances and have been willing to talk or write about him; the books he has written and the recordings he has made; the success or failure of the work he has done in the varying spheres of his ministry – this, of course, being fraught with difficulty in as much as spiritual values cannot be estimated with the exactitude that belongs to material things.

Anyone who writes the biography of a Church leader, if that biography is to be anything more than the bare narrative of a succession of events, must at least attempt an answer to such questions as these: What came first in the man's life and thought? What were his main ambitions and hopes? What was the foundation of his private life? What was the driving power behind his work and achievements? To put it crudely: What made him tick?

Talk to anyone about Cuthbert Bardsley and it will not be long before one hears the word "enthusiasm". A correspondent who had known Cuthbert from his Oxford days wrote about him in 1987 that he was "a remarkable personality, rather like a highly bred race horse". He has been described as "the superlative Bishop" because of his love of language which in others might be thought extravagant; where ordinary mortals, asked for a comment, would reply "That's O.K.", Cuthbert would answer with great conviction: "That is *wholly* good."

Nor does one have to wait for long before the word "dynamic" comes into the conversation. "Devoted, dynamic, explosive", said a priest who had shared in a mission which Cuthbert conducted in Toronto. "Dynamic and gracious" was the verdict of a woman who looked back over some forty years to her Confirmation by Cuthbert when he was Bishop of Croydon. A middle-aged priest remembers as a boy of seventeen hearing him say "Good morning" on the "Lift Up Your Hearts" programme of the BBC. Those two words alone, spoken with evident joy, made all the difference to his day, and he has never forgotten them. "There was an aura about him", said another priest. One of his franker clergy wrote: "Sometimes I want to kick Cuthbert. But I'd go to the ends of the earth for him." A parishioner said of him that, when he ceased to be Vicar, "it was as though the sun went in".

The cynic might say that this side of his character was frothy and effervescent, but he would be wrong. The criticism would show a lack of perception. Life to Cuthbert was good, and God was good in giving it to him. His enthusiasm, his dynamism sprang, not from a desire to be theatrical or histrionic (though he had the makings of an actor in him), but from the depths of his faith in the living God, his "Living, Loving, Liberating Lord of Today".

The point is important and we must try to get it right. It is not easy to express. The best way to get to the heart of this side of his character will be to quote from John Chrysostom, Bishop of Constantinople (347–407):

> The waters have risen and severe storms are upon us, but we do not fear drowning, for we stand firmly upon a rock. Let the sea rage, it cannot break the rock. Let the waves rise, they cannot sink the boat of Jesus. What are we to fear? Death? "Life to me means Christ, and death is gain." Exile? "The earth and its fullness belong to the Lord." The confiscation of our goods? "We brought nothing into this world, and we shall surely take nothing from it." I have only contempt for the world's threats, I find its blessings laughable. I have no fear of poverty, no desire for wealth. I am not afraid of death nor do I long to live, except for your good.
>
> Do you not hear the Lord saying: "Where two or three are gathered in my name, there am I in their midst"? Will he be absent, then, when so many people united in love are gathered together? Let the world be in upheaval. I hold to his promise and read his message; that is my protecting wall and garrison. What message? "Know that I am with you always, until the end of the world!"

If that be true, life has a certain exhilaration to it. And Cuthbert was not averse to giving exuberant expression to that exhilaration. Humour and a keen sense of fun are aspects of such exuberance. Charades after the Christmas dinner, with Cuthbert lavishly dressed for the part, were perhaps one of the more extravagant forms which this sense of fun took. But one has to see and hear him tell a story to get the full impact, nor should one be too extreme to mark where the historical ends and the apocryphal begins – as, for example, in the story which circulated about his visit to Dartington Hall, outpost of *avant-garde* education. He arrived at the door, so it is said, to be met by a five-year-old girl entirely naked, who said, "We don't believe in God here!", and slammed the door in his face. From a somewhat different setting, a priest who acted as Cuthbert's chaplain remembers his muttered aside as they neared the end of a three-hour Orthodox liturgy in Coventry Cathedral. Out of the side of his mouth, a weary Cuthbert said to the chaplain: "Don't they *ever* sit down in Greece?"

Cuthbert enjoys a joke against himself. He tells the story of how, in the early days of his ministry, he was taking the wedding of a girl, Rosemary, whom he had known for a long time, to a young man whom he had not previously known.

They came to the point in the service where the priest addresses the man by his Christian name. Cuthbert's mind went blank. He tried the letters of the alphabet, but nothing came. "Abraham" would have to do. "Abraham", he said, with great authority, "say after me: 'I, Abraham, take thee, Rosemary, to my wedded wife . . .' " Obediently but with great hesitation, the young man replied: "I, Abraham, take thee, Rosemary . . ." In the vestry they discovered that his name was Ernest. Twenty-five years later, a middle-aged colonel in the Middle East approached Cuthbert. "You won't remember me", he said. "I'm Abraham." Cuthbert had never forgotten! He never could.

Perhaps it was this sense of fun which, in part, enabled him to mix so easily with people from all walks of life. His own domestic team, the chauffeur of a close friend, the staff of a hotel in the Lake District where he and Ellen often stay – all treat him as their own friend because they know that to him they matter.

"He made it such fun to follow Christ", said Bill Williams whose work as Provost of Coventry with Cuthbert over many years enabled him to speak with authority. The widow of one of his clergy tells how her husband would take his problems to the Bishop and, on returning home, would say to her: "An hour with that man and you could move a mountain!"

Another word which recurs in conversation about the Bishop is "simplicity". There were those who said of him that he had a "simple faith", or that in his presentation of his message he "over-simplified" it. It is true to say that he was not subject to continual gusts of doubt about the fundamentals of the Christian faith. His was not a questioning mind in the sense that he constantly agonized over the problems of theological or philosophical thought. He was not a Charles Gore or a John Robinson, still less a Don Cupitt.

But, having said that, it is easy to use the word "simple" in a critical, even a pejorative, sense. To say that a man has a simple faith is not to say that he is therefore a "simpleton" or that his belief is "simplistic". Rather, as Charles Kingsley suggests, there is a "true wisdom that shows itself by simplicity", a wisdom which derives from spiritual insight. There is a perception, a penetration into truth, which is given to the pure in heart and sometimes denied to the professor of theology, and which, knife-like, can cut through complication and verbiage. To put it positively: openness to God's guidance and obedience to his will can lead to right decisions, where unaided intellectual ability does not.

A priest who lived very close to Cuthbert over many years spoke of his ability to "*detect by intuition* the things which were bugging people". What is "intuition" in this context? Is it the insight which is given by God to those who live in communion with him and make a habit of referring all things to him? Constantly, when problems arose, Cuthbert would say: "Our God rules and overrules" and, to the annoyance of men of lesser faith, would be content to leave the issue to him. The irritating thing was that so often it worked out all right! William Temple, who knew a thing or two about the complexities of life and conduct, offered, half humourously, the prayer: "God who made me simple, make me simpler yet!"

Donald Bradley, who was one of Cuthbert's staff at Southwark Cathedral, comments significantly on this aspect of his character:

Some may think of him as somewhat simplistic in his approach to the problems of the age and certainly we tend perhaps to look at things in a more sophisticated way these days, but there are signs that he may have been more penetrating than we once thought.

Perhaps we have been too clever by half! What always impressed me about Cuthbert was his transparent sincerity, his sensitive kindliness and courtesy and his very real humanity. He was utterly free of that pompousness which so readily afflicts the successful ecclesiastic and through all the vicissitudes of his ministry he remained open-minded and spiritually sensitive. He is fundamentally, I suspect, a profoundly devout man – the characteristic product of a long tradition of the best evangelicalism – and whatever he did was always coloured by this tradition. The fact that this was so will ensure the durability of his achievements and the continuing high regard of those who were privileged to be associated with him.

Eric James, in his *Life of Bishop John A.T. Robinson*, writes of the Bishop's contact with the kind of "simplicity" of which we are writing. He tells how John's daughter Catherine describes her father's visit, very near the end of his life, to Max Williman, the priest who had married John and Ruth:

> He is a man who lives from the heart, and he touched John's heart, in a way no one else had done, by his moving account of his own identical illness. [John was dying of cancer.] Through it, he learned to give himself totally into God's hands, with a simplicity and openness which released him from anxiety and fear. In his account he apologized frequently for his being only a simple parish priest with no learning. John would shake his head, close to tears, and urge him to go on . . . Williman spoke from a conviction and a trust which went way beyond intellect and ideas, and he held out a hand to John, showing him what a total acceptance of God's will could mean.[1]

There is the *true* simplicity. Let Cuthbert himself have the last word in this matter. In *Him We Declare*[2] he wrote:

> There is a simplicity . . . which we abandon, or smile at, or argue ourselves out of, at our peril. We must trust Christ, or not seek to walk with him at all. And trust must involve relying upon him in

[1] Collins 1987, pp. 301–2
[2] p. 79

particular situations, to the limit, to lift us up, and make us capable of actions in his name of which, unaided, we should be quite incapable. This is not a matter of the will or the intelligence, so much as a willing surrender of the heart and mind to Christ in the full trust that he will never let us down, but always hold us up. It is an essential element of encounter with him; to move in his service boldly in situations in which one knows that alone one would be lost.

Perhaps there were times when Cuthbert's love of people and his almost innate desire to see the best in them made him somewhat blind to their weaknesses and to the sheer naughtiness that is in man. There was a certain innocence about him. To bear in mind the apostolic saying that "charity . . . thinketh no evil" and at the same time to be a shrewd judge of character is to maintain an extremely difficult balance. He shared with William Temple a lack of judgement of character which exposed him to the danger of making wrong appointments, and of yielding to enthusiasm about the last man he had met rather than waiting to give a maturer judgement. After all, "love hopeth all things, believeth all things. . . ." Might not his geese be swans?

Cuthbert was an optimist. No doubt, the Christian's correct answer to the question: "Are you a pessimist?" is: "No. I am a proximate realist and an ultimate optimist. I can be no other, for I believe in a God who ultimately will have all things in subjection under him." Better, surely, to be optimistic, even sometimes over-optimistic, than as a pessimist to spread a fog of gloom.

*   *   *

Cuthbert Bardsley believed profoundly in the power of God to change a man or woman and to make new creatures out of them. Of course, he was not so naïve as to hold that, given enough "conversions", society would enter Utopia and the Kingdom of Heaven would have arrived. His work in the House of Lords showed that he realized that there were cancers in the heart of society which had to be excised, social problems which called for radical handling. His work in industrial mission in South London and in Coventry bore witness

[2] p. 79.

to this same fundamental belief. With Leslie Hunter, Bishop of Sheffield, and one of the prime movers in the world of industrial mission, he believed that

> it is unreasonable to suppose that the re-conversion of England . . . will proceed only by the attraction of individuals one by one from the non-Church group to the Church group. This, none the less, is the premise of those who see the Church's strategy solely in terms of individual conversions – a conversion which in effect requires them to break away from the solidarity of one neighbourhood unit to join another fellowship . . . As a matter of history that is not how Christianity has spread.[3]

Nor did Cuthbert neglect the central councils of the Church. He took his part in, for example, the work of the Church Assembly and the General Synod, though often his spirit rebelled at the slowness with which the wheels of such councils moved and at the sterility of so many of their committees. "The truly prophetic method of operation so often begins with an individual's initiative, the seeing of a need, the gathering of a group to see what could be done, and then experimentation and action."[4] To this approach he warmed, and by it he frequently worked. Peter and Paul actively decided to break down the middle wall of partition between Jews and Gentiles and *only then* to call the Council of Jerusalem. Would anything have happened had the Council met *first?*

It was not a case of either/or – *either* social work and Church Councils *or* individual conversions. What gave Cuthbert cause for deep anxiety was the undeniable fact that in a world and in a Church which put great trust in the first, the second so often got forgotten. Societies depend on the renewal and re-creation of individuals for their wholeness, their health, their holiness.

Hence the long hours which the Bishop gave to work with individuals in his study and in his chapel. Hence the directness of his preaching and the fearlessness of his appeal, for decisions. Hence the

---

[3] *Strategy for the Spirit: Leslie Hunter, Bishop of Sheffield 1939–1962* edited by Gordon Hewitt. Becket Publications 1985, p. 136
[4] See David M. Paton: *R.O. The Life and Times of Bishop Ronald Hall of Hong Kong*, 1985, p. 304

care which he gave in the preparation for missions in his own diocese and in other parts of Britain and of the world. Hence the central part that he himself took in these missions. He expected men and women to "turn from darkness to light and from the power of Satan to God" – and they did; and Cuthbert rejoiced. He preached for a verdict.

In his retirement he read with great appreciation Laurens van der Post's book *A Walk with a White Bushman*: "The individual must not wait for governments and he must not wait for groups and powerful people to do something."[5] "Real societies depend for their renewal and creation on individuals."[6] Cuthbert was wholly at one with van der Post in this. From his days with the Oxford Groups to his maturer work as a bishop and pastor of souls, he sought to bring men and women face to face with Christ, there to acknowledge his Lordship and by an act of will to enlist in his service.

If Cuthbert was adamant in refusing to accept the either/or of social action and personal conversion, he was equally adamant in refusing the either/or of "Catholic" and "Evangelical". He had been brought up under the ministry of his father who was not strictly a party man; if he had to be labelled, Norman Bardsley would probably have answered positively to the word "evangelical", certainly in the negative sense of opposition to Rome and its tenets as held and expounded in the days before Vatican II. As Cuthbert travelled and saw the Church at work, his own vision developed and, at a critical time in his life, his residence at Mirfield made a deep impression. He began, for example, to feel the importance of regular auricular confession. In 1957 he wrote:

Gradually all my distrust was broken down. Came a day when I knelt before our Lord in the presence of one of his accredited ministers, heard for the first time the royal words of pardon, received wise counsel, and rose up with a load off my back, able to look the world in the face again. Since that day, nearly twenty-five years ago, sacramental confession has been my regular habit. It has become central in my teaching.[7]

[5] Chatto & Windus 1986, p. 5
[6] *op. cit.*, p. 92
[7] In an Introduction to *The Double Cure*, by Eric James (Hodder & Stoughton)

Now in his retirement, the Bishop finds that he learns much from the sisters of St Mary at Wantage, some of whom, though he has ceased to visit them officially, still come to his home for "ghostly counsel and advice". He finds himself challenged by their community discipline. He refers to them, and to other Religious Communities, special problems which call for prayer, and special errands on which he goes and for which he needs special grace.

A friend of Cuthbert's writes:

> In many ways he is a strange mixture [one is compelled to ask why "strange"?] of churchmanship and theological perspective. A firm Evangelical in the pulpit and [in] his real zeal for personal conversion and individual commitment to the Lord, but also very Catholic in his real understanding and appreciation of sacramental life, and especially in his advocacy of such things as sacramental confession. And always a true man of prayer who never lost an opportunity to share his own deep and extensive experience of the efficacy and beauty of prayer and daily communion with God.

The artist in him and his concept of God as the author of all beauty made him eager to accept and incorporate into worship all that was beautiful in colour, design, architecture, music. He was equally at ease with the magnificence of Cathedral worship as with the fervour of an evangelistic rally in the Albert Hall. It is doubtful that he would want to add any addition to the label "Anglican" if his churchmanship were being described. But if he were pressed, he would give his assent to the hyphenated words "Evangelical-Catholic". Perhaps he has been mindful of the saying of that doughty Anglican and equally convinced Evangelical leader, Charles Simeon:

> The truth is *not in the middle* and *not in one extreme; but in both extremes* . . . so that if extremes will please you, I am your man; only remember that it is not *one* extreme that we are to go to, but *both* extremes.[8]

*   *   *

The title of this chapter includes the words: *Man and Mission*. It is impossible to separate the two. The man and the message, the man and the mission, were one.

[8] Quoted in William Carus' *Memoires of the Life of the Rev. Charles Simeon* (London 1847, p. 600)

Edward Patey, who worked so closely with the Bishop during the early years at Coventry, writes of him as a preacher:

If Cuthbert had not been a bishop he might have become a stage celebrity. He had the flamboyant style of the older generation of actors, and he could never tell a story without impersonating the people whom he was describing in voice and gesture. It was his histrionic ability and resonant voice which, with his deep personal devotion to Jesus Christ and his love of people, combined to make him one of the most admired and sought after preachers of his generation. He did not claim to be an academic nor an expert theologian. There was not a great deal of intellectual content in his sermons. He could sometimes lapse into naïvety. But his great ability to communicate the Christian faith in direct language to ordinary people attracted large congregations. He was particularly in his element when speaking to great assemblies of men such as at the annual conference of the Church of England Men's Society where he was absolutely in his element, and much hero-worshipped. There are many men today who encountered him in the Forces or in C.E.M.S. rallies who would testify to having received their faith through his ministry.

There are certain themes to which we find Cuthbert constantly recurring. For example, the basic importance of holiness, of prayer, of quiet, of withdrawal into the presence of Christ prior to advance in his service. He knew whereof he spoke. Simon Phipps writes:

He was a dedicated man of prayer – very much so. I think when a Bishop is really open to the Spirit in this committed way, all sorts of good things happen in his diocese, which he may not himself necessarily understand. Any diocese owes a great deal to a bishop who has been committed to that particular bit of hidden hard labour.

Constantly Cuthbert stresses – and again he speaks from experience – the sufficiency of God. "You cannot: God can, through you" is almost a refrain in his speaking and in his writing.

He is conscious of the ever-present danger of an inward-looking pseudo-Christianity. To him it is of the very essence of the Faith that its followers should be outward-looking: "Lift up your eyes and look on the fields." Evangelism is never far from his thinking and his preaching. Hence, to take but one example, his annual visits to St Aldate's, Oxford, over a period of twenty-three years, to challenge each new generation of undergraduates to respond to the call of Christ. Nor was he backward in telling them of his own experience of being found and won by his Lord. In *Him We Declare*,[9] a book he wrote in collaboration with Canon William Purcell, in a chapter entitled "This Happened to Me", he goes into some detail as to the way in which, down the years, God had led him on.

He could never be satisfied with the Church as it was. "Other sheep I have which are not of this fold, them also I must bring." The Church must always have an outward thrust, a concern for the outsider, a divine discontent. He feared for a Church which was strong on maintenance and weak and indecisive on mission. In a Charge to the Diocese of Coventry, he challenged his hearers, quoting Bishop Trevor Huddleston: "Is the message of the Gospel being proclaimed with 'a freshness, a stimulus, a shining sparkle?' Only rarely, I fear."[10]

Sometimes he found himself maddened by the slowness and the lack of vision of the Church of which he was a leader. But beneath that sense of occasional frustration, he had a deep love for the Church of England. *Sundry Times Sundry Places* contains a chapter, originally broadcast from St Martin's Church, Canterbury, entitled "Why I believe in the Church of England". In typical fashion, he spells it out alphabetically – "A for Apostolic; B for Bible; C for Catholic; D for Discipline; E for Evangelistic; F for Fight".[11] In that Church he had been brought up and in it he was content to remain and to serve. Constantly he acknowledges his debt to his father, and among others who had deeply influenced him he mentions B.K. Cunningham (from his Westcott House days), Tubby Clayton (All Hallows by the Tower), Father Algy Robertson of the Society of St Francis, Father Geoffrey Curtis of the Community of the Resurrection, and Father William of Glasshampton.

*　　*　　*

[9] Mowbrays 1967
[10] *Sundry Times Sundry Places*, p. 139
[11] pp. 89ff.

Canon William Purcell, Canon Theologian of Coventry 1959–66 and Canon Residentiary of Worcester 1966–76, has given permission to include in this chapter what he calls "an attempt to look at him as a man, as a person, from the viewpoint of one who has known him many years and loved him as a friend. It is", he says, "necessary to search for some of those characteristics which have always been part of him."

One of them is perfectly caught by a press photograph dating from the early 50s. It is before me now. The background of marquees and a country crowd fix the place as the Kent Agricultural Show held that year in Maidstone. On the right Archbishop Fisher is graciously receiving, for reasons long forgotten and probably, by his expression, slightly obscure to him at the time, a copy of a parish magazine. But it is the figure on the left of the picture which dominates. This is Cuthbert Bardsley of Croydon, wearing the gaitered rig of a bishop of those days. It is the manner which catches the eye, for he is presenting the magazine almost as though it were the Grail itself, and the smile with which he does so speaks of an all-embracing enthusiasm for everything around – the place, the day, the people, the enterprise.

What on earth is going on in this picture? It has to be turned over for the explanation, in fading pencil. "Canterbury Diocesan Publicity Committee. Exhibit at Kent Agricultural Show. Cuthbert Bardsley, Chairman." One is reminded, by the large enthusiasm of Cuthbert and the smallness of the occasion, of the remark by Samuel Johnson at the sale of Thrale's Brewery, that they were not there merely to dispose of a collection of vats and tuns, but to acquire wealth beyond the dreams of avarice. He was indicating the limitless possibilities in a commonplace occasion. In the same way and in his own manner, Cuthbert at the Show was indicating the riches he felt to be latent in even the most ordinary event. And in so doing, he was showing forth quite unconsciously that feature of his personality his many friends have noted, sometimes to their amusement – a striking capacity for enthusiasm. "All was", he would say of many things, people, situations, experiences, "wholly good." There was, and is, however, more in that expression than the occasion for an affectionate smile. Cuthbert liked God's world. But then, so did God when he made it; and said so.

Now here is another picture. This is Cuthbert as Bishop of

Coventry, scarlet-cassocked in a TV studio, just about to be interviewed. The years have passed by now, and the face shows it. But the camera has caught the same enthusiasm, the same undimmed enjoyment of the possibilities of the moment, and of the potential of what may be just over the horizon. The root and ground of this exuberance was indicated by an incident which comes into the memory of those times. He and I had been collaborating in the writing of a small book concerned with giving some expression to the faith which moved us. But we were stuck for a title. Then, one day, as we were in the middle of a round of golf, it came to him, and he went off down the fairway joyfully proclaiming "Him we Declare!, Him we Declare!", and that is how the book eventually appeared, and was well received.

So this enthusiasm was founded in an ardent love of Jesus as Lord, and in a "thankful remembrance of all other benefits of his Passion". This sense of the need for thankfulness has always gone deep with Cuthbert. Clearly, like everyone else, he has had his limitations, and it is part of the endeavour to get a whole picture to take note of them. Thus his faith could at times seem a little simplistic, and to fail to take sufficient note of the difficulties it presented to those less fortunately circumstanced. Maybe in this he has been influenced by his social background; reasonably comfortable in terms of this world's goods, and unmistakably officer class, with the privileges often associated with it. But these are surface matters. Like the process of panning for gold, which produces sand at the beginning, so any search for the true spiritual quality of Cuthbert Bardsley may fairly look upon these facts, then throw them away, then search among what remains for the shining specks which indicate the really precious.

Thus it is a bright fact that Cuthbert has always attracted many people, of all sorts and conditions, by something unusually luminous in his personality. It is as though, in a strange way, they felt warmed by him. This has been much more than a mere geniality. Enthusiasm and exuberance were a part of it, but by no means the whole. The truth is that he warmed people because it was evident that he loved them. And because he found them important in their own right, which is an often forgotten part of loving, so they responded, and felt warmed by this evidence of his manifest caring. It was, therefore, an essential part of his ministry to meet people, mix with them, talk with them, at a length and with an ardour which could be positively exhausting to less socially robust persons who might chance to be with him. This was something we talked of at times. Why did he take such pleasure in meeting people? To one who had always found sociability something of a trial the answer was illuminating – and humbling. He loved people because he felt a deep interest in what they were as children of God, and in what they had the potential to become. Their lives mattered because they mattered to God, and that was about the long and the short of it. So wherever he met with them, on some military base during his time with the Forces, in parish rooms over the tea-cups, in the privacy of their homes, and in his own study when people came to him, he would warm them in the glow of his concern and regard.

To those many who came to him in trouble, sorrow, need, sickness, or any other adversity, he would suggest, indeed he would press upon them, a simple exercise: that they should there and then, on paper, note down those things for which, in spite of all, they had reason to be thankful. It would surprise them how many such things there were. He wanted them, as part of a spiritually healing process, to regain a sense of gratitude "for all the blessings of this life". There were always some, however bleak or defeated the person concerned felt life to be. Was there not the natural world, God's creation, to enjoy? Was there not the love of friends, often overlooked or even spurned? Was there not the ever renew-able challenge of living in that world in a manner worthy of it, in spite of disappointment, in spite, as with so many who came to him, of the formidable challenges of pain and sickness? Above all, was there not always the offer of Christ's healing power, and ultimately the blessed hope of everlasting life? And then, when these truths had been considered, he would take the person across to his chapel, so that there, usually in total quiet, they would draw near to that divine presence which to Cuthbert was always so real. It is an interesting fact that, in all his houses, he would always insist on having his chapel close by his study, so that he could take people across to it with the minimum interruption of the counselling they were having together. Even at Cirencester, after his retirement, he felt it essential to have his private chapel similarly available.

Here it is necessary to go deeper in this search for the truth, or at any rate a little of it, about Cuthbert Bardsley. That word "enthusiasm", to start with, is clearly quite inadequate to describe the zest and warming ardour he brought to the business of living. Life can, of course, be a dreary business; it can be a predicament to be got through as best one can. But with Cuthbert it has clearly been, in the best sense, a joy. That is not to suggest that it has been for him always a pleasurable experience, by any means. But *joy*, in the New Testament sense, as a fruit of the Spirit, he does seem to have known and shown forth over the years. So that is the word to fix on; joy, joy and peace in believing, a deep sense that all will be well for those who love God.

This gift of the Spirit, this joy, it has seemed to this witness, has always had something to do with Cuthbert's healing powers. The woman with a cancer of the spine who struggled, severely bent, up the drive of Bishop's House in Coventry in order that he might lay hands on her, and left the place standing upright, was one of many who, in different degrees and at different times, experienced this gift of his. He said to me that it had always seemed to him that there was in everyone a kind of *élan vital* which could, through the power of the Spirit, in many cases where, sometimes for psychosomatic reasons it had been dammed up, be wonderfully released. This is an area of great mystery, as Cuthbert would be the first to acknowledge. But that he had powers in this area does seem beyond question.

In many ways he has been a simple person, certainly in his unquestioning faith in Jesus as Lord. He has never been a scholar. He has never been fond of administration, nor very good at it, as he himself would admit. What, then, is the essence of this man? That he has affected many lives for good is undeniable. That people of all sorts have loved him is a fact. But what is the real secret of his attraction? It needs, or so it has seemed to this witness, a moment of special revelation to perceive it. That moment came, for this writer, on 25th May 1962, the day of the Consecration of Coventry Cathedral. It fell to Cuthbert then to be at the centre of one of the greatest moments in the life of the Church of England in this century. He was at full stretch, sustained by the prayers of many friends, and splendidly impressive. But there seemed something special about him. A good place from which to note this special quality was from behind the TV cameras in the control vehicle, often a place singularly revealing of the truth about a person. When

257

the time came for Cuthbert to come into the view of one of the cameras, it seemed to this old friend that the real nature of this exceptional man was for once plain to see. That real nature can perhaps best be summed up in the words of the Shunammite woman who, as is told in the Second Book of Kings, had watched the prophet Elisha passing by several times. Then she had a moment of insight. "Behold now," she said to her husband, "I perceive that this is a holy man of God."

*   *   *

Cuthbert Bardsley, in the words of one of his friends, still "goes through the world with his arms wide open" – open to God, open to welcome men and women into His love.

Index of Names

Griffith, Harry 214

Haigh, Mervyn G. 126, 127, 129
Hall, Ronald 249 (note 4)
Hand, Peter 82
Handel, George Frederick 82
Hardy, Alister 204
Harland, Maurice H. H. 104
Harley, Ian 24
Harley, Thomas 23, 74, 192, 239
Hart, B. H. Liddell 94
Haynes, John S. 181
Hayter, William 33
Headlam, A. C. 13
Henley, Miss 25
Henson, Herbert Hensley 13, 39
Herbert, Percy Mark 21, 34
Hewitt, Gordon 249
Hitler, Adolf 59, 83
Hogg, Quintin 182
Horan, Forbes 43
Hough, Brenda 14
Howard, Robert T. 32, 127, 130,
    132, 133, 139, 140, 142, 151, 157,
    163
Hoyle, Fred 97
Huddleston, Trevor 253
Hughes, F. L. 100
Hulstrand, D. M. 214
Humphries, Donald 186
Hunter, Leslie 66, 146, 249
Hutton, John 141
Hyde, Douglas 211

Inge, W. R. 56, 87
Iremonger, F. A. 13, 58
Irenaeus, St 237
Islip, Kay 82

Jackson, Lawrence 153, 180, 181,
    182, 183, 208
James, Eric 247, 251
Jasper, R. C. D. 13
Jennings, Wentworth 137
Joad, C. E. M. 95
Jones, Jack 233

Kennedy, G. Studdert 26, 211
Kennedy, John 144
Kerin, Dorothy 201–3

Killick, Annie Mabel (*see* Bardsley,
    Annie Mabel)
Killick, William 22
Kindersley, R. F. 30
Kingsley, Charles 246
Kivengere, Festo 214

Lang, Cosmo Gordon 13, 19, 39,
    203
Lang, L. H. 66
Larkin, Peter J. 178, 181
Larkin, Philip 233
Lean, Garth 37
Leigh, Lord 183
Lightfoot, Kenneth 242
Linton, Sydney 43, 49, 50
Lippman, Walter 89
Lloyd, Roger 143, 201
Lockhart, J. G. 13
Lousada, Anthony 33
Loveitt, Percy 131
Lovell, Bernard 173
Lunn, Henry 56
Lunt, F. Evered 116

McClaughny, Victor 82
McCreery, Richard 110, 112
McKaye, Louis 186
McKie, J. D. 149, 192, 230
McKie, William 163
Maclagan, William Dalrymple 19
Maclaren, Archibald 26
Macnaghten, Robin 24
Maddocks, Morris 203, 243
Maitland, F. W. 13
Manley, H. 133
March, Lord 176
Margaret, Princess 163, 164
Marmion, Bishop 213
Marten, Henry 32, 34
Mary, Queen 96
Maud, John 173
Menuhin, Yehudi 166
Meredith, J. N. Michael C. 72, 95
Minshull, Lincoln 185
Mitchell, Elizabeth 191
Mitchell, Ellen (*see* Bardsley, Ellen)
Mitchell, Ellen Edith (née
    Shepherd) 190
Mitchell, Walter 191